The Future of Catholic
Biblical Scholarship

The Future of Catholic Biblical Scholarship

A CONSTRUCTIVE CONVERSATION

Luke Timothy Johnson
&
William S. Kurz, S.J.

WILLIAM B. EERDMANS PUBLISHING COMPANY
GRAND RAPIDS, MICHIGAN / CAMBRIDGE, U.K.

Wm. B. Eerdmans Publishing Co.
255 Jefferson Ave. S.E., Grand Rapids, Michigan 49503 /
P.O. Box 163, Cambridge CB3 9PU U.K.

Printed in the United States of America

07 06 05 04 03 02   7 6 5 4 3 2 1

Library of Congress Cataloging-in-Publication Data

Johnson, Luke Timothy.
    The future of Catholic biblical scholarship : a constructive conversation /
Luke Timothy Johnson & William S. Kurz.
        p.   cm.
    Includes bibliographical references.
    ISBN 0-8028-4545-2 (pbk.)
        1. Bible — Criticism, interpretation, etc. — United States. 2. Catholic Church —
Doctrines. I. Kurz, William S., 1939- II. Title.

BS511.3 .J64 2002
220′.088′22 — dc21

                                                          2002072187

www.eerdmans.com

CONTENTS

CONTENTS

PREFACE

The purpose of this book is to start a conversation concerning the future of Catholic biblical scholarship. We (the authors) set out on this project because we think that things are not entirely healthy in the present situation. We are not interested in blaming anyone. We are not even certain that blame is an appropriate category. We are anxious about the future, both because we are concerned about biblical scholarship, and even more because we are concerned for the church. We invite you (our readers) into a reflection on the present state of affairs, and, should we agree that things ought to be better, into a consideration of how we might move forward together. So we have called this a "constructive conversation." The double sense of the word "constructive" is deliberate. We want to be positive, and we want to figure out how the future might be constructed by our wise choices.

Our perspectives are particular and our focus necessarily narrow. Both of us write as middle-aged white males of the American Midwest. We are both New Testament scholars shaped by years in the religious life. Bill Kurz is a Jesuit of the Wisconsin Province. Luke Johnson was formerly a Benedictine monk. Kurz remains a priest and religious, teaching at Marquette University in Milwaukee. Johnson is a Roman Catholic layperson who teaches at Candler School of Theology at Emory University in Atlanta. We each received the Ph.D. in New Testament from Yale University. In fact, we were classmates. Both of us wrote dissertations on Luke-Acts. Inevitably, the view we have of the present situation is affected by our commitments and life-experiences. Because we choose, in Kierkegaard's terms, to "speak passionately," that is, out of our life and commitment, readers should know from the beginning that we are not relying on surveys, statistics, or any other paraphernalia of science. We can adopt no universal viewpoint but only the one legitimated by our respective lives and commitments. We are ill prepared, furthermore, to discourse about all biblical scholarship everywhere. Readers should expect here, then, a limited view of reality, and measure its worth accordingly. We know something about the New Testament, about the American academy, and about Roman Catholicism in this country. Others can help us discover whether what we say on these things (if itself correct) applies also to other spheres.

The form of the book, we hope, will also exemplify a "constructive conversation." The first section is written by Johnson, with Kurz responding with a short essay. After the second section written by Kurz, Johnson likewise responds with an essay. Then, both authors engage a series of questions in a more free-wheeling way, and close with a final statement. We hope that others will join the conversation.

Even in these preliminary remarks, you notice that we slip back and forth between "biblical interpretation" and "biblical scholarship." That slippage is not simply linguistic. It suggests a deeper ambiguity. "Biblical scholarship" is something that we ordinarily assume is carried out by people able to read the original languages, who are academically trained, and who publish books. "Biblical interpretation," however, is not simply to be identified with "biblical scholarship," for it is an ecclesial activity carried out at many levels and in many ways. We would like to find a way to think about biblical interpretation within the church that is not totally defined by academic conventions yet truly has a scholarly quality.

This book draws on earlier efforts and the help of others. A shorter version of Johnson's chapter, "What's Catholic about Catholic Biblical Scholarship?" was first delivered as a Plenary Address at the 1997 meeting of the Catholic Biblical Association of America in Seattle, Washington, and an epitome was published as "So What's Catholic about It?" in *Commonweal* 125/1 (16 January 1998): 12-16. His chapter, "Imagining the World That Scripture Imagines," is substantially the same as the article with that title appearing in *Modern Theology* 14 (1998): 165-80. His other three chapters were written as a Henry Luce III Fellow in Theology during 2000-2001, and he wishes to thank the Luce Foundation and the Association of Theological Schools in America and Canada for their support. Earlier versions of these chapters were delivered as the Clark Lectures at Duke Divinity School and as the Harry Vaughn Smith lectures at Mercer University in February 2001. Kurz's chapter, "Beyond Historical Criticism: Reading John's Prologue as Catholics," draws extensively from his article, "The Johannine Word as Revealing the Father: A Christian Credal Actualization," *Perspectives in Religious Studies* 28/1 (Spring 2001): 67-84, and sections of "Voices in the Church: Preunderstandings in Applying Scripture," and "Feeding 5000 in John 6 and the Eucharist," rely heavily on his article, "Ethical Actualization of Scripture: Approaches toward a Prolife Reading," *Fides Quaerens Intellectum* 1 (Summer 2001): 67-93. He would also like to express his special gratitude to his most recent Marquette University teaching and research assistants, who were helpful in the research and writing of his manuscript: Matthew McKinnon, Christopher S. Dorn, and Jeremy R. Holmes. Together, the authors thank Allen Myers and Wm. B. Eerdmans Publishing Co. for their interest in this project, and the communities of scholarship and faith that have supported them in this as in every other endeavor.

LUKE TIMOTHY JOHNSON
WILLIAM S. KURZ, S.J.

ABBREVIATIONS

AB	Anchor Bible
ABD	*The Anchor Bible Dictionary,* ed. David Noel Freedman
ABR	*Australian Biblical Review*
ABRL	Anchor Bible Reference Library
ANRW	*Aufstieg und Niedergang der Römischen Welt,* ed. Hildegard Temporini and Wolfgang Haase
BibInt	*Biblical Interpretation*
BRev	*Bible Review*
BTB	*Biblical Theology Bulletin*
CBQ	*Catholic Biblical Quarterly*
CBQMS	Catholic Biblical Quarterly Monograph Series
CCC	*Catechism of the Catholic Church*
DS	Heinrich Denzinger–Adolf Schönmetzer, *Enchiridion Symbolorum*
DV	*Dei Verbum*
EV	*Evangelium Vitae*
FG	Fourth Gospel
HBT	*Horizons in Biblical Theology*
HTR	*Harvard Theological Review*
ICEL	International Commission on English in the Liturgy
Int	*Interpretation*
JBC	*The Jerome Biblical Commentary,* ed. Raymond E. Brown, Joseph A. Fitzmyer, and Roland E. Murphy

JSNT	*Journal for the Study of the New Testament*
JSNTSup	Journal for the Study of the New Testament Supplement
LCL	Loeb Classical Library
LumVie	*Lumière et vie*
NJBC	*The New Jerome Biblical Commentary,* ed. Raymond E. Brown, Joseph A. Fitzmyer, and Roland E. Murphy
NRSV	New Revised Standard Version
NTS	*New Testament Studies*
PG	*Patrologia graeca,* ed. Jacques-Paul Migne
PL	*Patrologia latina,* ed. Jacques-Paul Migne
PRSt	*Perspectives in Religious Studies*
RSV	Revised Standard Version
SBLTT	Society of Biblical Literature Texts and Translations
ScEs	*Science et esprit*
SNTS	Studiorum Novi Testamenti Societas
SSEJC	Studies in Scripture in Early Judaism and Christianity
TD	*Theology Digest*
TS	*Theological Studies*
TT	*Theology Today*
VTSup	Supplements to *Vetus Testamentum*

ANCIENT WORKS

Ambrose
Paen.	*De paenitentia*

Augustine
Civ.	*De civitate Dei (The City of God)*
Conf.	*Confessions*
Cons.	*De consensu evangelistarum (Harmony of the Gospels)*
Doctr. chr.	*De doctrina christiana (On Christian Instruction)*
Enarrat. Ps.	*Enarrationes in Psalmos*
Enchir.	*Enchiridion*
Ep(p).	*Epistle(s)*
Faust.	*Reply to Faustus the Manichaean*
Gen. litt.	*The Literal Meaning of Genesis*

Retract.	*Retractions*
Serm.	*Sermons*

John Chrysostom
Sac.	*De sacerdotio (Priesthood)*

Clement of Alexandria
Strom.	*Stromata (Miscellanies)*
Did.	*Didache*
Ep. Barn.	*Epistle of Barnabas*

Eusebius
Hist. eccl.	*Historia ecclesiastica (Ecclesiastical History)*

Justin
Dial.	*Dialogue with Trypho*

Origen
Cels.	*Contra Celsum (Against Celsus)*
Comm. Cant.	*Commentarium in Canticum*
Dial.	*Dialogue with Heraclides*
Ep. Afr.	*Letter to Africanus*
Ep. Greg.	*Letter to Gregory*
Pasch.	*De pascha (Tractate on the Passover)*
Philoc.	*Philocalia*
Princ.	*De principiis (Peri archōn, On First Principles)*

Plutarch
Mor.	*Moralia*

Socrates
Hist. eccl.	*Historia ecclesiastica (Ecclesiastical History)*

Sozomen
Hist. eccl.	*Historia ecclesiastica (Ecclesiastical History)*

PART ONE

LUKE JOHNSON

CHAPTER ONE

What's Catholic about Catholic Biblical Scholarship? An Opening Statement

The 20th century saw a fundamental change in Catholic biblical scholarship. A symbolic start was the condemnation of Alfred Loisy for his espousal of historical critical methods in reading Scripture.[1] A symbolic ending is Rome's official stamp of approval on the historical-critical approach,[2] and the involvement of Catholic scholars in the quintessential historical-critical project, the quest for the historical Jesus.[3] The symbolic (and real) point of pivot was Pius XII's encyclical

---

1. Loisy's formal excommunication in 1908 under Pope Pius X followed several years of suppression, including the placement of some of his books on the Index of Forbidden Books. See Harvey Hill, *History, Theology, and the Crisis of Religious Authority: Alfred Loisy's Modernist Agenda in Context* (diss., Emory University, 1996).

2. On 18 March 1994, The Pontifical Biblical Commission issued a statement entitled *The Interpretation of the Bible in the Church*, with a Preface by Cardinal Joseph Ratzinger. The statement is written in response to the historical-critical method's being brought into question, in part because of the rise of new methods and in part due to the sense among some that the method is "deficient from the point of view of faith." While discussing the value and limitations of newer methods, and while acknowledging that reading the Scripture in faith requires more than history, the document nevertheless stresses the centrality of the approach: "The historical-critical method is the indispensable method for the scientific study of the meaning of ancient texts . . . proper understanding not only admits the use of this method but actually requires it" (1.A).

3. For quite different approaches, but each firmly within the framework of the historical-critical paradigm, see John P. Meier, *A Marginal Jew: Rethinking the Historical*

3

Divino Afflante Spiritu in 1943.[4] Coming at the mid-point of the century, it legitimated the use of the historical method for Catholic scholars, and changed everything. From the middle of the 19th century to the middle of the 20th century, the phrase "Roman Catholic biblical scholarship" would have been regarded by many as oxymoronic: it may have been Roman Catholic, but was it really scholarship? At the end of the 20th and the beginning of the 21st century, however, the phrase is equally oxymoronic: no one doubts the quality of the scholarship, but in what sense is it any longer "Catholic"?

An answer to this question can begin with some appreciation for Catholic biblical interpretation before *Divino Afflante Spiritu*, trace the expectations Catholic scholars had concerning the advantages of the historical-critical approach to Scripture, and then assess the consequences of a 50-year engagement with that approach. The version of these three stages that you are about to read should not be confused with history. What follows is not a matter of fact but of opinion shaped by experience. I write as a New Testament scholar who was born the year that the encyclical was issued, who grew up in the post-Tridentine church, who was a seminarian at 13 and a Benedictine monk at 19. I prayed the Divine Office in Latin for many years — and thereby inhabited the world shaped by patristic exegesis — but also did my theological studies in the immediate aftermath of the Second Vatican Council at a school (St. Meinrad School of Theology) that had recently revised its entire curriculum within a self-consciously historical paradigm. But I also write as a Catholic whose professional training as a New Testa-

---

Jesus, 3 vols. ABRL (New York: Doubleday, 1991, 1994, 2001); and John Dominic Crossan, *The Historical Jesus: The Life of a Mediterranean Jewish Peasant* (San Francisco: HarperSanFrancisco, 1991); *Jesus: A Revolutionary Biography* (San Francisco: HarperSanFrancisco, 1994).

4. Pope Pius XII issued *Divino Afflante Spiritu* on 30 September 1943 to mark the 50th anniversary of Leo XIII's *Providentissimus Deus* (18 November 1893). Although it clearly initiated a new era, the encyclical stresses continuity with earlier papal teaching and suggests that its directives are a logical development rather than a new approach. Pius XII opens the way for unfettered study of the original languages (16), text-criticism (17), and the study of the literal sense (23), defined as the meaning "intended and expressed by the original author" (26). The use of history for determining the circumstances of the composition (31-37, 40) and its literary expression (38) is approved.

ment scholar took place at Yale, the very belly of the Enlightenment beast, and whose career as a teacher has been entirely within the framework of the secular academy (10 years at Indiana University's Department of Religious Studies) and Protestant seminaries (6 years at Yale Divinity School and 10 years at Candler School of Theology at Emory University). These are my (perhaps idiosyncratic) perceptions of a story in which I have been a participant, not the detached analysis of a disinterested observer. *Caveat Lector!*

The Spirit of Catholicism and Scripture

For the sake of simplicity, I suggest that the spirit of Catholicity can be expressed as a preference for the conjunctive more than the disjunctive. To be Catholic is to think inclusively rather than exclusively. Catholics tend toward the "both/and" more than they do toward the "either/or." And before you rush to point out that my very proposal is couched in terms of the disjunctive, let me hasten to affirm that Catholics also have a high tolerance for paradox! The real point of my distinction will become clearer as we go. For the moment, I propose that the "both/and" applicable to the interpretation of Scripture consists in the affirmation simultaneously of the value both of Scripture and of Tradition.[5] There are at least three important ways in which this conjunction was expressed in the biblical interpretation that preceded 1943: in the connections between Scripture and liturgy, between Scripture and theology, and between Scripture and the history of interpretation.

With respect to each of these conjunctions between Scripture and Tradition, however, there was both good news and bad news. Let's be-

---

5. For the statement concerning Scripture and Tradition at the Council of Trent, Session IV (8 April 1546), see H. Denzinger and A. Schoenmetzer, *Enchiridion Symbolorum Definitionum et Declarationum,* 33rd ed. (Rome: Herder, 1965), par. 1501. For the statement of Vatican II, see the *Dogmatic Constitution on Divine Revelation* (1965) II, 7-10, in *The Documents of Vatican II,* ed. Walter M. Abbott, S.J. (New York: Association, 1966), 114-18. And, most recently, the *Catechism of the Catholic Church* (Washington: United States Catholic Conference/Vatican: Libreria Editrice Vaticana, 1994), pars. 74-84. A useful collection of Catholic statements on Scripture is James J. Megivern's *Official Catholic Teachings: Bible Interpretation* (Wilmington, N.C.: Consortium, 1978).

gin with the good news about the longest stage of Catholic biblical interpretation.

The first expression is the intricate and organic links between the interpretation of Scripture and the liturgical life of the church, expressed above all in the Eucharist and in the Divine Office, but to a lesser degree as well in all the sacraments and practices of piety. That Catholics have always been exposed to large amounts of Scripture through the Eucharist needs no demonstration and little reminder. The ordinary of the Mass is built up on the basis of biblical language, from the *kyrie* to the *agnus Dei*. Participation in the Eucharist meant an invitation to the world constructed by Scripture. The proper portions of the Mass included not only readings from Scripture in the Latin Vulgate and preaching on the basis of the readings, but also subtle interpretations of those readings through antiphons, responses, and prayers. Such tropes on Scripture did not fall from heaven. They were the work of skilled interpreters whose mastery of the Bible enabled them to combine fidelity and imagination in astonishing fashion. For those privileged to perform the *opus Dei* within the frame of monastery or religious house, the immersion in a world shaped by Scripture was even more complete, especially since the language of the psalter, the hymns and canticles, and the prayers was so completely interwoven. Likewise for the other sacraments and sacramentals, from the rosary to the stations of the cross. Catholics learned their Scripture through the practices of faith, and those practices also interpreted Scripture.

A second expression of both Scripture and Tradition was the connection between the study of the Bible and theology. Before the emergence of Scholasticism, theology simply *was* reflection on the sacred page *(sacra pagina);* just as there was no gap between study and prayer, neither was there between Scripture and reason. Even during the long reign of Scholastic theology, Scripture remained the basis of doctrinal and moral reasoning, just as the practice of theology ideally led to a deeper understanding of the Scripture. It was impossible to think of a disciplined study of Scripture that was *not* part of theology. There was also a sociological dimension to the unity between theology and Scripture, Scripture and the Liturgy: Scripture scholars were either priests or religious. Their professional language of Latin was the language also of Scripture, theology, and liturgy. Their study and teaching of Scripture took place in academies that were ecclesially defined and directed: monastic and cathedral schools, universities in which theology was the queen of the sciences, and (in later years) seminaries where the study of Scripture was entirely directed to preaching, piety, and prayer. Again, an "academy" that was sociologically distinct from "church," much less opposed to it, would have been as unthinkable as a Scripture scholarship that was not theological or transformative.

A third aspect of the Catholic "both/and" was the way that Scriptural scholarship in the church was nourished by a long tradition of patristic, medieval, and scholastic interpretation. There was no great chasm between the way in which Origen of Alexandria or Bernard of Clairvaux read the Song of Songs and the way in which more recent scholars did; all of them understood the ancient poem as more than a human love song, and saw in it truth about the relationship between Christ and the church, God and the soul. Patristic and medieval biblical interpretation continued to live and speak in the liturgy of the Eucharist and the Hours. Contemporary interpreters found little reason to eschew their readings and many reasons to imitate them. At the very least, Catholic interpreters of Scripture saw themselves as part of a continuous 2000-year conversation that included Augustine and Thomas and Estius and Calmet and Cornelius à Lapide, not a broken conversation whose themes were set only in the previous century.

I have described as "good news" some ideal connections between Scripture and Tradition in Catholic Scripture scholarship. In reality, those connections had, over the course of the centuries, themselves become unbalanced. Instead of Scripture and Tradition, it was all too often Scripture being swallowed by Tradition. The appropriate dialectical tension between Scripture and Tradition tended to be weakened, because Scripture lost its "otherness," and therefore its capacity to challenge rather than simply confirm Tradition. Yes, the liturgy was richly infused with biblical reading and language, but Scripture had little voice outside its liturgical mediation. Yes, Scripture was part of theology, but all too often provided a set of predictable proof-texts for theological positions, rather than provoked theology to deeper insight into the divine mystery in response to the work of God's Holy Spirit in the present. Yes, Scripture study was in conversation with ancient interpreters, but did so mainly through repetition of ancient readings rather than through a vigorous engagement with prior interpreters. Yes, the interpretation of the Scripture was directed completely to the church, but that church was dominated by a clerical class that alone had access to the Latin language uniting Scripture, theology, and liturgy. In effect, the "both/and" of Scripture and Tradition had paradoxically been collapsed into *"Sola Traditio"* ("Tradition alone"), in a manner that reinforced every sort of liturgical and theological precedent, while at the same time hardening an ecclesiastical caste-system that allotted power and privilege only to ordained males.

The Hope of Renewal

If the loss of Scripture's "otherness" had thrown the both/and balance of Catholicism out of whack, then the recovery of that otherness should also lead to the renewal of Catholicism. That was the hope that many found in the way opened up by Pius XII's encyclical, *Divino Afflante Spiritu*. In one way or another, that recovery of otherness was bound up with the recovery of *history*. To read the Scriptures in the original languages of Greek and Hebrew, and to seek for the biblical authors' original intentions, meant in some sense to engage in historical study. It was impossible to adequately translate into the vernacular from the Greek and Hebrew without a deep sense of how those languages were embedded in the cultures of ancient Israel and the Greco-Roman world. It was impossible to seek the original meaning of the composition without contextualizing that voice in its historical circumstances. For the first time, Catholic scholars were encouraged not simply to compile historical information — they had always done that superbly — but to engage in a way of reading Scripture that had been practiced among Protestant scholars for some 200 years, that is, historically-critically: using the methods of history to locate the specific circumstances of each biblical voice. For many, it seemed as though a brave new world, hitherto interdicted, had suddenly been opened to Catholic exploration and immigration.

At the most obvious level, there was joy at the simple pleasure of freedom. Catholic scholars had been allowed to study history, but they were forbidden to indulge in historical-critical judgments of the sort their Protestant colleagues had long made. Without that intellectual freedom, Catholic scholarship rightly was perceived by outsiders, and by the scholars themselves, as suspect: if every investigation must in the end come to the same preordained conclusion, then scholarship is scarcely either free or critical. The first half of the 20th century saw scholars who dared to challenge the interdiction on history (Alfred Loisy is the great example) be excommunicated, and other wonderful scholars (Albert LaGrange is the supreme example) suffer repression and profound frustration.[6] Pius XII allowed Catholic biblical scholars to join a game that was already well-advanced, to become perhaps equal partners with their Protestant colleagues in advancing a truly critical (meaning at least intellectually free) study of Scripture.[7]

More than the freedom of Catholic scholars was at stake. There was also the hope for the renewal of the church through the recovery, through history, of Scripture's "otherness." Certainly, Catholics would now contribute more positively toward ecumenism, not only because they could work with Protestant scholars using the same methods, but above all because the retrieval of the literal sense, stripped of the accretions of dogmatic and polemical interpretations, would help overcome historic antipathies. The methods of history, it was thought, are neutral and objective. The literal sense is recoverable through history. The plain sense of Scripture could therefore mediate theologically. Once Catholic and Protestant exegetes determined together what Paul really meant to say about justification through faith in Romans, then the hostilities of the Reformation period might finally be overcome. Catholic translations based on the original languages would also help to renew the liturgy and the practices of piety, eventually enabling all Chris-

6. A useful survey is provided by Gerald P. Fogarty, S.J., *American Catholic Biblical Scholarship: A History from the Early Republic to Vatican II.* Confessional Perspective Series (San Francisco: Harper and Row, 1989), whose account deals with a series of repressive measures carried out in the name of orthodoxy (35-198), and gives particular attention to the sad case of Henry Poels (85-119).

7. Fogarty shows how *Divino Afflante Spiritu* did not change things overnight. Systematic attempts at suppressing Catholic intellectual freedom were undertaken (especially by the *American Ecclesiastical Review*), leading to a major showdown between that journal and the Catholic Biblical Association in 1961 (see *American Catholic Biblical Scholarship*, 281-310). Especially in light of recent tendencies, this history is important to remember. And if "second generation" American biblical scholars seem obdurate in their position, it must be remembered that it was a position that was hard-won, and involved the unjust suffering of that generation's teachers.

tians to share a common lectionary in worship. Best of all, historical scholarship would make available to all Catholics in their own language the riches of Scripture, empowering them to read and be renewed by the reading of the Bible. Such ready access to Scripture was essential if the full dignity of the laity in the church, now understood as the People of God, was fully to be accomplished.

There was every reason for joy and for hope when Catholic biblical scholars were invited to explore the possibilities of a historical-critical reading of Scripture. There was no hint that an infusion of history would do anything but good. The goal was not the destruction of Tradition but the enlivening of it by restoring a healthier dialectic between the otherness of Scripture and the living Tradition of the church.

The Brave New World:
A Third-Generation Perspective

The world of historical-critical scholarship has turned out to be more ambiguous than anyone could have imagined, although not everyone has yet come to appreciate just how ambiguous it is, especially for Catholics. In fact, when I delivered a first version of these remarks to the Catholic Biblical Association meeting in Seattle in 1997, the response was far from uniformly positive. It is important to note, then, that mine is a "third-generation" perspective.

I am borrowing from the classic analysis of American immigrants from Europe, which shows how the first three generations have distinctly different views of their situation in the "brave new world" of the United States.[8] Spelling out the analogy will make my point clearer. First-generation immigrants to the United States from the "old World" — for the sake of cleverness, let's say Italy — tend to be full of enthusiasm for the practices of the new country, especially the privileges and responsibilities of citizenship. In a very real sense, however, they are culturally still in "the old World" of Italy: they cook as they used to, they still speak Italian in the home, their families and friends are in the old country, they find much in the new place strange. They are, in a

8. Will Herberg, *Protestant, Catholic, Jew: An Essay in American Religious Sociology* (Garden City: Anchor, 1960).

word, so Italian that becoming American citizens is simply a positive addition to a secure cultural identity.

The second generation, in contrast, tends to seek "americanization" in every respect. Not only do they learn English idiomatically and drop Italian, they are a bit embarrassed by the elders who speak Italian or English with a strong accent. They prefer baseball to bocci, hot-dogs to pasta, movies to opera. They don't want to hear about Italy or go there. They want to leave the past behind and move forward. And they want their kids to be even further along in the process of enculturation; they themselves went to Boston College, but their children are going to attend Yale.

The third generation of immigrants typically finds itself in a condition of increasing alienation. They are Italian mainly for purposes of the census. They are thoroughly American. Yet they are not sure whether they have not lost as much as they have gained. They are aware that "being American" is not without its ambiguities. What does it mean to become like everyone else, when the result does not seem to mean anything? Third-generation children of immigrant families tend to reexamine the process they have inherited, and seek to recover some of the cultural riches they have lost. They certainly do not want to return to Italy, would not know what to do if they were forced to return. They are at home in America. But at the same time, they want a richer existence than that offered by a derivative, lowest common denominator, new world identity. They may want to learn some Italian from Grandma before it is too late. They certainly want to preserve her ways of making pasta! They want to be able to find a way of being Italian-American.

By analogy, we can speak of three generations of American Catholic scholars who have immigrated to the world of scholarship previously inhabited mainly by Protestants. A "generation" as I speak of it here is not simply a matter of age, but also of degrees of assimilation into the dominant culture. The first generation was made up of those who grew to maturity in the "old world" of Catholic sensibility, whose theological education was traditional, and whose commitment to the church was expressed through vows or ordination. They eagerly adopted historical methods and rejoiced in the freedom of inquiry. They were so profoundly Catholic, however, that the exercise of historical methods was simply a positive addition to a robust and secure identity.[9] No surprise that we find among such first-generation scholars a large number of books that were popularizing, and the consideration of such theological topics as the inspiration of Scripture.[10]

The second generation consists of those who entered more whole-heartedly into the ethos of critical scholarship, not least by participating fully in the academic guilds and publishing volumes that bristled with learning.[11] These scholars were by no means faithless or negligent. Many of them remained clergy or religious. Many were still trained in Catholic institutions, although some began to acquire Ph.D.'s from secular universities. Many still took up theological issues. The main distinguishing feature of this generation is its uncritical acceptance of the dominant historical-critical paradigm, and a style of scholarship that was increasingly directed to . . . other scholars.

What no one in either the first or second generation noticed was the sociological revolution that was taking place within the new world they had so recently made their own. The revolution was twofold. First,

9. For each of these generations I give some few examples, simply to jog the memory and to pay small tribute to the scholars who made a huge impression on me personally. So, for the first generation, I would include such American names as Barnabas Ahern, Bruce Vawter, Carroll Stuhlmueller, John McKenzie, and such Europeans as Ceslaus Spicq, Lucien Cerfaux, Jean Daniélou, Albert Gelin, and Yves Congar.

10. See, for example, Pierre Benoit, *Inspiration and the Bible* (New York: Sheed and Ward, 1965); Karl Rahner, *Inspiration in the Bible* (New York: Herder and Herder, 1961); John L. McKenzie, "The Social Character of Inspiration," *CBQ* 24 (1962): 115-24; and Luis Alonso Schökel, *The Inspired Word* (New York: Herder and Herder, 1965).

11. The names everyone immediately thinks of here are those of Raymond E. Brown, Joseph A. Fitzmyer, and Roland E. Murphy, not least because of their landmark contribution through *The Jerome Biblical Commentary* (Englewood Cliffs: Prentice-Hall, 1968) — which marked the "coming of age" of American Catholic biblical scholarship — as well as their separate works. Many others, including John P. Meier and John Dominic Crossan, fit within this generation. Because this essay argues the need to move beyond that generation, it is important to note three things. First, addressing a mode of scholarship is not questioning the sincerity, integrity, or holiness of the scholar's life. Second, the contributions of such scholars have been remarkable on any number of fronts. Third, we would not be in a position to reconsider the present situation had such scholars not accomplished the sort of parity described here. Each generation can only stand where it stands and do the work assigned it. To argue the need for a reconsideration is not an expression of disloyalty to our forbears but is the mark of highest loyalty, for it continues their own dedication to critical inquiry.

there was a huge growth in the number of biblical scholars generally and in the size of professional biblical guilds, who increasingly democratized their procedures and encouraged the participation of diverse people and perspectives. Second, there was a shift from seminaries to universities as the locus for serious scholarship on the Bible, so that "academic" increasingly meant departments of religious studies whose main conversation partners were not the church or theology, but other disciplines in the social sciences and humanities.[12]

The third generation is made up of those who grew up in a post-Tridentine church, underwent the cultural change within Catholicism caused by Vatican II when in their 20s, studied theology — or didn't — in a period of upheaval (if not chaos), and, as a matter of course, fulfilled everyone's dream by getting their Ph.D.'s at Harvard, Yale, Chicago, and Vanderbilt, so that they could sit at the table with the best of Protestant and secular scholars and play the game of exegesis as complete equals. This is the generation that is now training still another generation of scholars and, at mid-life and late career, looks around and begins to ask whether the losses have not been as great as the gains. We cheered the progress of our predecessors, and were enormously proud of the parity they achieved and the patrimony they enabled us to inherit. We do not want to deny their accomplishments. But we want to be more aware of the implications of where we now are and be more critical and discerning about the next stage of our journey as scholars in service of the church. We are like the third generation of immigrants who do not want to go back to Italy, but would like to know Grandma's recipe for osso buco.

In a word, this generation of Catholic biblical scholars is far from feeling oppressed by the church — our freedom has been, at least to this point, extraordinary. I should add that freedom is a reality especially for those of us who are lay, or who teach outside of official Catholic institutions. This generation scarcely feels disenfranchised from the biblical guilds: Catholic scholars, indeed, are generously represented in major academic positions, prestigious publishing ventures, and guild

12. This shift is noted in Luke Timothy Johnson, *The Real Jesus: The Misguided Quest for the Historical Jesus and the Truth of the Traditional Gospels* (San Francisco: HarperSanFrancisco, 1996), 67-76; and again by Philip Jenkins, *Hidden Gospels: How the Search for Jesus Lost Its Way* (New York: Oxford University Press, 2001), 148-77.

leadership.[13] The characteristic of this generation is its disillusionment with the brave new world that is now so totally ours. Is this really where we want to be? And if we want to be here, is it in this fashion? Those in the present generation consider themselves in a better position to realize four things that the earlier generations of Catholic scholars, who fought for a foothold in a scholarship dominated by the historical-critical approach and then an ever more complete assimilation into that scholarship, were less able to appreciate. The first is that what is often called a "method" (the "historical-critical method") is instead a model or paradigm for the study of the Bible. It is not simply interested in studying as much history as possible in order to better understand the original voice of the writings. It is instead specifically concerned with historical reconstruction, with an interest in the literary compositions of the Bible mainly as (more or less usable and not uniquely valuable) sources for such reconstruction, whether of ancient Israel, Jesus, or early Christianity.[14]

The second is that this model has promised more than it can deliver and is, in Walter Wink's prescient characterization, "bankrupt."[15] There are actually two aspects of this bankruptcy. The more obvious is that the use of this approach has not in fact led to an agreed-upon historical reconstruction of ancient Israel, of the human mission of Jesus, or of the development of early Christianity. In fact, the opposite is true: the more scholars have pursued these questions, the more elusive such agreement appears. There are on offer today more versions of "the historical Jesus" and of "early Christianity" than are compatible with the perception of

---

13. Most revealing here is the place of Roman Catholic biblical scholars in leading Ph.D. programs usually identified as secular or loosely aligned with Protestant traditions, such as Chicago (Margaret Mitchell), Harvard (Elizabeth Schüssler-Fiorenza), Yale (Harold Attridge, Adela Yarbro Collins, John Collins), and Emory (Luke Johnson), as well as in such traditionally Catholic Ph.D. programs as Catholic University of America, Marquette, and Notre Dame. An earlier mark of parity was the election of Roman Catholics to the presidency of the Society of Biblical Literature: John McKenzie in 1967, Raymond Brown in 1977, Joseph Fitzmyer in 1979, Roland Murphy in 1984, Elizabeth Schüssler-Fiorenza in 1987.

14. See the discussion in Luke Timothy Johnson, *The Writings of the New Testament: An Interpretation,* 2nd ed. (Minneapolis: Fortress, 1999), 1-19 and 621-26.

15. Walter Wink, *The Bible in Human Transformation: Toward a New Paradigm for Biblical Study* (Philadelphia: Fortress, 1973).

history as a scientific discipline. The less obvious aspect of the paradigm's bankruptcy is its incapacity to feed the life of faith in a positive fashion. At the very best, historical reconstruction has provided alternative understandings to those offered by Tradition; at worst, historical reconstruction has been in service of challenging traditional faith.

The third realization is that the historical-critical paradigm is peculiarly hegemonic. It has claimed exclusive right to designate itself as "critical" and scientific, relegating other approaches to Scripture — at least by implication — to the realm of the uncritical or "imaginative." Even those newer academic approaches to the Bible known as the social-scientific and the ideological play within the framework established by the dominant paradigm. In subtle ways, the literal sense of Scripture has come to be more or less identified with the historical sense, and the historical sense has taken on a normative authority. It is not simply that all interpretations must respect the literal sense, a proposition to which all rightly and gladly agree. It is also that the "original" meaning of the text, a meaning that can be determined only by historical exegesis, functions as a limiting control to all other interpretations. In addition to falling short of its own goal, the historical approach has, by asserting scholarly legitimacy for itself alone, inhibited the development of other modes of critical engagement with Scripture.

The fourth realization is that the historical-critical paradigm is not, as advertised, theologically neutral. The model bears within it the specific theological presuppositions, which get spelled out in terms of consistent mental reflexes, of the Protestant form of Christianity from which the model derived.[16] In contrast to the conjunctive "both/and"

---

16. Although the pioneering text-critical work of the Roman Catholic Richard Simon (1638-1712) is sometimes taken as a starting point for the historical-critical approach, together with the biblical studies of the radical Jewish critic Baruch Spinoza (1632-1677), the paradigm took hold most firmly and explicitly within German Protestant universities of the 18th and 19th centuries, and combined "scientific historiography" with specifically Lutheran theological premises. See Luigi Salvatorelli, "From Locke to Reitzenstein: The Historical Investigation of the Origins of Christianity," *HTR* 22 (1929): 263-369; William Baird, *History of New Testament Research*, 1: *From Deism to Tübingen* (Minneapolis: Fortress, 1992); Stephen Neill, *The Interpretation of the New Testament, 1861-1961* (London: Oxford University Press, 1964); Werner Georg Kümmel, *The New Testament: The History of the Investigation of Its Problems*, trans. S. McLean Gilmour and Howard Clark Kee (Nashville: Abingdon, 1972).

that I have suggested expresses the spirit of Catholicism, the Protestant ethos is expressed in terms of the disjunctive, "either/or." The spirit of Protestantism demands a choice for one thing or another, with the clear implication that a choice for is at the same time a choice against. With respect to the interpretation of the Bible, it is clear that the slogan associated with Martin Luther, *Sola Scriptura* ("Scripture alone"), not only asserted the unique authority of the Bible as the guide to Christian life, but at the same time denied the authority of Tradition. For Luther, it was the recovery of the true voice of Scripture that enabled the reform of the corrupt Tradition. The two cannot be in dialectical harmony: one must rule the other, and it must always be Scripture. In similar fashion, the development of Christianity must be regarded as *opposed* to the spirit of its origins. In the same way, the literal sense of Scripture must be *opposed* to figurative interpretations.

A fairly obvious and noncontroversial example of the way in which these presuppositions actually operate in New Testament scholarship is provided by the interpretation of the parables from Adolf Jülicher through Joachim Jeremias to John Dominic Crossan.[17] I use this example both because it reveals the premises and also because it enjoys almost universal approval within scholarship. In parable research, the "historical method" means far more than acquiring historical knowledge about the world of the parables in order better to understand their point. From beginning to end, it has aimed at historical reconstruction. The goal has been to determine the earliest version of a parable and the course of its development. Closely connected to that goal is another: to draw conclusions concerning the "historical" Jesus in contrast to the portrayal of him by the church's Tradition, which in this case begins in the Gospel narratives themselves.

Fundamental to the exercise is the premise that "church tradition" as found already in the Gospels, can and must be distinguished from the original teaching of Jesus. It is either/or. The quest is not for "the parables of the church" as interpreted by figures like Origen and

---

17. Scholarship on the parables is huge. I offer these names as signposts: Adolf Jülicher, *Die Gleichnisreden Jesu,* 2 vols. (Freiburg: Mohr [Siebeck], 1899); C. H. Dodd, *The Parables of the Kingdom* (New York: Scribner, 1961); Joachim Jeremias, *The Parables of Jesus,* trans. S. H. Hooke, rev. ed. (New York: Scribner, 1963); John Dominic Crossan, *In Parables: The Challenge of the Historical Jesus* (New York: Harper and Row, 1973).

Augustine, who read the parables in light of the entire story of salvation in the Bible. Nor is it for "the parables of the Gospels," asking what the parables might mean in the context of the respective evangelical accounts.[18] The search is for the voice or (ideally) words of Jesus *in contrast* to these. For Jeremias in particular, the purportedly literary distinction between a parable (with only one point) and an allegory (with many points) becomes an ironclad criterion for distinguishing Jesus from the Tradition. Not only does Jeremias assume the intrinsic superiority of parable to allegory, but he assumes as well that Jesus could have used only one of these literary forms. It follows that the teaching of Jesus (as discovered through such historical excavation) is also superior to the teaching of the church, *even within the Gospels themselves*.[19] For Jeremias, the church betrays Jesus' message through allegory. Allegory in the Gospels is already the first step in a disastrous history of interpretation from which history alone can rescue readers. Parable versus allegory stands as a template for Jesus versus the Tradition of the church. History is the instrument of the either/or that separates the authentic from the counterfeit, the original from the copy, the pristine primitive from the corrupted development. Notice in this the assumption — in itself thoroughly mythic — that earlier is better than later, that chronology also corresponds to worth. Because history alone can accomplish such discrimination, it alone is criticism's legitimate instrument, and the historian is, in effect, the most genuine of reformers.[20]

I will return to the connection between the historical-critical para-

18. This approach to the parables has been characteristic of some contemporary Catholic scholars; see Madeleine L. Boucher, *The Mysterious Parable: A Literary Study.* CBQMS 6 (Washington: Catholic Biblical Association, 1977); John R. Donahue, *The Gospel in Parable: Metaphor, Narrative, and Theology in the Synoptic Gospels* (Philadelphia: Fortress, 1988); Luke Timothy Johnson, "The Lukan Kingship Parable (Lk. 19:11-27)," *Novum Testamentum* 24 (1982): 139-59.

19. See Jeremias, *The Parables of Jesus,* 48-114, esp. the conclusions on 113-14.

20. A fine example is provided by that most scientific of historians, F. C. Baur: ". . . the essential nature of Christianity is a purely historical question, whose solution lies only in that past in which Christianity itself had its origin; it is a problem which can only be solved by that critical attitude of thought which the consciousness of the present age assumes toward the past"; *Paul, the Apostle of Jesus Christ, His Life and Work, His Epistles and His Doctrine: A Contribution to the History of Primitive Christianity,* 1st ed., 1845; 2nd ed., ed. E. Zeller, trans. A. Menzies (London: Williams and Norgate, 1875), 2.

digm and Protestant theological premises later in this chapter, and in other chapters, because it is a complex subject that must be approached from several angles. Before moving ahead, however, it is important to clarify exactly what I intend by my contrast between the spirit of Catholicism and the spirit of Protestantism, and what I don't intend.

I certainly do not mean to suggest that the historical paradigm has not yielded great benefits for the interpretation of Scripture. Because of a sedulous pursuit of history, we know infinitely more about the world of Scripture than any generation prior to us. It would be ungrateful and even stupid to ignore such a wealth of knowledge. Moving forward does not mean reverting backward. The doing of history must remain a permanent aspect of biblical study. I would, however, make what I think is an important distinction between learning history in order to better understand the compositions of the Bible and dismantling the compositions of the Bible in pursuit of a (usually chimerical) historical reconstruction. The first remains an essential and valuable part of Scripture scholarship. The second is a mistaken detour that has, regrettably, characterized the past 200 years.

Nor do I mean to suggest that the either/or has not made a profound theological contribution. It did, after all, generate the Reformation! And because the church always stands in need of reformation, the either/or can always function as a sharper version of the Catholic both/and, and should be heard by Catholics. By addressing Catholic scholars and asking "what's Catholic?" I am not calling for a retrenchment or spirit of triumphalism, nor opposing the ecumenical spirit which has enabled Catholic and Protestant scholars to work together and join in the fellowship of biblical guilds. I am suggesting, rather, that ecumenism is best served when denominational and theological traditions speak to each other from within their deeply held commitments, rather than when they ignore or suppress those commitments for the sake of a false communion. I suggest, further, that the most authentic ecumenism is found in the willingness of each tradition both to affirm the validity of the other tradition's gift (while being open to receiving its benefit) and celebrating the value of its own gift (and being willing to share it). Calling Catholic scholars to consider their relationship to the Catholic tradition is in service to such an authentic ecumenism. One of the paradoxes of the present scholarly situation, indeed, is that at the very moment that many Protestant scholars, themselves aware of the limitations of the historical-critical paradigm, are looking to their Catholic colleagues for an alternative vision, Catholic scholars are in danger of forgetting the distinctive charism that is theirs to share with fellow believers.

In this spirit, I propose that what is distinctively "catholic" about Catholic biblical interpretation (scholarship) is to be found in its instinct for the both/and, and in its conviction that critical scholarship is not merely a matter of separating and opposing, but also of testing and reconnecting. I begin by sketching some of the ways a Catholic perspective might come into play and make a difference historiographically, theologically, and literarily.

Historiographical Perspectives

The either/or premise has dominated the study both of ancient Israel and of Christian origins. The historical study of the ancient Near East has revealed countless ways in which Israel shared culturally with its neighbors. Yet despite all the signs of similarity and even influence, the critical issue has frequently been posed in terms of how the religion of Israel (at least) was different from the circumambient cultures. The perspective has been even more obvious in the study of Christian origins, not least in the assumption that "origins" is itself of particular importance. Here again, the dominant tendency has been to show how New Testament Christianity stands apart from what precedes it as well as what follows it. More than that: the New Testament must also stand *against* what precedes and follows it. Of critical importance are the ways in which earliest (or primitive) Christianity is *distinct* from Judaism and Greco-Roman culture.

Concern for differentiation is at least understandable when the task is detecting new growth among older foliage. But what is the motivation when the subject is that new growth's maturation? Why would a botanist insist that the acorn, not the oak, is the point of perfection? Every study of natural or human development assumes just the opposite: that the developed form of a species is the more perfect specimen. Why, then, is so much New Testament scholarship so sharply separated, not only from the first part of Scripture (the Old Testament), but also from the second and subsequent centuries of Christianity?

Clearly, deep theological commitments are at work. Jonathan Z. Smith has shown brilliantly how the study of Christian origins has been shaped by Protestant — especially Lutheran — theological premises. Christianity's development into Catholicism is inevitably viewed in terms of a decline or the corruption of the pure gospel by a recrudescence of Jewish influence (through law and structure) and pagan culture (in the sacraments).[21]

A commitment to the notion of an original and pure good news, a moment of revelation so uniquely untouched by human influence that it is self-evidently divine, is, I must repeat, not a principle of history. It is simply a theological commitment. And it is a commitment that has generated a substantial portion of the scholarship that has been called, paradoxically, "historical-critical." It is this commitment that requires not only the isolation of the New Testament from its environment, but also the purging of the dross from the New Testament compositions themselves:[22] thus, the impulse to find "the historical Jesus," not as a human person of the past who is as complex and ultimately unknowable as any other historical person about whom we have partial and imperfect records, but as a fixed source of the good news — even if it turns out to be a bit trivial — untouched by the corruptions of church Tradition.[23] And to accomplish this historical-reconstruction-as-

21. See the sharp critique of such Protestant presuppositions in Jonathan Z. Smith, *Drudgery Divine: On the Comparison of Early Christianities and the Religions of Late Antiquity.* Chicago Studies in the History of Judaism (Chicago: University of Chicago Press, 1990), 1-35, 114-15. For a classic example of this picture of development, see Hans von Campenhausen: "In the course of these three centuries the ideal to which Christianity had originally been committed was impaired in various ways: not only do we find rigidities of attitude, curtailment of aspiration, distortion of insight, but also in every department — an indisputable trivialization" (!); *Ecclesiastical Authority and Spiritual Power in the Church of the First Three Centuries,* trans. J. A. Baker (Stanford: Stanford University Press, 1969), 3.

22. In *The Gospel and the Church,* trans. Christopher Home (London: Isbister, 1903), Alfred Loisy brilliantly identifies the theological tendentiousness of Adolf von Harnack's attempt to extract the "kernel" of essential Christianity from its historical "husk" by means of the historical method, in his *What Is Christianity?* trans. Thomas Bailey Saunders (London: Williams and Norgate, 1901).

23. Perhaps the best (because least camouflaged) example is provided by Robert W. Funk, *Honest to Jesus: Jesus for a New Millennium* (San Francisco: HarperSanFrancisco, 1996), esp. 297-314.

theological-project, the compositions of the New Testament themselves are variously suppressed, harmonized, or subjected to salvage operations:[24] thus also (using the same sort of criteria) the need to distinguish the authentic Paul from the inauthentic Paul, so that the sacred moment of Christian origins can be distinguished from the corruption of a profane development.[25] The bias is always in favor of either/or rather than both/and. Scholars do not show the ways in which the sayings of Jesus gain clarity and depth of meaning through the process of their transmission, but only how they are obscured and trivialized. Scholars do not show how Paul's perceptions are perhaps deepened by the Letter to the Ephesians, but only how they are flattened. And when it comes to the non-Pauline portion of the canon, the case is worse. Hebrews, 1 Peter, 2 Peter, James, and the Pastorals are all lumped together in a category called (revealingly) "early Catholicism," and are read only to be dismissed, since their very placement in history already determines their meaning, and that meaning, since they are later, must be a decline from the moment of origins.[26]

Real history (and responsible historiography), however, always works in terms of both/and. History certainly sees new developments, in religion as in other cultural forms. But every historical origin bears within itself, and passes on, elements of what preceded and helped shape it. To fixate only on distinctive moments of origin is to be driven by theological rather than historical principles, and theological principles specifically connected to the Protestant Reformation. Responsible historiography, I submit, concerns itself with all the ways in which the old and new intermingle. If history does offer lessons, one of them might be the inevitability of such admixture.

Despite the recent renewal of the search for the historical Jesus — the classic example of theology driving history past its competence — it is possible to detect encouraging signs that the defensive either/or posture of so much Christian investigation of early Christianity is being

24. See Johnson, *The Real Jesus*, 1-56.

25. The similarity of the methods used for the Gospels and for Paul is pointed out in Luke Timothy Johnson, "The Search for (the Wrong) Jesus," *BRev* 11/6 (1995): 20-25, 44. For a full discussion of the dissection of the Pauline corpus, see Johnson, *The First and Second Letters to Timothy*. AB 35A (New York: Doubleday, 2001), 19-90.

26. See, e.g., Rudolf Bultmann, *Theology of the New Testament*, trans. Kendrick Grobel, 2 (New York: Scribner, 1955), 95-118.

modified in the direction of a healthier both/and sensibility. Recent study of the Jewish context of early Christianity has rejected the reflex anti-Semitism that characterized so many standard works of New Testament scholarship,[27] and has moved toward a more nuanced — that is, a more appropriately historiographical — appreciation of the New Testament as a complex and powerful midrash on Torah analogous to other contemporaneous Jewish expressions driven by other powerful religious experiences.[28] From the Greco-Roman side, there is growing recognition of the ways in which the New Testament is thoroughly at home in the rhetoric and moral teaching of the Greco-Roman world, though a similar recognition of the influence of Greco-Roman religious impulses and practices is still mostly resisted.[29]

Roman Catholic biblical scholarship has been and should be at the front of such nonapologetic and thoroughly historical appreciations of the world that shaped early Christianity. Catholics above all have no theological motivation for suppressing such influences. The Catholic intellectual tradition owes far more to Irenaeus and Justin (and the ways in which they point to an inclusive vision) than it does to Marcion and Tatian (who identified the truth of Christianity with its exclusiveness). The truth of Christianity does not require the denial of truth and beauty everywhere else. Catholics celebrate God's capacity for self-disclosure both to Jews and pagans. Such traces of God's revelation are the surest pledge that God is also capable of revealing Godself to Christians. The affirmation of *both* continuity *and* distinctiveness (not the same as uniqueness, please note) is congenial to Catholic historiographical and theological instincts.

The same capaciousness of vision should enable Catholic Scripture scholars to embrace church history. The isolation of the New Testament from subsequent Christian life and literature makes as little sense as a botanist's neglect of oaks in favor of acorns. From a Catholic

27. See Charlotte Klein, *Anti-Judaism in Christian Theology,* trans. Edward Quinn (Philadelphia: Fortress, 1978).

28. See the discussion in Johnson, *The Writings of the New Testament,* 10-16, 608-13; as well as *Scripture and Discernment: Decision-Making in the Church* (Nashville: Abingdon, 1996).

29. For discussion and bibliography on this point, see Luke Timothy Johnson, *Religious Experience in Earliest Christianity: A Missing Dimension in New Testament Studies* (Minneapolis: Fortress, 1998), 1-37.

perspective, there is no reason to regard Christianity's development into the patristic period as either decline or corruption. There is every reason to regard it as an organic growth out of the same complex components of culture and religious experience that generated the New Testament itself, and therefore deserving of the same attention. Catholics should be concerned not only with the world that produced the New Testament but as well with the world that the New Testament itself produced.

What would the practical manifestations of such an enlarged vision be? At the very least dissertations and commentaries on the New Testament ought to include the entire history of interpretation in their *Forschungsberichte,* which now usually begin at best with the 19th century. This inclusion might balance the mythic view of the history of interpretation that treats everything written before the Enlightenment as unworthy of serious consideration by "critical" scholars. But such a view is based primarily on the premise that the recovery of origins is the point of historical scholarship. If this is perceived as a theological rather than as a properly historical principle, then the way is open to a wider view of the history of interpretation. The view is also based partly on ignorance of the earlier tradition. Anyone who has worked seriously with patristic and medieval scriptural interpretation knows that it cannot simply be dismissed as aberrant. Even at the level of the *sensus literalis,* the Venerable Bede offers at least as much insight as the average recent commentary.

An even more basic enlargement of vision is desirable. Just as text criticism of the New Testament becomes astonishingly more interesting once it shifts from trying only to establish the original text — as receding an ideal as finding the historical Jesus — and analyzes variants and versions as a form of *Receptionsgeschichte* ("history of reception/interpretation"), so that variants are perceived not as regrettable errors but also as sometimes impressive interpretations, so can the study of the New Testament compositions be enlivened when attention shifts from getting origins right to engaging the myriad ways in which these compositions were actualized in the life and literature of the church.

Why should scholars trained in the discipline of New Testament pay attention to this subsequent history rather than leave it up to colleagues in other fields? Besides the always attractive value of transcending disciplinary turf-boundaries, there are two excellent reasons for

New Testament scholars to work in this area rather than simply converse with patristic and medieval scholars. One is that those who are trained in the 1st-century milieu are in an ideal position to establish a conversation between the New Testament text and its appropriations in a manner that patristic and medieval interpreters themselves did not. Another is that New Testament scholars can discover from how a text has actually been understood how it also *can* be understood, and therefore also might have been understood, not only by 4th-century commentators, but as well by Paul and James and Peter and their first readers. Such insight can occur especially when the later writers are using the same Koine Greek as used by the New Testament itself.

Theological Commitments

The same either/or perspective that pits Scripture against Tradition has had the effect of positioning critical biblical scholarship against the church. The historical-critical paradigm's internal myth has consistently been told in terms of a struggle for free inquiry against the constraints of church tradition. This was the Enlightenment's refinement of the basic Protestant either/or. The Reformation challenged the Catholic myth ("this is the way things have always been") by an appeal to origins ("this is not the way things were in the time of sacred beginnings"). The Reformation, in a word, used one theology of history to displace another. The Enlightenment, however, especially as found among British Deists of the 18th century and German Lutherans of the 19th century who learned their criticism from them, turned the same instrument of history against every form of tradition, including Protestantism's own. The instrument of critical inquiry (and therefore the freedom of the scholar) was exclusively scientific history. The choice was thought to be clear: on one side there were dogma, law, sacraments, and miracles; on the other side there was free and critical inquiry as found in the historical method.

The 19th-century German scholarship that so attracted Alfred Loisy posited the either/or so explicitly that we can scarcely wonder at the Roman Catholic hierarchy's resistance to such perspectives. It was no slander to say that biblical critics might erode the miraculous dimension of faith — that was their express and often repeated goal! The social and ideological implications of this either/or could not, however, come fully to light so long as biblical scholarship remained at least nominally Christian and operated within an academic setting that was officially theological. When at the beginning of the 20th century the deans of the great American Protestant divinity schools sponsored German "Higher Criticism," they thought of themselves as reformers of the church, not as destroyers. It is only when the logic of this either/or took institutional form in the development of religious studies departments in secular universities that the implications for the church of a biblical scholarship removed from the life of the church (and synagogue) could begin to be assessed.

In hindsight, Roman resistance to history is understandable, even though we are also able to see the elements of political self-interest that complicated Rome's response. Although the Vatican's resistance was excessive and its methods of repression surely wrong by any measure, we can also see that its instincts were not entirely wrong. We can see all around us the consequences of a biblical scholarship that is more and more independent of a theological commitment to the church. It has not been uncommon in college or even seminary classes introducing students to the New Testament that the professor begins with the demand that students forget the way they have understood the Bible within the practices of the church. Students are asked to adopt a new set of dogmas concerning the writings of the New Testament, now not those dictated by a faith community (inspiration/authority) but those dictated by academic authority (dating/authorship). Students do not reach these positions by means of reason but by means of a changed allegiance. At least for the purposes of passing the course, the dogmas of Criticism are accepted in preference to the dogmas of Church. It has also happened that a New Testament scholar who has reached an opinion that happens to agree with church tradition is regarded by other scholars as lacking in critical intelligence or independence, as being an "apologist" for the faith.

The current battle within religious studies departments in the United States concerning the legitimacy of including theology as a part of the scientific study of religion[30] represents the logical end-point of

30. See the revealing article by Charlotte Allen, "Is Nothing Sacred? Casting Out the Gods from Religious Studies," *Lingua Franca* 6/1 (1996): 30-40.

the struggle between the church and critical scholarship that has been played out surreptitiously in seminaries and schools of theology over the past 150 years. The sharpness of the present debate is helpful because it clarifies the issues for both university and church. I mentioned earlier that the 1960s saw a major sociological shift: most advanced study in the Bible now takes place in academies that owe little or no allegiance to a faith community. In such academies, theology is either interdicted, or generic, or a minor partner to biblical studies. Advancement in the academic profession does not result from service to the church but from research published for other scholars. That research is increasingly shaped by the changed conversation, in which biblical scholars interact with ancient historians, literary critics, and a variety of social scientists.[31]

In short, the study of the Bible (not understood as "Scripture") is increasingly an academic activity that is removed from the existential concerns of communities of faith and responsive instead to the expectations of a profession that is not merely secular but often actively antireligious in character. The impact on the church is already felt in two ways. First, more and more seminary professors of Old Testament and New Testament are lay rather than clerical, are lacking in theological background, and are shaped by the academic expectations of the biblical guild: their loyalty and ambition is not directed to the church but to the profession. They are not well prepared to teach Scripture for the life of the church. Second, the writing of such scholars is less turned to the life of the church than it was even in the "second-generation." The ever-increasing demands of publication of a scientific sort in order to achieve tenure and promotion (critical if the scholar is a married layperson rather than a celibate religious) shifts the focus of energy into research that has little to do with transforming lives of Christians. Although like the Latin-reading clergy of old, then, the new academics enjoy a rich intellectual life centered in the Bible, the benefits to the vast lay population of the church is scarcely discernible.

31. A harbinger of this development is Patrick Henry's *New Directions in New Testament Study* (Philadelphia: Westminster, 1979), in which every approach except the theological is entertained, and the shift to a secular academic setting is conscious and deliberate.

What the partial divorce between the academy and the church has also revealed is the fallacy of the claim made for the historical-critical paradigm that it was objective and value-free. The reading of texts is always in substantial measure shaped by the premises and practices of a specific reading community.[32] No scholarship, and certainly no exegesis, is utterly disinterested. All scholarship, and certainly all biblical scholarship, is both socially located and ideologically committed. Two important consequences follow. One is the necessity of scholars to know and declare their loyalties. Now, everyone has multiple and mixed loyalties — thus it is all the more important to make the effort to identify and rank them! Another is the importance of expanding the concept of critical inquiry beyond the narrow understanding of "historical-critical." Catholic scholars today are well positioned to take up these challenges and offer leadership to their colleagues.

First, then, it is necessary to affirm the both/and of loyalty to the Tradition and criticism. Loyalty to the church's teaching and practices is no more incompatible with the free exercise of the mind than is loyalty to the norms of the academy. Loyalty is not the opposite of criticism but its condition. Loyalty (or faith) does not demand the sacrifice of the intellect to be genuine, nor does it demand the mind's assent to any one rendering (even one purportedly authoritative rendering) of the Tradition. But it does demand the affirmation of that Tradition as the starting point of any inquiry. It does require the most careful attention to authoritative renderings of that tradition. And it does ask that the task of criticism take place within the conversation of the community for whom the Tradition has deep and existential importance. Finally, it does ask that the critic participate in the Tradition's embodied practices. The advantage for Catholic scholars on this point is that, despite the alarms and confusions of recent decades, the Catholic tradition remains sufficiently coherent to command such loyalty. Criticism still has something to address, and does not yet have to bear the burden of replacing a living tradition. The distinctive challenge to Catholic scholars is to claim the honorable place of loyal criticism and even dissent within the large Catholic tradition, even in the face of

32. A witty statement of the principle is Stanley Hauerwas' essay, "Stanley Fish, the Pope, and the Bible," in *Unleashing the Scripture: Freeing the Bible from Captivity to America* (Nashville: Abingdon, 1993), 19-28.

those who — in the name of that same tradition — seek to suppress all diversity, and who equate loyalty with uniformity.

Second, Catholic scholars need to rediscover dimensions of critical inquiry broader than the historical. I use the term "rediscover" advisedly. The Catholic intellectual tradition has never utterly capitulated to the epistemological monism of the Enlightenment, which declared out of bounds any cognition that was not empirically verifiable (in the present, through scientific testing and replication; in the past, through historical criticism). Catholicism has continued to hold that criticism has philosophical, theological, moral, and aesthetic dimensions that are at least as legitimate and important as the historical. To include a broader array of criticisms is not to exclude the historical, but it is to limit its claims and uses. The historical moment does not exhaust the process of criticism. Historical determinations (even if we should agree on them) have no normative value on their own. Historical knowledge plays a limited role within a complex conversation enacted by a faith community. History is only one voice in the process of faith discernment that demands multiple critical perspectives. In a healthy state of affairs, the Scripture scholar's loyalty to the text allows (and demands) the most searching inquiry into both the positive and negative dimensions of a passage, and at the same time, the Catholic scholar's loyalty to the church allows (and demands) the most honest and persistent questioning of its own ethics of reading as well as the practices attached to such interpretation.

I return to the liturgy as an example. Let us agree that historical studies, including the historical study of Scripture, played a significant role in the renewal of the liturgy realized after Vatican II. But the study of liturgical origins and development, the recovery of ancient alternatives for anaphoras, and even the providing of a new translation of the Bible for use in the lectionary, do not exhaust the possibilities for critical conversation between Catholic Scripture scholars and the liturgical practices of the church. It is entirely appropriate, indeed, imperative, for New Testament scholars to continue to challenge the aesthetic, theological, and liturgical adequacy of translations. It is important for them to engage critically the selection, arrangement, and — a very troubling topic — editing of biblical passages in lectionaries. It is appropriate for them to recover better models for biblical preaching than presently seem available, and to interpret Scripture through commentaries in ways that are translatable to the act of preaching. Finally, it falls within the responsibility of Scripture scholars to join debates concerning the ways in which the liturgical employment of texts shapes Christian consciousness: is the best we can do with the hard texts of the New Testament to cut them out of lectionaries so they are not heard?

As for the liturgy, so for other ecclesial practices: decision-making in the church, catechesis, spirituality, morality. How does Scripture speak to the transformation of consciousness according to the mind of Christ? How does it challenge contemporary individualism and consumerism by its call to a communal consciousness and a radical sharing of possessions? How does Scripture challenge the supremacy of the social and political order by the announcement of God's Rule over the world? I do not suggest that these contexts should exclusively occupy every Catholic Scripture scholar all the time — mine is a plea for both/ and, after all — but I do suggest that Scripture scholars cannot excuse themselves from such engagement, and that the absence of such critical engagement by Scripture scholars is good neither for themselves nor for the church.

To put these two challenges together: Catholic scholars have the opportunity to reverse the present odd situation, in which academics now occupy the former privileged position of the clergy, and enliven both their vocations and the life of the church. They can do this by bringing both the deepest loyalty and the deepest intelligence to the task of interpreting Scripture. And they can do this by engaging Scripture critically in a variety of ways that matter to the practices of the believing community.

Literary Imagination

One of the more bizarre manifestations of the either/or impulse has been the literary dismemberment of the Bible. In the name of history, compositions have been chopped into sources. Sources, in turn, have been sliced into ever finer layers of redaction and placed on slides. Then, like some home laboratory experiment in cloning, these textual tissue samples are used to reconstruct the putative histories of hypothetical communities. Not only is a hypothetical source named Q, but Q is sliced into the layers Q1 and Q2 and Q3, which then are thought to yield the history of the "Q community."[33] To find the history of the Corinthian community, Paul's letters to that church are broken into as many as six sources. The course of the "Philippian controversy" is thought to be traceable once Paul's letter to the Philippians is broken into three sources which can then be arranged in sequence.[34] Small wonder if the casual reader of commentaries concludes that biblical studies has little to do with the actual Bible.

The passion for savaging and then scavenging sources has, blessedly, waned a bit. Engagement with contemporary literary criticism and with ancient rhetoric has helped scholars regain some sense of the biblical compositions in their literary integrity. It is surely a sign of sanity to hear discussions about "the voice" of biblical compositions and the need to hear "the diverse voices" of canonical writings, even if such conversations have not yet made significant progress toward the renewal of a theological reading of these compositions.[35]At least in some circles, particularly in America, it is again possible to discuss the literal meaning of the text with the shared perception that such meaning is to be found within a consideration of a composition's literary integrity and literary form.

Having been in the forefront of that stage of recuperation,[36] perhaps Catholic scholars are sufficiently healthy to consider another look at their own right tradition of polyvalent interpretation. In a final application of the both/and perspective, I suggest that Catholic scholars ought to embrace both the literal sense of Scripture and figurative senses.

The obsession with a single, historically-fixed, objectively determined, textual meaning is a direct expression of the either/or principle called *Sola Scriptura* ("Scripture alone"). If the biblical texts alone secure identity, then they must contain one meaning that is universally accessible. The stakes are even higher when Scripture is set against Tradi-

33. The egregious example is Burton Mack, *The Lost Gospel: The Book of Q and Christian Origins* (San Francisco: HarperSanFrancisco, 1993).

34. For discussion of such theories, see Johnson, *The Writings of the New Testament,* 312-24, 369-81.

35. I discuss the complications for theology presented by literary readings of the New Testament in *Scripture and Discernment,* 45-58.

36. Credit must be given to the efforts of Luis Alonso Schökel to link literary and theological sensibilities, in such works as *The Inspired Word.*

tion. Historical exegesis is needed to secure the "truth of the Gospel." Catholicism, in contrast, valorizes Tradition in all of its richness as the context for identity. Sacraments, sacramentals, spiritualities, laws, customs — all regarded as consonant with Scripture even when not arising directly from it — shape Catholic identity together with Scripture. Although its role is a privileged one, Scripture is not the only mediator of Catholic identity.

In this respect, Luther was surely right when he saw Catholicism as closer to Judaism than to Protestantism. An observant Jewish community is structured by *halakah*. So is Catholicism. Jewish scholars are freed by the strong identity-formation accomplished by *halakah* to engage Torah *haggadically*, that is, not only as a collection of rules but above all as a source of wisdom. So are Catholic biblical scholars free to engage Scripture in a variety of imaginative ways as a source of transforming wisdom. Jewish scholars would not allow the legitimacy of a choice between *halakah* and *haggadah*, for these modes of interpretation are both mutually dependent and serve distinct functions. So also a Catholic scholar ought to resist the choice between either the literal sense or the allegorical, for the Catholic scholar also recognizes that these modes of reading are both interdependent and serve distinct functions.

The literal sense of the text remains always of supreme importance for the life and practice of the church, and historical study remains always pertinent to the analysis of the literal sense, establishing its range of possible meanings, locating its sense within the grammar, rhetoric, and social circumstances of each composition. But such historical analysis does not even constrain completely the literal sense. Even at this level, we have learned how illusory is the quest for a single "right" reading. We recognize how polyvalence is unavoidable even with the literal sense, because of the multiple perspectives of readers and the diverse kinds of questions they put to the text.[37] We have come to appreciate that exegesis can determine some "bad" or "wrong" readings — those that clearly cannot be supported by the text — but can also give rise to an indeterminate number of "responsible" and "good" readings.

37. Some direction concerning the pertinence of personal story and social location for interpretation is given by Brian K. Blount, *Cultural Interpretation: Reorienting New Testament Criticism* (Minneapolis: Fortress, 1995); and Fernando F. Segovia and Mary Ann Tolbert, eds., *Reading from This Place*, 2 vols. (Minneapolis: Fortress, 1995).

We properly look, then, not for a single right reading that is locked in the past, but for a variety of good readings that are responsible both to the text and to the community of other readers. Understood as the most publicly available meaning, the literal sense thus serves as the indispensable basis for discernment and decision-making in the church (its *halakah*). Historical criticism here retains its role as maintaining the "otherness" of the text against all efforts at manipulation or suppression by the Tradition.[38]

By no means every reading of the text within the church, however, is for the purpose of deciding *halakah*. Much reading is for wisdom and delight, for the transformation of the mind and the conversion of the heart. In such reading, both communities and individuals can enter into the imaginative world constructed, not simply by this composition or that, but by all the voices of Scripture, and all the voices of faith that have also lived before us in the world imagined by the Bible. Allegory and typology may no longer be to our taste — although we would be foolish, even as critical scholars, to deny that we might have something to learn from them. It is legitimate to ask, for example, whether some of the purposeful playfulness found in some postmodernist readings of Scripture might not rightly claim a share in the noble heritage of allegory. Perhaps the path before us is to explore more deeply some of the root metaphors of Scripture that help create a world in which we can live as creatures shaped in the image of God. How we might discover and celebrate Scripture's prolific capacity to create meanings is a task that lies before us. But it is surely a Catholic sensibility to affirm both the enduring importance of the literal sense and the life-enhancing poetry of the figurative.

The Way Forward

My "third-generation" perception of the state of Catholic biblical scholarship in the United States combines elements of discouragement

---

38. Sandra M. Schneiders, *The Revelatory Text: Interpreting the New Testament as Sacred Scripture* (San Francisco: Harper Collins, 1991), is particularly helpful in showing the limits to the historical method for serious theological engagement with the world of the text.

and hope. I sense that a too-eager assimilation to the dominant histori-cal-critical paradigm has brought with it some unfortunate corollaries of the Protestant ethos of either/or and a weakening of the distinctive Catholic instinct for the both/and. I have a strong sense of urgency, precisely as a third-generation scholar who is involved in the education of another generation, because I think that what we are in danger of losing altogether is even more precious than what we have gained. As I have said repeatedly, I am far from questioning the value of historical studies for the interpretation of the Bible. But I am convinced that we need to find a way forward that enables us to share the distinctive Catholic gift for the both/and with our Protestant colleagues who are themselves searching for it. The present moment therefore also con-tains hope, for it is a moment in which the possibility for change and renewal is still available. But the time is short. And the future is not one to be charted by any one person or any single committee. It will require the best efforts of this and the next generation.

Two aspects of this conversion are political and pedagogical. I am convinced that they are central to any real effort, but although I am working on them in my own life and teaching, I will not expand on them in practical terms in my portion of this book. The first is the turning of Catholic scholars themselves toward the life of the church in their scholarship. This will require deliberate and decisive will, for there is nothing in the life of the contemporary university that encour-ages such commitment, and little in the contemporary church that in-vites such participation by the scholar. I mean of course writing for the church. But I also mean deeper and broader levels of participation. The second is the shaping of a pedagogy within the church that will em-power a lay readership of the Bible that is capable and responsible, and can provide the sort of rich soil out of which future Catholic scholars can arise. Such pedagogy requires work. It is one of the tasks to which scholars dedicated to the future of the faith community can give them-selves.

Two other aspects of this conversion are more properly conceptual, and I will develop them in the chapters that follow this opening state-ment. A major and difficult task is opening up a conversation that has been shut down for too long, namely the conversation between so-called precritical and critical scholarship, or, to use more appropriate terms, between premodern biblical scholarship and that of modernity.

33

The next three chapters of the book are dedicated to this task. A second and even more daunting challenge — though not unrelated to the first — is recovering a sense of how Scripture might play a role in theology. The last chapter of this part of the book addresses the question of how to imagine the world that the Scripture imagines.

There are other aspects that I have not dealt with, or even thought about. But I am convinced that there is urgency to the task, that it requires the best efforts of this generation, and that it will require both commitment and much more creative conversation.

CHAPTER TWO

Rejoining a Long Conversation

For Catholic biblical scholarship to recover something of its distinctive identity, it is necessary to move forward by engaging a more distant past, when Scripture was interpreted by people at least as intelligent as contemporary scholars, often as learned, and frequently holier. This long history of interpretation is part of our story; ignorance of it is an impoverishment of our present. In this chapter I suggest some reasons why rejoining a longer conversation concerning Scripture can help show us a way toward the future.

The past is not literally a place to which we can travel. But through imagination and decent historical knowledge, we can hear voices from the past still speaking through literary compositions from long ago and far away. Hearing those voices, we can also speak, if not directly to the ancient writers, at least to each other about them. And we can join those ancient authors in speaking about the texts of Scripture that both they and we are reading. To some extent, then, through the same activity that carries the old writings into our present mental world, our imagination can carry us from the present time and place back to an earlier place and time. Our imagination is helped by our sharing so much with the ancient interpreters. They were as convinced as we are that their lives were defined by the life, death, and resurrection of the Lord Jesus, were committed as we are to the Sacred Scripture as a revelatory text that spoke truly to them about this Lord Jesus, enacted these convictions (as I hope we do) through participation in the liturgy and the practices of piety, and spent even more time and energy than we do (I would wager) interpreting the Scripture. Because they are ancient and foreign, their voices may strike us as strange, but because they are deeply Christian, they should also strike our ears with a strange familiarity.

Rejoining a conversation that has long been abandoned requires hard historical labor and theological imagination. It is not easy or automatic. The point is not an easy nostalgia about the good old days (there is much in ancient interpretation that is unattractive) nor a simple imitation of perfect models (there is much in ancient interpretation that is inadequate). The point, rather, is a critical engagement that can enrich the present and enable a future. We need a good reason to do this. It is not only a demanding task, it also goes against the grain of the present ethos of scholarship, which has made the model of science its own. In science, knowledge progresses incrementally. Newer knowledge is always superior to older. To plausibly engage the literature of the distant past, we need another understanding of biblical interpretation, one that does not deny its character as *scientia* (science/knowledge) but places even more emphasis on its character as *sapientia* (wisdom).

Seeking a conversation about Scripture as wisdom means declaring dissatisfaction with the present understanding of it simply in terms of science. To put it as boldly as possible, we need to learn from the past because our own way of doing business is in bad shape. The way we have been doing things for the past several hundred years seems to have brought us to a dead end. And we don't know how to move forward. Our desire to learn something about and from the past, then, is intimately connected to the present crisis in biblical scholarship. It is not a crisis solely for Catholic Scripture scholars, but it is one that was reaching a climax precisely in those years when, freed by Pius XII to join the critical methods of the 20th century, Catholics eagerly sought assimilation into a profession dominated by Protestant scholars and (as I tried to demonstrate in the previous chapter) Protestant theological premises. Since Catholics have so wholeheartedly embraced the dominant ethos, therefore, it is also now very much a crisis for Catholic scholars as well.

The Present Crisis in Biblical Scholarship

Some will contend that my analysis of the situation is entirely wrong, or shaded much too negatively. And considerable evidence supports the position that, in many respects, biblical scholarship flourishes. There are undoubtedly more people with Ph.D.'s in Bible today than throughout all of previous history. They bristle with languages and lore. They are capable of exegeting an ancient scroll or a flinty inscription before breakfast. National and international societies dedicated to biblical scholarship gather in major cities for conferences that host thousands of participants and feature hundreds of presentations, discussions, and expense-account lunches. These armies of scholars produce prodigious amounts of research and publication. The past century has been one of unprecedented and exciting growth in sheer knowledge about the world of the Bible. Archaeological discoveries have opened entire libraries to contemporary analysis. Because of the pace of discovery, editing, translating, and publishing, more sheer information about antiquity is now available to the average college sophomore than was available even to the greatest scholar a mere 80 years ago. At the level of sheer *scientia,* things have never been so good.

So much is written, however, that no one scholar today can possibly read everything, or even everything important. The volume of production is overwhelming the capacity of scholars to absorb or even observe it all. As a direct result, biblical scholarship is increasingly divided and subdivided into specialties. Old and New Testament scholarship have for some time faced in different directions and encompassed quite different sorts of conversation partners.[1] Within the testaments, moreover, specializations become ever smaller and more arcane. As in medicine some doctors deal only with tibias, so some biblical scholars command all there is to know about Philemon or Daniel but will not venture beyond the safe boundaries of that expertise.

The sheer amount of scholarship is therefore part of the crisis. There is much product, indeed much admirable product, but is there any point to the production? The present generation approaches the

---

1. A small but scarcely irrelevant bit of evidence is that virtually all my examples are drawn from New Testament scholarship. I simply do not know the contemporary literature in Old Testament well enough to assess it.

state of *idiots savants*, people who know everything about some small aspect of the Bible, but nothing about the Bible as a whole, or its good and destructive uses. Not only is it increasingly difficult to find a professionally identified biblical scholar capable of engaging theological issues with any sophistication, much less creativity, it is hard even to locate a biblical scholar today who is truly a scholar of the entire Bible. The question therefore presses for answer: is there any real conversation among scholars, or is there only a self-generating machine of publication and review? It's not only volume, it's also tone. Conventions of biblical scholars reveal the less admirable dynamics of academic competition. Scholars posture and score recognition points, reminding everyone that much research is produced (and written in a style) to impress tenure and promotion committees within universities. There is reason to worry that biblical scholarship in the university is primarily shaped in service to a professional academic career.

The word university points us to a second aspect of the present crisis, which is the sociological shift of such scholarship from the church to the academy. As I mentioned in the previous chapter, this shift was a long time coming, but is now complete. The secular academy is now the dominant place where scholarship on the Bible is carried out, and it increasingly sets the rules for the game. The study of the Bible is therefore more and more removed from communities of faith, and is carried out in academic contexts that are at best neutral and at worst positively hostile to the religious communities that claim ownership of these books.

The graduate programs in religious studies that draw the "best and brightest" of this generation — an ever decreasing number of the best and brightest do advanced work in any form of the humanities, with religious studies coming at the tail end of desirable academic fields for the most talented — are located in universities that debate internally about the legitimacy of studying theology within their programs. Biblical scholars trained in such programs are primarily students of antiquity and literature who find their conversation partners elsewhere than in theology or the church. The situation poses a real question to the university: why should so much energy be devoted to the Bible as Bible? Why should an entire Ph.D. program be devoted to a collection of writings (like the New Testament) that one can read in an afternoon? The university can justify such commitment only within the frame of a comparative or interdisciplinary program in which religious texts are read from the perspective of the humanities or social sciences. For schools of theology and seminaries dedicated to the preparation of ministers for the church, the problem takes another form: how can scholars whose education paid no attention to the concerns of the church now teach pastors how to interpret Scripture in and for the church? The challenge for Protestant (and increasingly Catholic) seminaries is to draw the Biblical faculty (notoriously the most guild-defined of all fields) into the theological and pastoral goals of the school rather than the expectations of a professional guild whose standards have nothing to do with the church. The academy, in short, is in danger of losing its heart, and the church is well along in the process of losing its mind.

The tendencies I describe show no signs of changing anytime soon. There is every reason to suppose that inertia will carry scholarship further in the same direction. The estrangement between secular academy and church promises to become greater and more entrenched. Since my commitment in the present book is to the future of Catholic biblical scholarship, I leave aside the crisis as it affects the university. But the church must come to realize that if it is to recover the soul of biblical scholarship as a form of wisdom, it cannot look to the academy for salvation. The church must therefore begin to look to its own resources, must somehow discover again how mind and heart can be united in the study of God's word. Chief among those resources is a tradition of reading Scripture as a form of wisdom rather than simply of science, a tradition that extended across the first 1600 years of the church's life.

The Possibility of Conversation

Renewing conversation with the interpreters of antiquity requires more than disenchantment with the present state of affairs. To take on the difficulties inherent in such conversation, scholars must be convinced that engagement is both possible and worthwhile. They can begin by honestly facing the resistance that is embedded deep within the outlook we now call "modernity," an outlook given perfect expression by the dominant historical-critical paradigm used in the study of the Bible. Those whose work is defined by the standards of modernity — a group that still includes many among us and perhaps some substantial part of each one of us — find ludicrous the notion that we can be instructed by ancient interpreters.

Many scholars who are otherwise highly trained still carry within them the unreflective conviction that ancient Catholicism was not based on the Bible in the same way that Protestantism is. Expressed most crudely, "those people did not read the Bible, or, if they read it, did not read it well." The first part of this statement continues Reformation polemics: Catholics don't read the Bible, whereas Protestants do. The second half of the statement expresses the self-justifying myth of modern biblical interpretation: even when the ancients read Scripture, they didn't read it well. Premodern interpretation is dismissed as a kind of dark ages where typology and allegory blinded people from the prophetic power of the literal meaning. The Reformation restored the principles of scriptural supremacy, the individual power to read, and the single literal sense as authoritative. Critical biblical scholarship, refining these reformation principles through Enlightenment, slowly climbed out of the darkness into the light by means of the historical-critical method, which eventually liberated itself even further from the shackles of the church and gained its complete liberty and autonomy in a scholarship that defined itself in terms of opposition to traditional belief and practice.

Although there are elements of historical fact in this self-interested account, its power over contemporary interpreters rests in its simple opposition (again the either/or) between premodern and modern. The opposition is problematic not only because it serves to justify the present state of affairs but also because, by over-simplifying, it distorts reality. This account serves to justify the neglect of any biblical interpretation before the Enlightenment. Such neglect leads to even greater ignorance of that tradition, and ignorance, in turn, reinforces the bias. We don't seek to learn from the ancient interpreters because there is nothing to learn. These dismissive attitudes are given specific expression within historical-critical scholarship in New Testament, about which I can speak most confidently.

One example is the "history of research" section required in all Ph.D. dissertations, in which students demonstrate the distinctiveness of their own contribution by showing how previous scholarship prepared for but did not preempt their project. Among New Testament dissertations produced in the United States today, it is rare to find a dissertation that reviews interpretation of the passages in question before the 19th century. New Testament scholarship's state of creeping amnesia is shown by the failure in many surveys even to consider anything earlier than the 20th century.

A second example is even more telling, because it suggests the reasoning behind the first example. A standard scholarly treatment of the history of New Testament scholarship — read by all Ph.D. students in the field — is a large volume of over 500 pages.[2] The entire history of New Testament scholarship in Christianity's first 1500 years is covered in seven pages.[3] This amounts to about a half-page a century. Such scholarly dismissal is a form of contempt. It says that there is nothing to learn from the earlier period that is in the least pertinent to present scholarship; all the important questions are formed by the period of the Enlightenment. There is an absolute divide between modernity and premodernity. The attitudes of modernity toward the first 1600 years of biblical scholarship within the church can thus be summarized: the Bible was either not read, or not read well, and in any case, there is nothing in those readings that is useful to scholars today.

It is important to remove some of the ignorance of the past that supports such bias and easy dismissal.[4] The truth is quite other than

2. Werner Georg Kümmel, *The New Testament: The History of the Investigation of Its Problems* (Nashville: Abingdon, 1972).

3. Kümmel, 13-19. This is not an isolated case. William Baird's *History of New Testament Research* (Minneapolis: Fortress, 1992) is revealingly subtitled *From Deism to Tübingen,* and the first sentence reads, "The critical study of the New Testament began in the eighteenth century" (3). In his Introduction, Baird devotes seven pages to the entire history of interpretation before the Enlightenment (xiii-xix). There are, to be sure, major works devoted to patristic and medieval interpretation. The point here is the communication of a message about worth in standard works that shape future scholars.

4. A sense of the history of biblical interpretation in the premodern period can be gained from Robert M. Grant and David Tracy, *A Short History of the Interpretation of the Bible,* rev. ed. (Philadelphia: Fortress, 1984); James L. Kugel and Rowan A. Greer, *Early Biblical Interpretation.* Library of Early Christianity (Philadelphia: Westminster, 1986); *The Cambridge History of the Bible,* 3 vols. (Cambridge: Cambridge University Press, 1963-1970), 1: *From the Beginnings to Jerome,* ed. Peter R. Ackroyd and Christopher Francis Evans (1970); 2: *The West from the Fathers to the Reformation,* ed. G. W. H. Lampe (1969); 3: *The West from the Reformation to the Present Day,* ed. Stanley Lawrence Greenslade (1963); and Richard A. Muller and John L. Thompson, *Biblical Interpretation in the Era of the Reformation* (Grand Rapids: Wm. B. Eerdmans, 1996).

the popular stereotypes suggest. In the first 1600 years of the church's life, Christians were intensely engaged with Scripture in a variety of ways, in a context that was far more "scriptural" than at any time since, not least because the great divide between the narrative world of Scripture and the empirical world of science and exploration — a divide of critical importance for the formation of modernity — had not yet been revealed.[5] In Eastern Christianity, preachers and teachers continued to think, speak, and write in the same *Koine* Greek that Paul had employed in his letters, and every form of Christian discourse was based squarely on Scripture not only in substance but also in style: preaching was biblical preaching, Scripture was read extensively in the divine liturgy of St. John Chrysostom, scriptural diction appeared in letters, poetry, and theological tractates.[6] Nobody could have conceived of a theology that was not a biblical theology.

The same was true for the Latin West. Together, the Vulgate translation of the Bible by St. Jerome and St. Augustine's *City of God* shaped a scriptural perception of society itself as the body of Christ. The power of Scripture in Christian imagination was all the greater because it had no real rivals. In the West, classical culture was a diversion for the most learned.[7] Islam was a threat from far away, and Judaism was a marginal-

5. See Hans Frei, *The Eclipse of Biblical Narrative: A Study in Eighteenth and Nineteenth Century Hermeneutics* (New Haven: Yale University Press, 1974). A sense of the impact made by world-exploration on the formation of modernity is given by J. Samuel Preus, *Explaining Religion: Criticism and Theory from Bodin to Freud* (New Haven: Yale University Press, 1987).

6. The world of Eastern Christianity remains seamless for 1500 years, and its literature shows remarkable consistency in language and in perspective. So naturally does it take place that one must be jarred into the realization that Clement of Alexandria, writing his *Stromata* in the 3rd century C.E., is debating authors (like Plato and Aristotle) who lived six centuries earlier. Emperor Leo in 911 writes an oration "In Praise of St. John Chrysostom," who lived in Constantinople five centuries before Leo (*Oratio* XVIII, PG 107:228). Certain literary forms remain constant: the *Loci Communes* of Maximus the Confessor in the mid-7th century (PG 91) and the *Sacra Parallela* of John Damascene in the mid-8th century (PG 94) and the *Loci Communes* of Antonius Melissa in the mid-12th century (PG 136) are all basically the same work, and continue with respect to Scripture the anthological impulse applied to secular literature in Stobaeus's *Anthologium Graecum* (of the 6th century).

7. See Helen Waddell, *The Wandering Scholars: The Life and Art of the Lyric Poets of the Latin Middle Ages* (New York: Doubleday, 1955).

ized remnant. With the partial exception represented by the introduction of scholastic philosophy in the high Middle Ages as a second theological diction, all learning, all art, even all music, was scripturally based.[8]

Such is our general ignorance of our own Christian past that even scholars need to be reminded of the different circumstances, contexts, and forms of interpretation in the premodern period. Here is where some historical imagination is helpful. Our immediate mental image for "reading Scripture" is of an individual sitting in a chair or at a desk, silently reading a book called the Bible. Our mental image of "biblical study" is of the isolated scholar sitting at a desk in an office or library, with that same book (in the original languages) and other reference books, also reading silently, but also taking notes. To grasp the way Scripture was read before the time of the Reformation, we must remember something both of technology and of social setting. Printing was invented only in the 15th century. Before that, all Bibles were in the form of manuscripts, books copied by hand, usually by skilled monks who devoted their lives to this thankless and anonymous task. Copying a Bible is a slow, difficult, and expensive task. Before the 15th century, a Christian community that had more than one or two complete Bibles in its possession would have been exceptional. Before printing with movable type made the reproduction of books relatively rapid and relatively inexpensive, it was literally unthinkable for individual Christians to have their own Bibles. The Protestant principle of individual interpretation, in other words, depends not a little on the technological advance represented by the printing press.[9]

The way Scripture was engaged before the invention of printing was therefore primarily communal and oral, rather than private and written. Scripture was engaged in the public activities of worship.[10]

---

8. A classic study of interpretation in the Latin West is Beryl Smalley, *The Study of the Bible in the Middle Ages*, 3rd ed. (Oxford: Blackwell, 1983). See also the magisterial 2-volume study by Henri de Lubac, *Medieval Exegesis: The Four Senses of Scripture*, trans. Mark Sebanc and M. E. Macierowski (1959; Grand Rapids: Wm. B. Eerdmans, 1998-2000); and now also Gilbert Dahan, *L'Exégèse chrétienne de la Bible en Occident médiéval, XII-XIX siecle*. Patrimoines Christianisme (Paris: Éditions du Cerf, 1999).

9. For a helpful guide, see D. C. Greetham, *Textual Scholarship: An Introduction* (New York: Garland, 1994), esp. 47-75.

10. See, e.g., Charles Renoux, "The Reading of the Bible in the Ancient Liturgy of

The Eucharist was woven from the words of Scripture, and included readings, prayers, and psalms as well as preaching from Scripture. Also of great importance was the *Opus Dei* performed by monks and members of cathedral chapters from the 4th century onward. In the divine office, monks spent at least four hours every day reciting the entire Psalter and other readings of Scripture. Scripture reading was primarily an ecclesial, that is, a churchly activity. The individual reading called *lectio divina* was not a replacement for but an extension of such communal practice. Scripture was consequently also experienced primarily orally-aurally, rather than simply visually. Memorization was more frequent because more necessary. Much of the Eucharist and the Divine Office was sung, and the combination of singing and of ritual movement meant that the words of Scripture took on kinetic associations that deepened the sense of reality ascribed to the world imagined by Scripture.[11]

The scholarly interpretation of Scripture took place within this context and in service to the practices of the faith community. Thus, a great deal of disciplined exegesis was involved in the composition of liturgical antiphons and hymns.[12] Scriptural interpretation was expressive and not simply explicative. Similarly, Scripture was used extensively in letters, sermons, theological treatises, poetry, and meditations. In such literary forms, the text of Scripture was not regarded as the problem to be explicated. Instead, the text of Scripture was brought to bear on some other problem or value in the Christian life. The most imaginative and original and important biblical interpretation of

---

Jerusalem"; and Douglas Burton-Christie, "Oral Culture, Biblical Interpretation, and Spirituality in Early Christian Monasticism," in *The Bible in Greek Christian Antiquity*, ed. and trans. Paul M. Blowers (Notre Dame: University of Notre Dame Press, 1997), 389-414 and 415-40.

11. For an appreciation of the liturgical context of Scripture in the medieval period, see Daniel J. Sheerin, "*Sonus* and *Verba:* Varieties of Meaning in the Liturgical Proclamation of the Gospel in the Middle Ages," in *Ad Litteram: Authoritative Texts and Their Medieval Readers*, ed. Mark D. Jordan and Kent Emery, Jr. (Notre Dame: University of Notre Dame Press, 1992), 29-69; and L.-J. Bataillon, O.P., "Early Scholastic and Mendicant Preaching as Exegesis of Scripture," in Jordan and Emery, 165-98.

12. William T. Flynn, *Medieval Music as Medieval Exegesis* (Lanham: Scarecrow, 1999), shows brilliantly how liturgical tropes represent careful and artful readings of Scripture.

Scripture in Christianity's first 1500 years, in other words, did not take place in biblical commentaries, but in other literary and liturgical expressions. Biblical commentaries tended to have an explanatory function. In them, the literal sense of Scripture was explicated. Commentaries then, as now, quickly became encyclopedic, as one generation borrowed lexical and grammatical and historical information from another.[13] Commentaries rarely had anything original to say. This is one reason why modern scholars find so little of interest in ancient interpretation. They assume that the commentary is where interpretation is to be found. But it is not. The most vibrant forms of interpretation in antiquity occur when the Scripture is *used* to explicate the Christian life. The way such uses bear within them an implicit understanding also of the biblical text requires careful analysis. Until contemporary scholars engage such readings of Scripture in the vast Christian literature of the patristic and medieval period (and of course, one should add as well the riches of Reformation interpretation, much of which continues in the same vein), they cannot say that they have yet learned what that interpretation involves.

Our access to this ancient form of scriptural performance — if we do not visit a monastery or participate in the Eastern Orthodox liturgy — is through the pale representation available through what was written down and preserved in monastic libraries, a tiny fraction of that public and oral expression over a period of 1600 years. Yet even those literary remains are enormous. The standard edition of the *Patrologia Graeca* (The Fathers of the Church in Greek) and the *Patrologia Latina* (The Fathers of the Church in Latin) consists of more than 380 very large volumes with multiple columns.[14] This is a huge repository of lit-

13. Venerable Bede already strews references to his predecessors throughout his pithy commentaries; similarly, the commentaries of the 11th-century Theophylact the Bulgarian represent an expansion of the 10th-century commentaries of Oecumenius of Tricca, who in turn made heavy use of the *Catena,* or chain of comments drawn from still earlier interpreters.

14. Jacques-Paul Migne, *Patrologia cursus completus: Patrologia graeca [PG],* 161 vols. (Paris: Migne, 1857-1866); *Patrologia latina,* 221 vols. (Paris: Garnier, 1844-1891). The editions in Migne are not the most critical. For the Greek patristic writers, critical editions are found in *Die Griechischen Christlichen Schriftsteller der Ersten Drei Jahrhunderte,* 53 vols. (Leipzig: Hinrichs, 1897-1969). Latin critical editions are found in *Corpus Christianorum: Series Latina* (Turnhout: Brepols, 1953-); and *Corpus Scriptorum Ecclesi-*

erature, vaster by far than the Babylonian Talmud, and equally complex in its engagement with Holy Scripture. This collection is only a small part of what was written, and what was written was only a small fraction of what was said through prayer and preaching and teaching. Jacques-Paul Migne's collection, for example, contains only the Latin and Greek texts; the Coptic and Syriac church also produced its own literature.[15]

Learning to engage again this long and complex conversation with Scripture will demand overcoming our bias and also our ignorance. Indeed, the two impediments are mutually reinforcing. A simple appreciation for the past is one thing. Serious and critical conversation with it will demand more than good will. Here the present state of language education causes discouragement. Only a small portion of this vast literature has been translated into modern languages.[16] Some New Testament scholars learn Coptic and Syriac — probably more than ever, because of the contemporary fascination with apocryphal writings — but few turn their attention to the history of interpretation. And the decline in competence in Latin and Greek means that the ignorance of patristic and medieval interpretation for the majority of New Testament scholars is not quickly going to be reversed. The effort to learn the languages required for a serious conversation with the past will not be undertaken by those who think of this literature as not worth reading, because, even if those authors did use Scripture, they used it wrongly!

I have spoken of these voices heard in premodern interpretation as

---

asticorum Latinorum (Vienna: Hoelder-Pichler-Tempsky, 1866-). These represent only a portion of what is in Migne, which therefore remains the most important source for Greek and Latin patristic and medieval literature.

15. See *Corpus Scriptorum Christianorum Orientalium* (Louvain: Peeters, 1903-).

16. There is an understandable tendency to begin each series with the best-known and "most important" texts, leading to a situation in which Augustine is available in many places but Oecumenius nowhere except in Migne. The most comprehensive translation from all ancient languages into a modern language is the French series *Sources chrétiennes* (Paris: Éditions du Cerf, 1941-), which translates from critical texts and has produced over 339 volumes, still only a small fraction of Migne. Readers in English can find important compositions in such series as *The Fathers of the Church* (New York: Fathers of the Church, 1947-); *Ancient Christian Writers* (New York: Paulist, 1946-); *Ante-Nicene Fathers*, ed. Alexander Roberts and James Donaldson, 10 vols. (repr. of 1885 edition by Wm. B. Eerdmans, 1979).

being both strange and familiar. They are familiar because they share with us the Christian experience and the same set of texts. But they remain strange because their approach to those texts differs significantly from that of modern scholarship. The difference lies less at the level of textual analysis than at the level of basic construal of the task. Modern and premodern construals are distinguished above all by the premises operative in interpretation. A condition for a fruitful conversation, then, is a candid assessment of the different premises at work in each approach. In what follows, I identify five aspects of premodern interpretation (here meaning mainly patristic and medieval) that are widely if not universally attested.[17] Premises by definition are those things that are assumed, that "go without saying," so they are not always or even frequently stated. Yet their influence is everywhere observable. They take on even sharper definition when they are contrasted with the presuppositions that are operative in today's historical-critical scholarship on the Bible.

The Premises of Premodern Interpretation

The first premise of premodern biblical interpretation is that Old and New Testaments form a unity that is grounded in the singleness of divine authorship.

For the earliest Christian writers of letters and Gospels, "Scripture" *(graphē)* meant the texts of law, prophets, and writings that fellow Jews reading in Hebrew called Torah. Christian authors like James and Paul and Luke, however much they used the same interpretive methods as Palestinian Jews did on the Hebrew text of Torah, read and interpreted the Greek translation of Torah called the Septuagint (LXX). This trans-

17. My five premises closely resemble (and certainly agree with) the "four assumptions" identified by James Kugel, *The Bible as It Was* (Cambridge, Mass.: Harvard University Press, 1997), 17-23. Kugel's list: (a) the Bible is fundamentally a cryptic document; (b) Scripture constitutes one great Book of Instruction; (c) Scripture is perfect and perfectly harmonious; (d) all of Scripture is somehow divinely sanctioned, of divine provenance, or divinely inspired. The consonance between Kugel's assumptions and my premises is the more impressive because his survey includes both Jewish and Christian interpreters of the Bible.

lation from Hebrew to Greek was widely used among Hellenistic Jews, and was regarded by at least some of them as divinely inspired.[18] When Paul says "all Scripture is divinely inspired" (2 Tim. 3:16), then, he refers to what Christians came to call the Old Testament.[19] The conviction of the first Christian authors that God spoke truly through this translation is reflected in their use of it to interpret the meaning of God's work in their own time through the death and resurrection of Jesus Christ. It is possible, in fact, to see the composition of the New Testament as arising out of the need to resolve the cognitive conflict between Scripture and the experience of a crucified and raised Messiah, and as consisting in a midrashic reinterpretation of Scripture in the light of this new experience of God in the lives of believers.[20]

In the 2nd century of the Common Era, a sharp dispute arose within Christianity concerning the relationship between that earlier *graphē* and the new set of Christian writings that had quickly been circulated and formed into a loose collection. Is the authentic teaching of Christ and about God to be found only in the new collection of writings, or is it found also in the older collection? The sharpest challenge was put by the heretic Marcion, who regarded the Old Testament as the revelation of a malicious God of wrath.[21] The response of the teachers we now call orthodox was to attach the Christian writings (as a New Testament) to the ancient Jewish writings (now designated as Old Testament) as a single Scripture.[22] From the end of the 2nd century, therefore, mainstream Christianity was distinguished by a strong commit-

---

18. The legend of the translation by the "seventy" is found in *The Letter of Aristeas* 303-11 and Josephus, *Antiquities of the Jews* 12:101-107 and *Against Apion* 2:46, without any intimation of divine guidance. Philo, however, clearly regards the LXX as divinely inspired (see *Life of Moses* 2:37), and the same view may have been held by Aristobolos (see *Fragment* 2).

19. That the LXX is divinely inspired is found in Justin Martyr, *To the Greeks* 13; and Irenaeus, *Against Heresies* III, 21, 2.

20. See Luke Timothy Johnson, *The Writings of the New Testament*, 2nd ed. (Minneapolis: Fortress, 1999), 1-19, 595-619.

21. Our most important source for Marcion is Tertullian's five books *Against Marcion* (207), in which description and rebuttal are intertwined.

22. See, e.g., *The Muratorian Canon;* Eusebius, *Ecclesiastical History* 3.25, 1-7; Cyril of Jerusalem, *Catecheses* 4, 35; Athanasius of Alexandria, *Paschal Letter* (367); The Council of Carthage (397), article 39; Augustine, *On Christian Doctrine* II, 8, 12-13.

ment to a closed canon of Scripture and a conviction that the writings of both testaments were inspired by the Holy Spirit.[23]

Implicit in this canonical decision was the recognition that the revelation of God in Torah and the revelation of God through Jesus Christ are the revelation of the same God.[24] But Scripture — which everyone recognized was composed by humans — was regarded not only as "revealing God" in the sense that it spoke truly *about* God, but also as "revealing God" in the sense that through Scripture *God* speaks in human words.[25] We will see in the next chapter how Origen exploits Paul's distinction in 1 Cor. 10:11 between "the things that happened to them (people in the past)" and "the things written (in Scripture)," putting his emphasis on Paul's insistence that the things written were "for our instruction" (see also Rom. 15:4). Now, if there is a single divine author at work through the literary compositions of Moses and Solomon and David and Paul and Matthew, then despite the diversity among these voices, there is a single revealer seeking to be heard. This deep conviction was liturgically reinforced by the reading from both testaments in sequence, and identifying all such lections as "The Word of the Lord."

The decision to read Old and New Testaments as one Scripture — and as one process of revelation — by no means relieved the difficulties inherent in trying to read them as one. How do the testaments relate to each other? Are all parts equally normative? Can all parts be read the same way? At the very least, however, all of Scripture was heard as speaking not only to the past but also to the present. Scripture speaks in each of its parts prophetically, not as predicting the future, but as speaking for God. So long as the Greek Septuagint remained the version of the Old Testament used in the churches, the unity of Scripture was linguistically reinforced. The New Testament authors not only

23. E.g., *First Letter of Clement* 45:2; Justin, *To the Greeks* 8; Theophilus of Antioch, *To Autolycus* 3, 12; Irenaeus, *Against Heresies* III, 28, 2; Clement of Alexandria, *Protrepticus* 9, 2, 1; Origen, *Commentary on the Psalms* 1, 4; *Homilies on Jeremiah* 8.1; Gregory of Nyssa, *Against Eunomius* 1.8; Ambrose, *On the Holy Spirit* 3, 16, 112; Theodoret, *On the Psalms,* Praef.; Gregory the Great, *Moralia,* Praef. 1, 2.

24. On the unity of revelation in Scripture, see, e.g., Irenaeus, *Against Heresies* IV, 12, 3; Epiphanius, *Panarion* 33, 9; Augustine, *Against Adimantus* 17, 2; *Against the Opponents of the Law and the Prophets* 1, 17, 35; Leo the Great, *Sermon* 63, 5; for the medieval period in the West, see de Lubac, *Medieval Exegesis* 1:225-67.

25. See de Lubac, "Scripture and Revelation," in *Medieval Exegesis* 1:24-39.

used the same language, but imitated and appropriated the words of the Septuagint in their compositions. That literary unity remains seamless today in the Greek Orthodox church. When Jerome (beginning in 382) translated the entire Bible into Latin for the West, he decided to translate the Old Testament directly from the Hebrew rather than from the Septuagint. The implications of this innovation did not for a long time become evident, since his translation of the whole tended to mask the differences that could result from a translation from the Hebrew.[26] For a millennium and a half of Christian interpretation, in short, Scripture could be and was read as a unified whole in such fashion that each part could be used to interpret every other part, and each part could be read in light of the whole. All of Scripture, in short, was the interpretive context for all of Scripture.

Contrast this with the premise suggested by the practice of contemporary biblical scholarship. The premise of divine inspiration and therefore of ultimate divine authorship is rarely made explicit even when (in some minimal fashion) it is maintained.[27] More tellingly, convictions about divine inspiration do not affect interpretation, which is carried out entirely at the level of human authorship. Modernity's commitment to the literal sense alone has been narrowed to mean the sense intended by the historical human author. What is sometimes taken to be a methodological concentration on the human voice has

26. Thus, Jerome's rendering of Matt. 1:22-23 faithfully echoes his own translation of Isa. 7:14, which has a *virgo* conceiving (as in the LXX) rather than a maiden (*'almah*), as in the Hebrew (and "young woman" in the NRSV). Likewise, in Mark's Passion account, the Vulgate's *diviserunt vestimenta eius* (Mark 15:24) faithfully echoes the *diviserunt sibi vestimenta mea* of Ps. 21:19 (Eng. 22:18), just as *mittentes sortem* (Mark 15:24) replicates the *mittentes sortem* of Ps. 21:19. Similarly, Jerome's version of Ps. 108:8 (Eng. 109:8), *et episcopatum eius accipiat alter,* and the citation of it in Acts 1:20, *et episcopatum eius accipiat alter,* follows the sense of the LXX rather than the Hebrew; compare *munus eius accipiat alter* in the 1959 translation authorized by Pius XII.

27. It is perhaps an indication of the direction of things that *The Interpreter's Dictionary of the Bible* (Nashville: Abingdon, 1962) has an extensive article on "Inspiration and Revelation" by G. W. H. Lampe (2:713-18), whereas the *Anchor Bible Dictionary* (New York: Doubleday, 1992) has none. Similarly, the article by Richard F. Smith, S.J. on "Inspiration and Inerrancy," in the *Jerome Biblical Commentary,* 499-514, has a sensitive treatment of the question of the inspiration of the LXX (511-12), but the article by Melvin K. H. Peters, "Septuagint," in the *Anchor Bible Dictionary* (5:1093-1104) makes no mention of its inspiration even as a historical oddity.

often become, in effect, a theoretical exclusion of the possibility of any other voice speaking through these texts.

As for reading the Bible as a unity, few scholars claim to be able to interpret even all of one testament much less the Bible as a whole. Old Testament scholarship, furthermore, is carried out in complete isolation from the New Testament. Interpretation of the Old Testament — now, revealingly, designated as "the Hebrew Bible" or "the Hebrew Scriptures," or "the Prior Testament" — interacts with other ancient Near Eastern literatures and contemporary Jewish interpretation, rather than the continued life of these texts in New Testament interpretations. It is considered a matter of integrity to construct a "theology of the Old Testament" without respect to the distinctive readings of those writings by New Testament authors.[28] New Testament scholarship is in a somewhat different position. It must take some form of the Old Testament into account, simply because the New Testament makes such heavy use of the Septuagint. Apart from identifying such uses, however, New Testament scholars are largely undecided as to what actual difference it makes whether the New Testament itself used the Hebrew text or the Greek of the Old Testament. Scholars make use of the Old Testament mainly to explain how the human authors used the earlier testament for their own rhetorical and ideological purposes. How God might be speaking through such uses does not arise, except by the implication to be derived from the studious avoidance of the issue. If pressed, most biblical scholars today would be embarrassed by the question concerning the revelatory character of the New Testament's use of the Septuagint.

The segmentation of study extends even further. Apart from the brave souls who continue to assay introductions or theologies of the respective testaments, and therefore are forced to some sort of synthetic vision, the tendency in scholarship is to consider each literature in terms of its individual books. Scholars study Paul or John or Luke, and try to find the voice of those ancient writers — even their theologies —

---

28. Even though there are real differences between the two major representatives of "Old Testament Theology" in America today, Brevard S. Childs, *Biblical Theology of the Old and New Testaments: Theological Reflections on the Christian Bible* (Minneapolis: Fortress, 1993), and Walter Brueggemann, *Theology of the Old Testament: Testimony, Dispute, Advocacy* (Minneapolis: Fortress, 1997), are similar in the level of the discomfort caused by an exclusive commitment to the literal sense of the text.

rather than to hear the voice of God that might speak through them in concert. Even the integrity of the individual authors is put in question by the logic of a historical model that specializes in fragmenting literature in service of historical reconstruction. The construal of interpretation as a form of history has also led to the effective elimination of canon as a meaningful term: if the goal is the reconstruction of ancient Israelite history, or the historical Jesus, or early Christian development, then, it must be granted, all available sources must be used, and the canonical texts *as* canonical can enjoy no special privilege.[29] In short, the unity of the Bible as based in a unity of divine authorship is so absent from today's scholarship that one would be laughed from the room if one were to suggest it as a serious option in a gathering of scholars.

The second premise of premodern interpretation was that Scripture speaks harmoniously.

Two aspects of this premise deserve attention. The first is that despite its many inconsistencies, differences, and even contradictions, Scripture as a whole can be understood as consistent with respect especially to the central matters of faith and morals. Ancient readers were not blind to problems in the text, and identified a wide range of apparent contradictions.[30] They noticed, for example, that Paul and James seemed

29. In New Testament scholarship, the primacy of the canonical texts as historical sources was first threatened by F. C. Baur's use of the Pseudo-Clementine literature in his reconstruction of Christian origins, in *Paul, the Apostle of Jesus Christ,* 2 vols., 2nd ed., ed. Eduard Zeller, trans. Allan Menzies (London: Williams and Norgate, 1875); and *The Church History of the First Three Centuries,* 3rd ed., 2 vols., trans. Menzies (London: Williams and Norgate, 1878-79); this was given great impetus by Walter Bauer's *Orthodoxy and Heresy in Earliest Christianity,* ed. Robert A. Kraft and Gerhard Krodel, trans. Paul J. Achtemeier et al. (1934; Philadelphia: Fortress, 1971), and granted programmatic status by James M. Robinson and Helmut Koester, *Trajectories through Early Christianity* (Philadelphia: Fortress, 1971).

30. The chapter on Origen will show how fastidiously he identified all such tensions at the literal level. The concern for harmony made ancient readers even more attuned to theological inconsistencies than are contemporary scholars. The apparent contradiction between the words of Jesus, "Lead us not into temptation *(peirasmon)*" (Matt. 6:13), and the exhortation of Jas. 1:2, "Count it all joy when you fall into various testings *(peirasmois),*" for example, led patristic interpreters to seek a resolution; see e.g., Athanasius, *Epistulae Heorasticae* xiii, 6 (PG 26:1417); Cyril of Jerusalem, *Catecheses*

to say opposing things with respect to faith and works.[31] Their instinct, however, was to find a way in which contradictions might be resolved in a higher harmony. Note that harmonization requires the maintenance of both passages, rather than the discarding of one in favor of another. In the case of Paul and James, the tension tended to be resolved in terms of the two authors addressing different contexts: Paul's insistence on faith rather than the works of the law was addressed to those coming to baptism, and James's insistence on the works of faith was addressed to baptized Christians.[32] As so often, a third passage is used to achieve the harmony, in this case, Paul's statement in Gal. 5:6 that what counts is neither circumcision nor lack of circumcision but rather "faith working through love." The basic sensibility at work in the effort to find a resolution to scriptural conflicts is expressed beautifully in a letter of Severus, the Patriarch of Antioch (ca. 465-538), to Julian, Bishop of Halicarnassus (after 518), concerning James and Paul. After an exquisitely argued exposition of the two passages in light of the story of Abraham as recounted in Genesis, Severus concludes, "The holy writings and the fathers have always handed on to us a harmonious teaching."[33]

Severus's conclusion points to the second aspect of this premise, namely, that Scripture speaks harmoniously with Tradition. Readers understood Scripture as a dimension of Tradition rather than as opposed to it. As the church created the New Testament through a rereading of Torah, so was the church continually shaped by both Old and New Testaments. The truth spoken by Scripture concerning faith and

---

5, 17 (PG 33:1121); Maximus the Confessor, *Questiones ad Thelassium* LXVIII (PG 90:594); Gregory Palamas, *Homilia* XXXII (PG 151:401-9).

31. For a full discussion of the passages and their interpretation, see Luke Timothy Johnson, *The Letter of James*. AB 37A (New York: Doubleday, 1995), 58-65, 143-56, 236-52.

32. See Origen, *Commentarii in Epistulam ad Romanos* II, 12-13; IV, 1-3; IV, 8; VII, 1; IX, 24 (PG 14:900, 908, 961, 970, 989-90, 1159, 1226). That James's exhortation is addressed to the baptized is emphasized by John Damascene, *De Fide Orthodoxa* IV, IX (PG 94:1121); see also Theophanis of Sicily, *Homilia* XXVIII (PG 132:617); John of Antioch, *Oratio de Disciplina Monastica* (PG 132:1120); Isidore of Pelusium, *Epistularum Liber IV,* LXV (PG 78:1121); Cyril of Alexandria, *Commentarium in Epistulam ad Romanos* IV, 2; VII, 16; VIII, 26 (PG 74:781, 812, 825); Theophylact of Bulgaria, *Expositio in Epistulam ad Galatas* V, 6 (PG 124:1012).

33. The correspondence is found in Zachary the Rhetorician, *Capita Selecta ex Historica Ecclesiastica*, Sect. IX (PG 85:1176-78).

morals, then, must in some deep fashion correspond to the belief and practice of the church. The church's rule of faith (the creed) and codes of behavior (ethics) can therefore also help to guide the reading of Scripture.[34] A simple example makes the point. In 2 Cor. 4:4, the plain sense of Paul's Greek is disconcerting, even troubling. Literally, he says, "The god of this world has blinded the minds of unbelievers so that they cannot see the light of the gospel of the glory of Christ, who is the image of God." Apart from the issue of divine mercy suggested by God blinding people from the truth, what are we to make of the phrase "the god of this world"? Here was a statement in Paul that clearly seems to support the argument of Marcion that the creator god was in rivalrous combat with the God of the New Testament. But Christian interpreters, sometimes at the cost of extreme exegetical ingenuity, understood the text in another fashion, because according to the rule of faith (drawn from the entirety of Scripture) there can be but one God. The creed plainly declares, "we believe in one God," and Scripture must conform (and be made to conform) with that truth.[35]

The tendencies of modern biblical interpretation reveal the exact opposite premise. The differences, inconsistencies, and contradictions found within the biblical writings are used to oppose compositions and authors. James and Paul, for example, are viewed not as sharers in a common faith who address slightly different concerns when they speak about faith and works, but as representatives of opposing forms of Christianity that struggle for dominance.[36] The differences between

34. For early expressions of the *Regula Fidei*, see Irenaeus, *Against Heresies* I, 10, 1; I, 22, 1; Tertullian, *On the Prescription of Heretics* 13 and esp. 19, for the right relation between Scripture and the Rule of Faith; *Against Hermogenes* 21; *Against Praxeas* 2; Origen, *On First Principles* I Praef. 4.

35. See Tertullian, *Against Marcion*, 5, 11 and 5, 17.

36. The polarizing instincts of Luther were rendered historically by F. C. Baur in his portrayal of earliest Christianity as an arena of conflict between Judaizing and Pauline Christianities. That tendency is now expressed not only in seeing Paul and James as opponents — as in Martin Hengel, "Der Jakobusbrief als antipaulinische Polemik," in *Tradition and Interpretation in the New Testament*, ed. Gerald F. Hawthorne and Otto Betz (Grand Rapids: Wm. B. Eerdmans, 1987), 248-78 — but in fragmenting earliest Christianity into a variety of competing movements — as in Burton L. Mack, *A Myth of Innocence: Mark and Christian Origins* (Philadelphia: Fortress, 1988). For comment, see Luke Timothy Johnson, "Koinonia: Diversity and Unity in Early Christianity," *TD* 46 (1999): 303-13.

Gospels serve not to draw the reader to the essential point they hold in common, but serve to discredit their value as historical witnesses to Jesus.[37] Even thematic or stylistic differences within biblical compositions are taken as signs of discordant traditions that must be separated into distinct sources.[38]

As for harmony between Scripture and Tradition, that is even more emphatically rejected within modern biblical scholarship, whose distinguishing feature is its constant opposition of historical reconstruction to the teachings of Tradition (whether doctrinal, moral, or sacramental). As I suggested in the previous chapter, this opposition began with Luther's theological use of Scripture to challenge the corruptions of Tradition in late medieval Catholicism, but in the Enlightenment the same opposition expressed the standpoint of a rationalistic criticism that defined itself by opposition to all forms of traditional faith and, eventually, by opposition to the authority of Scripture itself.

The third premise of premodern interpretation of Scripture is that the Bible, as the Word of God, is authoritative.

The third premise of premodern biblical interpretation is that the Bible is authoritative in the strongest possible sense. As divinely inspired, it is God's Word. Therefore through the agency of human speech, it reveals God and God's will for humans. Precisely in and through its literary configuration, Scripture is a "revelatory text."[39] As the vehicle of God's self-disclosure — not uniquely, of course, for God is not contained in the book in the manner that a jewel is enclosed in a locket — Scripture is the measure for humans, rather than humans being its measure. The Scripture heard as the Word of God makes a claim

37. See Luke Timothy Johnson, *The Real Jesus* (San Francisco: HarperSanFrancisco, 1996).

38. For a sense of source-criticism in the Old Testament, see Pauline A. Viviano, "Source Criticism," in *To Each Its Own Meaning: An Introduction to Biblical Criticisms and Their Applications,* ed. Steven L. McKenzie and Stephen R. Haynes, rev. ed. (Louisville: Westminster John Knox, 1999), 29-51; for its application to the Gospels, see Robert H. Stein, *The Synoptic Problem: An Introduction* (Grand Rapids: Baker, 1987).

39. I borrow the title of the wonderful study by Sandra Schneiders, whose perceptions derive from the heart of this tradition: *The Revelatory Text: Reading the New Testament as Sacred Scripture* (San Francisco: Harper Collins, 1991).

on readers unlike the claim made by any other literature. Prior to any question readers might put to the text is the question that the text puts to the readers, or, perhaps better, the fact that the text puts readers in question. The human reader of Scripture therefore always assumes that there is wisdom to be found in each of its pages, even if the shape of that wisdom is not immediately obvious or must be approached by circuitous routes. Readers of Scripture do not view it from the vantage point of superior intelligence or cultural context, but view it as a text that can disclose the mind of God. The reader therefore approaches the text of Scripture not with arrogance, but humbly as a suppliant. Prayer and fasting are needed before reading the text to prepare the mind and heart for right reading.[40] Human reason seeks to be conformed to the mind of Christ in order to grasp how all of Scripture teaches us the mind of God. The fundamental reading attitude is therefore docility, the willingness to be taught, to be shaped, the glad eagerness to obey what God reveals to God's people.

Since the Enlightenment, the opposite premise has governed the critical study of the Bible. Human reason is the measure of all things, even of claims to divine revelation. Now Scripture must answer at the court of a human reason that is constituted, not on the basis of the mind of Christ, but on the basis of a rationalistic worldview.[41] Ancient readers were like peoples who were convinced that if one lived in harmony with nature then nature would bless them with lives of harmony. Enlightenment readers were like people who bulldoze forests to build shopping malls because all blessing comes from what they can control and sell. Rather than seek to serve the text, the text is inquired as to how it might serve. Rather than approach with the assumption that readers need to learn and obey, the text is considered worthy only when it meets our cultural or religious standards of acceptability. And more often than not, the Bible is seen to fall short of meeting the intellectual or moral standards of contemporary readers. Biblical scholarship since the Enlightenment therefore has been one of the main in-

40. See the discussion of "Discipline," in de Lubac, *Medieval Exegesis* 1:15-24.

41. See Henning Graf Reventlow, *The Authority of the Bible and the Rise of the Modern World,* trans. John Bowden (Philadelphia: Fortress, 1985), who stresses the influence of Deism in particular on the formation of German theology and biblical study in the mid-18th century (see 411-14).

struments by which the world imagined by Scripture has been dismantled bit by bit, in order to provide a few interesting pieces of decoration in a world constructed in fundamental opposition to that of Scripture. Ancient readers started with the conviction that Scripture's meaning could and should become our own; modern readers start with the conviction that our meaning dictates what we select to salvage from Scripture.

The fourth premise of premodern biblical interpretation is that Scripture speaks in many ways and at many levels.

Because Scripture is composed by humans inspired by the Spirit of the living God, it speaks God's Word as well as human words. The meaning of the Bible cannot, therefore, be restricted to what the human authors intended to say in the past, although that meaning is always important and to be taken into the most serious consideration. God's meaning transcends the limits of human intentionality. God finds ways of addressing not only the past — when the texts were written — but also our present, and the future as well. The strong understanding of inspiration that characterized premodern interpretation grasped that God's Spirit is at work not only in the ancient author, but at work also in the present reader, prodding and guiding human reason into the wisdom that God seeks to reveal here and now about the present and future world.

Ancient interpreters found such convictions confirmed by their reading of the New Testament itself. In other words, their hermeneutical premises were themselves grounded in the words of Scripture. Paul and the author of the Letter to the Hebrews read parts of the Old Testament typologically, so that events of the past (like the wandering of the people in the desert [1 Cor. 10:1-11; Heb. 4:1-11] and the worship of the tent in the wilderness [Heb. 9:1-28]) spoke warnings and encouragements to the people of today, and also read parts of the Old Testament allegorically (such as the story of Hagar and Sarah [Gal. 4:21-31] and the story of Melchizedek [Heb. 7:1-10]). These New Testament authors also provided explicit hermeneutical warrants for such interpretive moves (1 Cor. 10:11; Rom. 15:4; 2 Cor. 3:4-18; Col. 2:16-17; Heb. 10:1-18). The example set by the New Testament authorized patristic interpreters to seek deeper levels of meaning in all the texts of Scripture, especially in cases when the literal or historical meaning of the text seemed to present difficulties, scandals, or impossibilities.[42] When the text seemed not to make sense, it was not abandoned. Instead, the conviction that God was trying to teach them precisely through the text impelled such readers to regard the scandals of the literal sense as an invitation to seek other senses. So in addition to telling the story of what happened in the past and bearing the record of prophecy and exhortation to people long ago, Scripture was regarded as continuing to speak, first to the lives of individual believers at the moral level — instructing them in the virtuous life — as well as at the spiritual level — showing them the path of transformation according to the image of Christ. All of Scripture taught this way. Ancient readers also heard Scripture continuing to speak at a deeper than literal level to the church, the people of God considered as the body of Christ. Scripture portrayed in mysterious fashion what the church should be in the present and the eschatological hope of what the church might be in God's fully realized kingdom.[43]

Contrast this to the premise of modern biblical scholarship, which has, as I have suggested, either bracketed or denied divine inspiration, leaving only the human author to speak in the texts of Scripture. In the world of modernity, there are no deeper meanings, there are no mysteries to be revealed.[44] There is only the literal sense, which is more or less equated with the intention of the ancient author. Biblical scholarship is defined therefore by its historical character. Interpretation is discovering what the text meant back then, not what the text signifies now. Asking about present significance is not the business of scholarship, it

42. The literal sense remained important throughout the entire period of premodern interpretation. In addition to de Lubac, *Medieval Exegesis,* 2:41-82, see the essays in Jordan and Emery, *Ad Litteram.*

43. See all of de Lubac, *Medieval Exegesis,* but esp. "Multiple Meanings," 1:75-115.

44. It is rare to find a scholar so explicit on such matters, but the statements of Jonathan Z. Smith can be taken to express the sentiments of many: "I stand squarely in the rationalist tradition. I have an uncompromising faith in realism and intellection"; and "For me, things are surface: there simply is no depth; there simply is no original; and there is no concealment. It's all out there, it's plain, it's ordinary, it's largely uninteresting, and it's utterly — in fact, overwhelmingly, that's the problem for a scholar — accessible." See *Violent Origins: Walter Burkert, René Girard and Jonathan Z. Smith on Ritual Killing and Cultural Formation,* ed. Robert G. Hammerton-Kelly (Stanford: Stanford University Press, 1987), 206, 211.

is the business of piety. Small wonder that contemporary scholarship should at once accumulate such mountains of learning about antiquity and have so little to say to the life of the church. Small surprise that the perfect exemplification of Enlightenment interpretation is the quest for the historical Jesus, a search for historical knowledge about a dead man of the past through a savaging and salvaging of ancient sources, rather than a quest for obedience to the will of the living Lord Jesus who is revealed everywhere in the New Testament, and a search for being conformed to the image of the human Christ, who is so variously yet consistently displayed in the narratives of the Gospels.[45]

The fifth premise of premodern biblical interpretation can be called a hermeneutics of generosity or charity.

This is not so much a separate premise as a summary of the others. Readers approached the text with love, and expected from the text to be built up in love within the body of the church. This does not mean that ancient interpreters were not critical in any number of ways — the next chapters will show some of them. But their critical inquiry was always within the context of a profound submission to the rule of faith and the authority of the text. They assumed that the text was right, rather than their own opinions; therefore they needed to pray and seek and knock in order to discover what God had to teach them. They were open to mutual criticism in order to grow in wisdom. They understood that the point of their reading was their transformation in the image of Christ.[46] And they considered that reading of the text as best that gave rise to the greatest love among believers.[47]

The hermeneutical standpoint of modernity has been characterized from beginning to end by suspicion rather than generosity, by a concern for how Scripture has torn down readers rather than built them up. In the classic form of the historical-critical paradigm, the hermeneutics of suspicion has expressed itself in challenges to every

---

45. See Luke Timothy Johnson, *Living Jesus: Learning the Heart of the Gospel* (San Francisco: HarperSanFrancisco, 1999).

46. We shall see this emphasis especially in the next chapter, in the work of Origen of Alexandria.

47. As we shall see, the principle is stated explicitly by Augustine in *On Christian Instruction* I, 26 [40], but it clearly expresses the attitude of the entire Tradition.

claim made for the text (its inspiration, authority) and many of the claims made by the text (ascribed authorship, the witness to Jesus, God, and the world).[48] The more recent form of the hermeneutics of suspicion — sometimes designated as ideological criticism — approaches the text with moral outrage, seeking to find all the ways in which Scripture has wounded the contemporary psyche, rather than the ways in which Scripture can heal the contemporary soul.[49]

This far-too-rapid survey of premises serves to suggest three summary observations. The first is that the five premises of premodern interpretation work together. Beginning with the perception of all of Scripture as inspired by the divine author, everything else follows logically: the unity and harmony of Scripture's witness, its capacity to speak wisdom beyond its historical sense, and the need to seek that wisdom in a spirit of humility, generosity, and charity. The second is how dramatically opposed the interpretation of modernity is at every point. If Scripture contains only the perceptions of ancient authors and we restrict ourselves to studying those past views, why should we not emphasize diversity rather than harmony, why should we not think ourselves superior to people who lived so long ago and far away? Why, indeed, should we expect to find wisdom in those texts at all? The third observation is that seeking to renew conversation with ancient interpreters will not be a matter simply of comparing techniques. Genuine conversation will demand the willingness to question and be questioned by the deep assumptions about Scripture that we may no longer share.

Premodern, Modern, Postmodern

Conversation with our Christian past must take place at a deeper and more specific level than that of generalization — a level that all too easily either idealizes or condemns. Conversation must engage individual

48. For the manifestations of suspicion in the classic historical-critical paradigm, see Johnson, *TD* 46 (1999): 303-13; and *The First and Second Letters to Timothy* (New York: Doubleday, 2001), 42-54.

49. Bibliography for the several forms of ideological criticism is provided by Johnson, *The Writings of the New Testament*, 625-26.

readers of the past. Closer examination of these ancient interpreters will reveal the ways in which we can and should disagree with them on any number of issues. But the general observations in this chapter are enough, I hope, to show that these ancient interpreters are our appropriate conversation partners if we seek to restore the soul of biblical scholarship as a scholarship in, of, and by the church as the community of the faithful. For patristic and medieval interpreters, the Bible was the Scripture of the church in terms of its setting in liturgy and teaching. It was the Scripture of the church in terms of the practices to which it was connected: communal reading, study, prayer, and preaching. It was the Scripture of the Church in terms of focus: the Bible spoke not only to the past but also to the present and future, not only to individuals but also to the church as the body of the risen Christ. And it was the Scripture of the church in terms of goal: the point of reading is transformation of the individual in holiness and the edification of the church in love.

I think the proper starting point is conversation with patristic rather than medieval interpreters, especially those patristic authors who lived and wrote before the Constantinian era was firmly established, that is, during the first 300-350 years of the church's existence. In fascinating ways, their situation has enough elements analogous to our own to make the conversation particularly challenging and instructive. I suggest that the period of biblical interpretation dominated by the historical-critical paradigm has taught us many things but has also led us to an ecclesial dead end. The period of modernity is now over for many of us, precisely because we can no longer accept the assumptions of modernity as self-evident.[50] In terms of biblical scholarship, the assumptions of modernity are those of the historical-critical paradigm, with its emphasis on a single, objectively realizable meaning of the text, its commitment to a referential understanding of truth, its implicit claim to universal reason. As soon as we are able to use the term "modernity," we find ourselves, willy-nilly, in the posture of postmodernism. Despite some impulses toward a "postmodern" reading of the Bible, however, what this new state of affairs might mean is

50. See Jean François Lyotard, *The Postmodern Condition: A Report on Knowledge,* trans. Geoff Bennington and Brian Massumi (Minneapolis: University of Minnesota Press, 1984).

not clear.[51] My suggestion is that the postmodern church can learn what it might mean to be postmodern in its biblical interpretation by means of a serious conversation with the premodern church.

In three important ways, the situation of the premodern interpreters of the first four centuries resembles our own. The first point of similarity is political. We are in the post-Constantinian era. Christianity is no longer the state-established and supported religion, as it had been from the time of Constantine and Theodosius until the 19th century. Although some Christians today bemoan the situation, grieving the loss of privilege and fearing the threat of social ostracism and even legal repression, most recognize it as a condition that will not be reversed, and many of us see it as a great blessing. The earliest Christian interpreters lived in a world that was politically pre-Constantinian. Christianity was still a minority religious cult. It was mostly despised and politically vulnerable to measures harsher than social ostracism. Confessing Jesus as Lord meant the possibility of persecution and martyrdom.

The second point of similarity is cultural. We live in a world that is intensely and explicitly pluralistic. We are aware as never before how Christianity is but one competitor among world religions, and that religion itself is but one competitor for human allegiance. To be Christian today means to make a choice among powerful and attractive options. The earliest Christian interpreters of Scripture lived within a cultural and religious pluralism almost as real and in some respects even more visible. Greco-Roman religion and philosophy dominated the world of the empire. Philosophy offered a variety of schools of thought and practice. Religion offered a variety of cults and practices, exoteric and esoteric. Judaism was an ancient, powerful, and growing tradition that provided rival interpretations of the sacred texts. Christianity was itself fractured into multiple parties (heresies) by the 2nd century, and itself helped generate another world religion (Manichaeism). Then as now, Christianity was fundamentally a diaspora religion, surviving without political support or cultural dominance. It was

51. E.g., Edgar V. McKnight, *Postmodern Use of the Bible: The Emergence of Reader-Oriented Criticism* (Nashville: Abingdon, 1988); Stephen D. Moore, *Poststructuralism and the New Testament* (Minneapolis: Fortress, 1994); A. K. M. Adam, *What Is Postmodern Biblical Criticism?* (Minneapolis: Fortress, 1995).

forced to make its way as an intentional community, drawing adherents but also generating resentment.

The third point of similarity is intellectual. We live in an intellectual world that is increasingly post-Enlightenment. The certainties of modernity — that reason is the measure of all things, that truth is accessible to empirical verification, that the universal is better than the particular — have lost their convincing character for many. The world that some call postmodern is more deeply aware of the constructed character of human meaning, how much it is connected to faith commitments, how profoundly it is rooted in community traditions. The earliest Christian interpreters lived in a world that was pre-Enlightenment, premodern. They certainly valued reason and were more than capable of critical thought, but their assumptions, as we have seen, were distinct from those of modernity, not least in their appreciation of the superiority of divine revelation to human reason, and their perception that understanding works best when it is grounded in faith and practice.

I do not suggest that being postmodern is the same as being premodern. People in today's world have a sense of the largeness and complexity of the universe (both cosmological and personal) unavailable to ancients, and we have (some of us) a sharper sense of critical history and of being "historical creatures." We have learned, and are unwilling to unlearn, the benefits of empirical testing in the realms of science and technology. We have a commitment to political liberty and to the equality of persons that ancients did not have. These are all gifts of Enlightenment, and we would be churlish (and stupid) to scorn them. But in important ways, we are closer to the earliest Christian interpreters than we might at first imagine, and it is this closeness that enables a conversation across centuries.

In the next two chapters, I will engage in some detail two interpreters, Origen of Alexandria and Augustine of Hippo. Their choice was not difficult. They are both towering figures, both of great influence, both men of great holiness of life. I am conscious that, by picking the best of the past, I might distort the conversation, but am willing to take that risk, especially since, on other counts (e.g., their love of allegory) Origen and Augustine would seem not to be people from whom we could learn much.

CHAPTER THREE

Origen and the Transformation of the Mind

A Scripture scholarship of, by, and for the church can have a future not by turning to the academy for help, but by looking to the resources offered by its own tradition. Biblical scholars must go back in order to get to the future, by reading the best of ancient interpreters of Scripture, seeking to learn again some of the things they ought not to have forgotten. Origen of Alexandria (185-253 C.E.) is an obvious first choice as a conversation partner because of his historical situation, his life, and his stature as interpreter of Scripture.[1] Origen was not only pre-Constantinian,

---

1. In this and the following chapter, most of the supporting evidence will be drawn from primary rather than secondary sources. For treatments of Origen, see Johannes Quasten, *Patrology, 2: Ante-Nicene Literature after Irenaeus* (Westminster, Md.: Christian Classics, 1992), 37-101; R. P. C. Hanson, *Origen's Doctrine of Tradition* (London: SPCK, 1954); Jean Daniélou, *Origen*, trans. Walter Mitchell (New York: Sheed and Ward, 1957); Henri de Lubac, *Histoire et Esprit* (Paris: Aubier, 1950); Henri Crouzel, *Origen*, trans. A. S. Worrall (San Francisco: Harper & Row, 1989); G. L. Prestige, "Origen: Or the Claims of Religious Intelligence," in *Fathers and Heretics* (London: SPCK, 1963); Joseph Wilson Trigg, *Origen: The Bible and Philosophy in the Third-Century Church* (Atlanta: John Knox, 1983); Karen Jo Torjesen, *Hermeneutical Procedure and Theological Structure in Origen's Exegesis* (Berlin: de Gruyter, 1986). Selections can be found in Hans Urs von Balthasar, ed., *Origen, Spirit and Fire: A Thematic Anthology of His Writings*, trans. Robert J. Daly, S.J. (Washington: Catholic University of America Press, 1984); and R. B. Tollinton, trans., *Selections from the Commentaries and Homilies of Origen* (London: SPCK, 1929). Tollinton has a particularly good essay on Origen as exegete in his Introduction, ix-xl.

he lived under persecution. His father Leonides was martyred under Severus in 202.[2] Origen himself was tortured nearly to the point of death under Decius in 253.[3] Christianity had already survived a long while in such difficult diaspora conditions. When Origen visited Rome in 212,[4] the death of Paul the Apostle was as far past for him (144 years) as the inauguration of James Buchanan is from that of George W. Bush.

Origen grew up and spent his life in a pluralistic culture. He first taught in the Hellenistic city of Alexandria, whose great library enabled a substantial tradition of learning in all the branches of philosophy.[5] One of those philosophers, known to us only as Celsus, wrote a sustained attack on Christianity called "The True Doctrine," about seven years before Origen's birth.[6] The Jewish population of Alexandria was not only large, but had produced the Greek translation of the Old Testament called the Septuagint — a translation that Origen regarded as divinely inspired — as well as an extensive apologetic literature based on that translation.[7] Christianity in Alexandria was so shaken by the Gnosticism advanced by Marcion, Valentinus, and Heracleon some 35 years before Origen's birth[8] that Origen had these heretical teachers constantly in view.[9]

2. Origen's life is treated extensively by Eusebius of Caesarea in *Ecclesiastical History,* Book 6. For the death of Leonides and Origen's youthful fervor for martyrdom, see *Hist. eccl.* 6.1, 1.

3. *Hist. eccl.* 6.39.

4. *Hist. eccl.* 6.14, 10.

5. The larger library at Alexandria had been damaged or destroyed in the Roman Civil War, ca. 48 B.C.E. The smaller ("Daughter") library under the patronage of Serapis continued in existence until the temple (and probably with it, the library) was destroyed by the order of Theodosius in 391. See Socrates, *Ecclesiastical History* 5.16.

6. Celsus's work is known to us through Origen's rebuttal, *Contra Celsum (Cels.),* but Origen quotes enough for a substantial version to be published separately; see Celsus, *On the True Doctrine: A Discourse Against the Christians,* trans. R. Joseph Hoffmann (New York: Oxford University Press, 1987).

7. In addition to the Wisdom of Solomon, 3 Maccabees, 4 Maccabees, and the extensive writings of Philo, other writings that can be safely ascribed to Alexandrian Jews are the *Letter of Aristeas, Joseph and Aseneth,* the *Sentences* of Pseudo-Phocylides, and the fragments of such authors as Aristobulus, Ezekiel the Tragedian, and Pseudo-Orpheus.

8. Origen's predecessor, Clement of Alexandria (150-215), already did battle against gnostic teachers such as Valentinus (*Strom.* 2.8; 2.11; 4.13; 5.1), Marcion (*Strom.* 3.3-4), and Basilides (*Strom.* 3.1; 4.12; 4.24).

9. Origen did not write any anti-heretical tractates, but takes care always to dis-

Origen's thought-world is certainly premodern. His idealism is that of Plato, not that of Descartes, Kant, or Hegel.[10] His physical world was smaller — his extensive travels never brought him outside the realm of the ancient *oikoumenē* — but Origen's cosmology is a more open system than that of moderns: souls enter bodies from a heavenly realm and exist after the death of those bodies;[11] miracles happen on every side;[12] and demons as well as angels play real roles in the affairs of humans.[13]

Origen lived the life of a saint. The fact that he was never given the title, or that versions of his thought known as Origenism created controversy for several hundred years, leading finally to a condemnation of his teaching by the Second Council of Constantinople in 553, tells us much more about ecclesiastical politics than it does about Origen.[14]

---

tinguish his position from those whom he variously designates as "heretics" (*Cels.* 6.72; *John* 1.40; 2.23; *Luke* 1.2; 7.4; 14.4; 14.7; 17.4; 25.5; *Jer.* 1.16.2; 11.3.1; 12.5.1; 17.2.1; *Comm. Cant.* 3.5; 3.6; *Num.* 9.1; *Josh.* 12.3), "Gnostics" (*Cels.* 6.31; 8.15; *John* 2.19), Ebionites (*Cels.* 5.21; 5.65; *Matt.* 11.12; 12.5), or Ophites (*Cels.* 6.24; 6.28; 6.30; 7.40) or Docetists (*John* 10:4), naming some heretical teachers explicitly, such as Marcion (*Cels.* 5.54; 6.53; 6.74; 7.18; *John* 5.4; 10.4; *Matt.* 11.14; 12.23; *Luke* 16.6; 16.4; 20.2; 29.4; *Exod.* 8.6; *Jer.* 10.5.1; *Lev.* 5.1.3) and his student Apelles (*Cels.* 5.54; *Gen.* 2.2), Valentinus (*Cels.* 5.61; 6.35; 12.23; *Jer.* 10.5.1), Basilides (*Matt.* 12.23; *Jer.* 10.5.1), and Heracleon (*John* 1.8; 2.15; 6.2; 6.8; 6.12; 6.13; 6.15; 6.23; 6.24; 6.38; 10.14; 10.19).

10. Origen thinks of Plato as the best Greek philosophy has to offer (see esp. *Cels.* 6.3-16), but he still considers Scripture to know more and better than Plato (*Cels.* 6.3; 6.5-6; 6.18; 7.42); he thinks it probable (as did some Hellenistic Jewish authors) that Plato learned the best in his teaching from Scripture (*Cels.* 7.19).

11. The origin and final destination of the soul are among the things left undefined by the apostolic teaching (*Princ.* I Praef. 5) and are topics diligently pursued by Origen in *First Principles*.

12. See, e.g. *Cels.* 1.38; 1.68; *John* 6.17.

13. Angels act for the good of humans (*Princ.* 1.8; *Josh.* 23.4). Demons can possess the soul of an evil person (*Princ.* 3.2.3; 3.3.4) and sponsor pagan worship (*Cels.* 7.31; 7.69; 8.63).

14. There are two stages to "Origenism." Evagrius of Pontus (345-399) developed some of Origen's ideas in *De principiis* far more systematically than Origen himself, pushing especially the notions of the pre-existence and transmigration of souls, and the final reconciliation of all beings (*apokatastasis*). The first episode was Epiphanius's attack on Origen ca. 391-392, leading to a rancorous personal dispute between Jerome and Rufinus, both of whom had begun as champions of Origen. The second stage took place in the 6th century and again involved disputes between

Though having some measure of controversy,[15] his public career as well as his private life was marked by deep piety and a most profound loyalty to the church, as demonstrated not only by his unflagging dedication to daily preaching but also by his confessing Christ under torture.[16] No one reading anything of his beyond *On First Principles* can doubt that he was a man in love with God, devoted to "our Lord Jesus Christ" (as he characteristically called him), a servant of the church,[17] and consumed with zeal for the transforming power of God's Holy Word.

Above all, Origen commands our attention for his astonishing achievements as a scriptural theologian. Ancient writers variously attribute to him 6000, or 2000, or only a mere 800 treatises.[18] Since Origen himself observed a strict evangelical poverty, the financial cost of such a prodigious literary output was borne by his good and wealthy friend Ambrose, who supplied writing materials and secretaries to take dictation.[19] All these resources were needed to keep up Origen's nearly

---

monks, leading to a condemnation of Origen as among the most pernicious of heretics by the Emperor Justinian and a council at Constantinople that condemned a list of Origenistic errors. Origen's teaching was subsequently condemned by the Second Council of Constantinople in 553. See Henri Crouzel, "Origenism," *New Catholic Encyclopedia* 10 (New York: McGraw-Hill, 1967): 771-74; G. Fritz, "Origénisme," *Dictionnaire de Théologie Catholique* 11 (Paris: Letouzey et Ane, 1931): 1566-87.

15. Eusebius recounts the story of his self-mutilation in obedience to the evangelical command to become a eunuch for the kingdom of heaven (*Hist. eccl.* 6.8, 1-3), and the controversy surrounding Origen's ecclesiastical status (6.8, 4-5; 6.19, 16-17).

16. Eusebius tells of his remarkably ascetical life (*Hist. eccl.* 6.3, 11-12) and the heroism of his witness under torture (6.39).

17. Two statements made in passing in his homilies express Origen's sentiment perfectly: "I want to be a man of the church. I do not want to be called by the name of some founder of a heresy, but by the name of Christ, and to bear that name which is blessed on the earth. It is my desire, in deed as in spirit, both to be and to be called a Christian" (*Luke* 16.6); and "I bear the title of priest, and, as you see, I preach the word of God. But if I do anything contrary to the discipline of the church or the rule laid down in the Gospels — if I give offense to you and to the church — then I hope that the whole church will unite with one consent and cast me off" (*Josh.* 7.6).

18. See Quasten, *Patrology*, 3: *The Golden Age of Patristic Greek Literature* (1960): 43.

19. Eusebius, *Hist. eccl.* 6.23, 1-2. Eusebius tells us that shortly after the martyrdom of his father, when the family lost all its property, Origen was sustained by a wealthy woman in Alexandria (6.2, 13). Origen wrote the massive *Contra Celsum* in response to Ambrose's request (*Cels.* 1.1), and apparently wrote the commentary on John also to

superhuman energy and never-flagging creativity. Because of his later reputation, only a small portion of this great outpouring escaped destruction, and that mainly in Latin translation.[20] But that small portion still astonishes and is more than enough to support the judgment that Origen is the greatest mind and most original imagination of Christianity's first three centuries, one of its last and greatest apologists, its first and most courageous systematic theologian, its most wide-ranging preacher, and the exegete who virtually by himself invented biblical scholarship, influencing directly or indirectly, through imitation or opposition, all subsequent interpreters.

Origen's Scriptural World

No Christian theologian ever more fully embraced Scripture as revealing the mysteries of God, or ever had a clearer perception of the intellectual difficulties involved in such an embrace. Raised in a Christian home, Origen learned the Scriptures hand in hand with secular learning.[21] Because he started teaching at the age of 18[22] in a city where those Scriptures were vigorously disputed — scorned by cultured despisers, controverted by hostile Jewish readers, read in dramatically divergent ways by gnostic Christians, clung to piteously by the fearful and noninquisitive pious — Origen never took Scripture as something

---

please Ambrose (see *John* 6.1), who had formerly been enamored of heretical writings (*John* 5.4).

20. Of the extant homilies, we have only the 20 on Jeremiah and 1 on 1 Samuel in Greek; the rest are in the form of Latin translations by Rufinus (16 on Genesis, 13 on Exodus, 16 on Leviticus, 28 on Numbers, 26 on Joshua, 9 on Judges, 9 on Psalms) and Jerome (2 on Canticles, 9 on Isaiah, 14 on Jeremiah, 14 on Ezekiel, 39 on Luke). Of the commentaries on Matthew, John, Romans, and Canticles, we have only 8 on the book of Matthew in Greek, the rest in Latin. Only the fragments of *On First Principles* that were included in the *Philocalia* assembled by Gregory of Nazianzus and Basil the Great in 358-359 are in Greek; the rest are in Rufinus's Latin translation. The *Contra Celsum* is extant in Greek, as are the remaining smaller compositions. For the translations of Rufinus and Jerome, see Quasten, *Patrology*, 4: *The Golden Age of Latin Patristic Literature, from the Council of Nicea to the Council of Chalcedon*, trans. P. Solari, O.S.B. (1986), 195-209.

21. See Eusebius, *Hist. eccl.* 6.1, 7-8.

22. Eusebius, *Hist. eccl.* 6.3, 3.

given, but rather as an arena for competing interpretation. To the task of an interpretation conformed to the piety and practice of his church he brought all the power of his remarkable mind.

In all his writings, Origen displays a rare combination of intellectual fearlessness and generosity. Such qualities may owe something to his bone-deep commitment to the faith and practices of the church, something to his distinctive and decisive temperament, and something to the clarifying effect of persecution. Whatever the reasons, Origen was the least anxious of all theologians. He had the willingness to risk his mind together with a cheerful openness to being corrected by the reading of others. He positively celebrates diversity of interpretation. In response to Celsus's charge that Christianity cannot be true because it has so many heresies (or versions), Origen says the fields of medicine and philosophy also have many conflicting theories. The more important the subject matter, Origen suggests, the more people of strong intelligence will disagree. He quotes Paul (1 Cor. 11:19), "there must be heresies among you so that the sound (or tested) among you might be revealed," and applies it to his situation: pluralism and controversy have the beneficial effect of testing the genuineness of our faith (*Cels.* 3.12-13; see also *Cels.* 5.61; *Num.* 9.1). Origen embraces truth wherever and however it is to be found:

> If the doctrine be sound and if the effect of it good, whether it was made known to the Greeks by Plato or any of the wise men of Greece, or whether it was delivered to the Jews by Moses or any of the prophets, or whether it was given to the Christians in the recorded teaching of Jesus Christ, or in the instructions of his apostles, that does not affect the value of the truth communicated. (*Cels.* 7.59)

Origen's two largest extant nonexegetical works give us a sense of his perception of Scripture as an arena for disputed interpretations. The first is his pioneering work of speculative theology, *Peri archōn (De principiis)*, usually translated as *On First Principles*. Written in Alexandria between 220 and 230, when Origen was between 35 and 45 years old, it made his name during his lifetime and destroyed his reputation after his death. Attention is usually paid to the elements that led to later controversy: his speculations concerning the origin of the souls and the final restoration of all things *(apokatastasis)*, which inevitably raises the question of just how Platonic a philosopher Origen was.[23] I want rather to stress two other features of this work that, quite literally, invented Christian systematic theology.

The first feature is Origen's discussion of his goal and method in the preface to Book I. After stating that the knowledge of the good and blessed life is available only from the teaching of Christ (I Praef. 1), he recognizes immediately that Christians themselves disagree on both trivial and great matters (I Praef. 2). Despite these disputes, he asserts, "The teaching of the church, handed down in unbroken succession from the Apostles, is still presented and continues to exist in the churches up to the present day." And further: "We maintain that that only is to believed as the truth which in no way conflicts with the tradition of the church and the apostles" (I Praef. 2). Then, in an early version of the rule of faith (or creed), Origen lists the doctrines that the apostles delivered in plain terms, concerning God, Christ Jesus, the Holy Spirit, the soul, spiritual powers, the world, and the scriptures (*Princ.* I Praef. 4). For each topic, he indicates first what must be believed, and then the issues yet to be settled.

Concerning souls, for example, he says that it is clear they have freedom and will share in the resurrection. It is not yet defined, however, what the origin of the soul is; that topic is open for further examination. Likewise, concerning the world: it clearly began to exist in time and will suffer dissolution. But what existed before the visible world, or what might exist after it, has not been plainly revealed. These matters also can be debated within the boundaries of the faith (*Princ.* I Praef. 5-7). So also with the Scriptures: they are inspired by the Holy Spirit, have both an obvious and hidden meanings, and the church accepts the law as spiritual. All of this is part of the Tradition. But what the hidden meanings of Scripture are is to be discovered through the grace of the Holy Spirit by interpreters of Scripture (*Princ.* I Praef. 8).[24]

As Origen sets out to create a "single body of doctrine" out of the connections between these fundamental principles and speculations concerning those matters not yet defined but locked mysteriously in Scripture (*Princ.* I Praef. 10), then, he regards himself as utterly loyal to

---

23. See, e.g., Daniélou, 73-98, 203-8; Trigg, 87-129.

24. For the Holy Spirit as the one who guides to a deeper meaning, see also *Cels.* 2.2.

the rule of faith proclaimed in the church. He cannot consider as true whatever is in conflict with that open teaching. He intends his interpretation of Scripture, then, not only to be consonant with the church's faith but a means of giving it intellectual coherence. And there was a real urgency to that task. Please remember that gnostic speculations — already circulating in Egypt — were at that very time providing highly seductive theories concerning the origin and fate of the world, the origin and future of the soul, theories seriously at odds with the rule of faith.[25] Within his context, then, Origen can best be understood, not as a speculative thinker who had little regard for the Tradition, but as a theologian responding to a pastoral crisis created by the need for a philosophically informed rendering of doctrine that did not fall into the irresponsible vagaries of Gnosticism.

Origen returns to the subject of the interpretation of Scripture in Book 4 of *Peri archōn*. He provides a discussion of hermeneutics more sophisticated than any up to — and quite possibly including — those of the 20th century. A popular impression of Origen is that he championed allegory and despised the literal sense of the text, once more because of a deeply ingrained Platonic outlook. The famous statement connecting a threefold reading of Scripture to a Platonic anthropology can certainly give that impression: "For just as man consists in body, soul, and spirit, so in the same way does the Scripture, which has been prepared by God to be given for man's salvation" (*Princ.* 4.1, 11). But the matter is more complex. A closer reading of the entire discussion shows that Origen's call for multiple meanings in texts is grounded less in a predilection for a philosophical system, than in the existing practice of the church, in Scripture itself — above all the Apostle Paul — and, once more, his pastoral perception of the disasters attendant upon a strictly literal interpretation.

1. In his preface to Book 1, Origen had already pointed to the wider practice of the church regarding the spiritual interpretation of the Jewish law: "respecting which, there is one opinion throughout the whole church, that the whole law is indeed spiritual" (*Princ.* 1 Praef. 8).

---

25. As examples, take the *Gospel of Truth* I, 16.5–18.10; the *Tripartite Tractate;* the *Apocryphon of John; On the Origin of the World,* all found in *The Nag Hammadi Library in English,* ed. James M. Robinson (Leiden: Brill, 1981).

2. Paul not only himself interprets Torah spiritually (as in 1 Cor. 9:9 when he applies the feeding of animals to the financial support of ministers), but he provides programmatic guidance. Of particular importance is 1 Cor. 10:11: "These things happened to them typologically, but they were written for our instruction." Origen seizes on the distinction between what happened in the past and the textual character of Scripture. Scripture was inspired by the Holy Spirit (so the church teaches). Therefore *in its language* it inevitably teaches; *in the way it is stated,* it is meant for our instruction, whatever its relation to "what might have happened" (*Princ.* 4.1, 12-13).[26]

3. More than any other ancient or modern interpreter, Origen saw the logical consequences of a literal reading that had no room for a moral or spiritual interpretation. He saw around him members of the circumcision who did not believe because they looked for a literal fulfillment of prophecies (*Princ.* 4.1, 8); what he does not mention here is that if the Old Testament legislation were read literally by Christians then they would continue to be under circumcision, that is, be Judaizers. He also knows of heretics, like Marcion, who conclude from a literal reading of the Old Testament that the creator God is malicious and unjust, and that the God of Jesus must be opposed to that God as mercy is to wrath (*Princ.* 4.1, 8). Finally, he sees "even the simple of those who claim to belong to the church, while believing indeed that there is none greater than the creator, in which they are right, yet believe such things about him as would not be believed of the most savage and unjust of men" (4.1, 8).

What makes Origen radical is his insistence that all Scripture has a spiritual meaning even when it does not make sense literally, and that the same thing applies to the New Testament as to the Old Testament (*Princ.* 4.1, 16). But he does not reach such conclusions arbitrarily. It is precisely because he is so deeply committed to the inspiration of Scripture (*Princ.* 4.1, 1) that he maintains its power to instruct even when humans are incapable of yet reaching the Spirit's intention. And it is pre-

26. Origen also finds warrant for spiritual readings in Moses' intended twofold meaning (*Cels.* 1.18) and in the Proverbs of Solomon (*Cels.* 7.34).

cisely the fact that he is so clear-eyed and unswerving a reader of the literal sense that he sees its limitations: "For our contention with regard to the whole of Scripture is that it all has a spiritual meaning, but not all a bodily meaning; for the bodily meaning is often proved to be an impossibility" (*Princ.* 4.1, 20).

This is particularly the case with historylike narratives. Origen sees that they contain some things which did not happen, or could not happen, or might have happened but did not, and this is all woven together with narratives that do correspond to what really happened; in some cases "a few words are inserted which in the bodily sense are not true, and at other times a greater number" (*Princ.* 4.1, 15). He does not deny that there is real history in the Bible; in fact, he thinks there is more rather than less (*Princ.* 4.1, 19). And the literal sense itself most often bears a useful moral meaning for the simple believer (*Princ.* 4.1, 19). When read carefully, however, the literal sense can be seen to present any number of difficulties to the understanding, "stumbling-blocks, hindrances, and impossibilities." But because the Holy Spirit seeks to instruct us through the text exactly as it is written, these stumbling blocks are actually the signal to "go deeper" and seek the spiritual meaning (*Princ.* 4.1, 15). In the law, for example, some precepts are useful for our own sake and others for the time they were given; but some precepts are not useful at all; and even impossibilities are recorded in the law . . . and indeed the New Testament as well (*Princ.* 4.1, 17-18). These textual aporiae are not the occasion for abandoning Scripture, but of seeking its deeper wisdom: they are "for the sake of the more skillful and inquiring readers, in order that these, by giving themselves to the toil of examining what is written, may gain a sound conviction of the necessity of seeking in such instances *a meaning worthy of God*" (*Princ.* 4.1, 15, emphasis added). The last phrase is one that echoes throughout Origen's work: the interpretation of Scripture must not be unworthy of the God who inspired the text and who is revealed through the text.[27]

On First Principles looks mainly inward to the life of the church. In his apologetic work *Against Celsus*, written ca. 246, we see Origen the public theologian facing outward toward the threat posed by the pagan philosopher's massive attack on Christianity. In this nonexegetical work as

---

27. See *Cels.* 4.71; 5.14; 5.24; 6.61; 6.62; 6.70; 7.12; *Josh.* 12.3; *Philoc.* 20.1.1; 28.2.3.

LUKE JOHNSON

well, we find Origen constantly engaging Scripture as the defining symbolic world of Christians, but one that is actively controverted. Here, his discussions of Scripture are necessarily even more complex than in *Peri archōn,* where he mainly read for doctrine. At issue in *Contra Celsum* are the Christian claim to a place in Greco-Roman culture and the legitimacy of the claim to being the authentic Israel spoken of in Scripture. On one side, Origen faces the philosophical challenge in the form of a somewhat eclectic Epicureanism (*Cels.* 1.8-9). But Celsus has cleverly made Jewish rebuttals of Christian claims his own (*Cels.* 1.8). Origen must therefore also engage the front represented by Jewish interpretations, in a form far more aggressive than those posed a century earlier to Justin by Trypho.[28] And, as always, he must bear in mind that in the eyes of pagans and Jews, Christianity is not one thing, but many: the heretics also have their readings of Scripture (*Cels.* 5.54, 65). *Contra Celsum* is notoriously difficult to read both for its length (eight large books) and its method of argumentation, which is the opposite of systematic. Readers sensitive to the shifting sands on which Origen was trying to place his scriptural foundation can appreciate his own need to keep turning in one direction and another and to keep his feet nimble.

I want to isolate only two features of this massive work for special attention. First, *Contra Celsum* shows how the literal sense can be meaningful, indeed critical, for Christian self-understanding. In disputation with Jewish opponents, the literal fulfillment or nonfulfillment of prophecy is obviously going to play a significant role.[29] Origen reads the prophetic texts straightforwardly as pointing to the messianic age, and he makes three powerful arguments.

1. Jewish claims that the prophecies refer to them as a people are false, for historical events have removed the possibility of their ful-

28. Justin's *Dialogue With Trypho* records a long dispute between the Jewish teacher Trypho and the Christian philosopher Justin shortly after the final destruction of the city of Jerusalem by the Romans (135 C.E.). The debate involves the rival claims of Jews and Christians to the heritage of Scripture, and therefore the fulfillment and nonfulfillment of prophecy, as well as the proper text (Hebrew or Septuagint) on which to base the respective claims. Trypho gets to make some good points, but, not surprisingly, Justin dominates the debate.

29. For the importance of the literal fulfillment of prophecy for Christian claims, see also *Princ.* 4.1, 3-7.

fillment (*Cels.* 2.8; 2.78). Remember that Origen is born within 50 years of the final destruction of Jerusalem in 135, a period equivalent to the space between us and the Holocaust. When he says that there is now no earthly Zion, no land, no people on the land, and no possibility for a messiah to gather them, he is not being a polemicist, but is taking the facts as seriously as some Jewish theologians have taken the Holocaust in the 20th century: things seem to have radically and forever changed.[30]

2. The Gospel narratives show that the prophecies concerning the Messiah's birth, ministry, and suffering have been literally fulfilled in Jesus. Those that speak of the Messiah's triumph — and not fulfilled in the Gospels — point to the second coming (*Cels.* 1.55-56; 2.29; 4.1-2). Here, Origen borrows a page from Justin.[31]

3. Most telling, the things that have befallen the Jews in their history are in literal fulfillment of the sayings of Jesus, who spoke of the destruction of the temple and the calamities to fall upon the land and the people. Not only that, Jesus also prophesied the spread of the gospel to all the nations, exactly as it has happened (*Cels.* 2.13; 4.22).

Today, we have little appetite for supersessionist arguments, but I invite your historical imagination to appreciate how powerful they would have been in Origen's time, and to consider as well how his careful use of the argument from prophecy is based entirely on the literal sense of the text.[32]

The second instructive feature of the *Contra Celsum* is the picture it gives of Origen the philosopher. Given Origen's education and early responsibilities as a teacher, we should not be surprised to find him thoroughly conversant with the entire range of Greek literature, religion,

30. E.g., Richard L. Rubenstein, *After Auschwitz: Radical Theology and Contemporary Judaism* (Indianapolis: Bobbs-Merrill, 1966); and Emil L. Fackenheim, *The Jewish Bible after the Holocaust: A Re-reading* (Bloomington: Indiana University Press, 1990).

31. See Justin, *Dial.* 32-34.

32. For examples of close reading at the literal level in the *Contra Celsum* apart from the fulfillment of prophecy, see Origen on the resurrection in Paul (*Cels.* 2.66) and on the Gospel accounts of Jesus' death and burial (*Cels.* 2.69), and the Genesis account of Lot's daughters (*Cels.* 4.45). Origen states in *Cels.* 7.10 that the literal sense addresses conduct, whereas the spiritual sense addresses understanding.

and philosophy. The depth of his knowledge, however, is impressive. Although his letter to Gregory Thaumaturgus suggests that secular knowledge is useful mainly as it can be used for Scripture,[33] the *Contra Celsum* shows that his own engagement was more than casual, and scarcely derived from handbooks. In seven successive chapters of Book 6, for example, he leads the reader through close analyses of Plato's *Timaeus, Apology, Laws, Phaedrus,* and *Epistles* (*Cels.* 6.9-17). More striking is the way he defines Christianity as a philosophical school, and thereby stakes out a recognizable place for the church within Greco-Roman culture.[34] Christians are, to be sure, better than the philosophers (7.47), but philosophy is the closest analogy, especially as found in Plato (3.81). Origen compares the "School of Jesus" (7.41) to the schools of Greeks and Jews (4.31) across a wide range of points: Jesus is like the founder of a philosophical school (1.65), not least in the way that he was betrayed and suffered (2.12); Christianity has sects as do other schools (2.27; 5.61) that generate disputes like those between philosophical parties (6.26). Christianity has stages of initiation like the Pythagoreans (3.51); must struggle with false philosophers who talk but don't walk (4.27, 30); resists local customs on the basis of principle like other philosophers (5.35); has traditions of Jesus' appearance such as are found attributed to other philosophers (5.57). Jesus can be compared to Socrates (2.41), and the speech in the Gospels can be called closer to the discourses of Epictetus than to the dialogues of Plato (6.2). Christian teaching is a form of healing in the way that philosophy claims to be (3.75), and the goal of Christianity is that humans become wise (3.45).[35] It is consistent, then, that Christians should follow the lead of Greek and Jewish philosophers (like Philo) and read Scripture

---

33. "I wish to ask you to extract from the philosophy of the Greeks what may serve as a course of study or a preparation for Christianity, and from geometry and astronomy what will serve to explain the sacred Scriptures"; *Ep. Greg.* 1.

34. See Robert L. Wilcken, "Collegia, Philosophical Schools, and Theology," in *The Catacombs and the Colosseum: The Roman Empire as the Setting of Primitive Christianity,* ed. Stephen Benko and John J. O'Rourke (Valley Forge: Judson, 1971), 268-91.

35. Origen compares the "schools" or "heresies" within Christianity to those within philosophy and medicine (*Cels.* 3.12-13), and consistently employs the standard medical metaphors widely used by philosophers of the period (*Cels.* 3.60-62, 74-75; 4.18). See Martha C. Nussbaum, *The Therapy of Desire: Theory and Practice in Hellenistic Ethics* (Princeton: Princeton University Press, 1994).

"philosophically" (3.58; 3.79).[36] The most fascinating aspect of this extended analogy between Christianity and philosophy is the way Origen uses it to counter Celsus's charge that Christians accept things on faith without evidence. In a response that sounds astonishingly postmodern, he points out that all members of philosophical schools begin with unproven assumptions and start with *believing* (1.10).

Origen's language about philosophy places him squarely within the world of Greco-Roman moralists, the popular philosophers of the early empire, whose concern was not theory but therapy, whose passion was not epistemology but ethics.[37] For Christians to "seek to become wise" meant not the acquisition of knowledge but the changing of their outlook and behavior. It meant the healing of the passions by good teaching. It meant battling vice and learning to practice virtue. Like Plutarch a century earlier, Origen saw the philosophical life as a progressive transformation of the soul.[38] As I will try to show, Origen's spiritual reading of Scripture had very little to do with a platonic realm of forms, but had everything to do with moral conversion. Plutarch sought to save the dignity of the religious myths about Isis and Osiris by reading them not literally but "philosophically" *(philosophikōs)*, that is, about human transformation.[39] For Origen to read the traditional

36. Origen claims that the story of Adam and Eve can be interpreted allegorically in exactly the same way that the myths of Hesiod were among the Greeks (*Cels.* 4.38), and he appeals to the practice of Plato in this matter (4.39).

37. See Abraham J. Malherbe, "Hellenistic Moralists and the New Testament," *ANRW* II, 26, 1 (1992): 267-333.

38. Plutarch, *On Progress in Virtue (Mor.* 75A-86A).

39. See Plutarch, *Isis and Osiris:* "If, then, you listen to the stories about the gods in this way, accepting them from those who interpret the story reverently and philosophically, and if you always perform and observe the established rites of worship, and believe that no sacrifice that you can offer, no deed that you may do will be more likely to find favor with the gods than your belief in their true nature, you may avoid superstition which is no less an evil than atheism" *(Mor.* 355D); trans. Frank Cole Babbitt. LCL (Cambridge, Mass.: Harvard University Press, 1959), 31. Likewise the Jewish philosopher Aristobulus, writing from Alexandria, speaking of the law of Moses: "I urge you to accept the interpretation in the 'natural' sense, and grasp a fitting conception about God and not lapse into a mythical, popular way of thinking" *(Frag.* 2.2). And further, "All philosophers hold that it is necessary to hold devout convictions about God" *(Frag.* 4.8). Translations are those of Carl R. Holladay, *Fragments from Hellenistic Jewish Authors,* 3: *Aristobulus.* SBLTT 39, Pseudepigrapha Series, 13 (Atlanta: Scholars, 1995), 137, 185.

texts of Christianity "philosophically" meant reading them as concerned with the transformation of the mind, for only such a reading is truly "worthy of God."

The only real problem is the degree to which a specific scriptural passage allows such a moral understanding. This leads us to a consideration of the ways in which Origen is not only scriptural but also critical. Before taking up that important topic, however, it is proper to respond more fully to the popular perception of Origen (largely derived from *Peri archōn*) that he was little concerned with the literal sense. I have already shown how he uses the literal fulfillment of prophecy in both *Peri archōn* and the *Contra Celsum*. When we turn to his other extant nonexegetical works, we find the same natural and straightforward handling of the literal sense. In his instruction *On Prayer* and his *Exhortation to Martyrdom*, we find an Origen deeply enmeshed in the practices of his community,[40] supporting those practices on the basis of a literal rendering of the Scripture.[41] It is no accident that these are moral topics to which the Scripture can speak in direct fashion at the literal level. We find the same thing, however, in his *Dialogue with Heraclides,* which discusses the doctrines concerning the Father, the Son, and the soul, and stays within the framework of the literal meaning (and the rule of faith!).[42] Likewise, the second of his surviving letters, in which he responds to Africanus's challenge to Origen's use of the History of Susanna when discussing the book of Daniel, takes up linguistic and literary issues entirely at the literal level.[43] His *Tractate on the Passover,* in contrast, gives careful attention to the literal sense, but also elaborates on the spiritual meaning.[44] And all of his exegetical work, both his commentaries that sought primarily to explain the text, and his homilies

40. See, e.g., *On Prayer* 28 and 30.

41. Note his struggle with the conflict between the texts of Ephesians and Hebrews, and his nonallegorical resolution of them, in *On Prayer* 27:15, and his demand for a literal fulfillment of the command to leave family behind in *Exhortation to Martyrdom* 37.

42. See *Dialogue of Origen with Heraclides and His Fellow Bishops on the Father, the Son, and the Soul* 1.25 and 10.15.

43. The *Letter from Origen to Africanus* is a glittering example of Origen's critical capacities, as he engages everything from text-criticism to canonicity to the details of Hebrew and Greek philology.

44. *Pasch.* 38-50.

that sought primarily to edify the hearers, paid an almost painfully precise attention to every nuance of the text.[45] When the literal sense yields powerful meaning, so does Origen's interpretation of the literal sense, as in his superb reading of the Abraham and Isaac story (see *Gen.* 8). And Origen uses all his skill to explicate the literal sense in a worthy fashion (see *Gen.* 6.2.3 5). But as the discussion of *Peri archōn* indicated, it was precisely Origen's close reading of the literal sense that helped persuade him of the need for higher senses (see *Lev.* 14.1.1).

Origen as Critical Scholar

Pre-Enlightenment scriptural interpretation is sometimes dismissed as "precritical," meaning, in effect, prehistorical-critical. The term precritical in any sense, however, does not apply to Origen. He saw it as his vocation to inquire (*Cels.* 4.8-9; 6.37), convinced that truth is truth wherever it appears (7.59). I can only review briefly some of the ways in which he engaged the text of Scripture with critical intelligence and learning. First, he was text-critical. His massive edition of the Old Testament in six columns (the *Hexapla*) not only enabled comparison between the Hebrew and four Greek translations (the Septuagint, Theodotion, Aquila, and Symmachus),[46] but made use of critical marks

45. It is possible to suggest a distinction in the kind of interpretation Origen tended to practice according to genre. The ancient *Commentarium* had basically an explanatory function; it was intended to aid the reader in understanding the meaning of a text by providing information. Origen tends to follow this practice in his extant commentaries (on Matthew, John, and Romans). His *Commentarii in Epistulam ad Romanos*, e.g., keeps a steady focus on exposition, making heavy use of the concordance to establish the meaning of Paul's terms. The commentaries on Matthew and John, likewise, tend to deal straightforwardly with problems presented by the literal sense. The exception among his extant commentaries is the *Commentary on the Song of Songs*, which lends itself particularly to a figurative exposition. The *Homilia* ("homily") in contrast is something of a "conversation" *(homilein)*, and has a more dialogical and exhortatory character. We find by far the greatest amount of Origen's spiritual interpretations in this preaching format. Note that in his commentary on the Song of Songs he deals with the question of literary form and the literal progress of the story, whereas in his extant homilies on the same book he is much more focused on the spiritual level.

46. The *Hexapla* remains our main source for those other ancient Greek translations. The final column was a transliteration of the Hebrew into Greek letters.

indicating lacunae and additions. In his exegetical work, moreover, he makes constant reference to variant manuscript readings in both the Old and New Testaments.[47] Rather than seek to discard readings in favor of the quest for a single prototype — the instinct of modernity — Origen uses such textual variations as a means of honoring local textual traditions and entertaining new possibilities of meaning.[48] Contemporary text-criticism is just catching up to that perspective.

His interpretation is linguistically informed. His Greek is native, but his Hebrew is constantly in play.[49] He makes use of Jewish learning,[50] sometimes at first hand,[51] and enters into conversation with Jewish readings that differ from his own.[52] He makes use of natural science, as well as political and social history, to inform his interpretations.[53] He did first-hand research into Palestinian geography.[54] He is critical with respect to canonicity, making use of apocryphal writings for a variety of things but never according them the authority of Scripture.[55] He is willing to challenge traditional attributions of authorship. Only one letter of Peter is genuine, the second is doubtful (*John* 5.3). All three letters of John are probably genuine, although some question the second and

47. See, e.g., *Ep. Afr.* 2-5; *Cels.* 1.62; *Commentary on the Gospel of John* (= *John*) 1.40; 2.13; 6.24; *Commentary on the Gospel of Matthew* (= *Matt.*) 12.15; 13.14; 13.19; *Commentary on Song of Songs* (= *Cant.*) 1.4; 2.1; *Homilies on Leviticus* (= *Lev.*) 21.13; 12.5.5; *Homilies on Luke* (= *Luke*) 7.3; *Homilies on Jeremiah* (= *Jer.*) 8.1.1; 14.3.1; 15.5.2; 16.5.2; *Homilies on Numbers* (= *Num.*) 12.1; 13.1; 17.3; 18.4; 24.1.

48. See, e.g., *Jer.* 14.3.1; 15.5.2.

49. See *Ep. Afr.* 6 and 12; *Cels.* 6.25; *John* 6.13; *Matt.* 12.21; *Jer.* 16.10.1; *Cant.* 2.4; *Homilies on Joshua* (= *Josh.*) 18.2-3; 20.2; 24.1; *Num.* 12.1; 13.6; 19.3; 20.3.

50. He is familiar with the writings of Josephus (*Cels.* 4.11; *Matt.* 10.17), Philo (*Cels.* 6.21), Aristobulus (*Cels.* 4.51), and the *Prayer of Joseph* (*John* 2.25).

51. *Ep. Afr.* 7; *Cels.* 1.45; 1.55; *John* 6.24; *Matt.* 11.9; *Cant.* Prol. 1; *Num.* 11.5.

52. *Cels.* 2.4; 2.5; 2.38; 2.79; 5.43; 5.60; *Luke* 5.1-4; 22.8.

53. For social and political history, see *Cels.* 1.24; 2.30; 5.29; 5.48; 6.19; 7.2-3; 7.30-31; *Ep. Afr.* 13-14; *John* 6.6; *Matt.* 10.21; *Jer.* 4.2; for natural science, see *Cels.* 1.33; 6.73; *Num.* 12.1; 17.1; 27.1.

54. See *John* 6.24.

55. Origen provides a canonical list of Old and New Testament in *Josh.* 7.1, and everywhere makes a sharp distinction between "the Scriptures that are current in the churches" and those that are not (*Ep. Afr.* 9; *Cels.* 5.54; 6.21; 6.36; *John* 5.4). In addition to his awareness of gnostic writings of various kinds, he makes reference to the *Gospel of Peter* and the *Protevangelium of James* (*Matt.* 10.17), the *Ascension of Isaiah* (*Matt.* 10.18), and "one of the apocryphal books among the Hebrews," the *Prayer of Joseph* (*John* 2.25).

third (*John* 5.3). He recognizes the Letter of Jude (*Matt.* 10.17). He generally treats Hebrews among the Pauline letters, although he has doubts about that ascription.[56]

Origen's commentaries contain many acute literary observations,[57] ranging from the nuances of grammar (*John* 2.2; 2.6) to the sequence of sentences (*John* 2.1) to the use of Greek rhetorical devices.[58] He knows the importance of genre and of literary context.[59] Borrowing from the practice of Jewish midrash, he makes lavish use of verbal comparison. He is a living concordance, and consistently seeks to clarify the meaning of specific terms at the literal level, drawing linguistic parallels all over the Bible with unerring accuracy.[60] He distinguishes all the possible meanings of key terms, such as *archē* ("beginning") in the prologue of John's Gospel (*John* 1.16-21). He is meticulous in the patient cataloguing of all the ways in which the Synoptic Gospels differ from John and among themselves.[61] His purpose in this is not to find the earliest Gospel, or to discredit any version. Rather, like modern redaction criticisms, he exploits these differences to find what each version enables us to learn.

Two final ways of being a critical reader might be thought of as particularly modern, namely ideological and historical criticism. Ideological criticism is really a form of moral criticism of the text. And Origen exercises this in a high degree. Origen's sensitivity on this

56. For treating it as Pauline, see *Princ.* I Praef. 1; for the doubts of others concerning authorship, see *Ep. Afr.* 9; for a statement of his own doubt, see the quotation in Eusebius, *Hist. eccl.* 6.25.

57. E.g., *Ep. Afr.* 15; *John* 6.24; 6.30; 10.5; *Matt.* 10.1; 10.4; 11.4; 11.15; 11.22; 12.43; 14.16; *Num.* 11.1; 20.3; *Gen.* 8.

58. Although Origen insists that the apostles and evangelists didn't use rhetoric (*Cels.* 1.69; 2.20), and that Jesus' language was adapted to the multitude (*Cels.* 7.61), he recognizes the use of devices such as personification (*Cels.* 7.36-37; *John* 6.5), hyperbole (*John* 1.40), and synecdoche (*Matt.* 12.38).

59. He insists as a matter of principle on determining who is speaking in a specific passage and in what context (see *Cels.* 3.20; *John* 2.29; 6.3; 6.5; *Num.* 18.2); on genre, see his identification of the Song of Songs as an *epithalamium*, *Comm. Cant.* Prol. 1.

60. Among countless examples, see *Num.* 3.4; 6.2; 11.3; 18.3; 24.2; *Lev.* 5.8.2; *Ep. Afr.* 11; *Cels.* 6.25; *John* 1.23; 1.24; 1.25; 1.26; 1.27; 1.28; 1.29; 1.30; 2.20; *Rom.* II, 4; II, 5; *Matt.* 10.15; 10.24; 12.22; 12.34; 12.35; 13.2; 13.20; 13.22; *Comm. Cant.* Prol. 2; *Philoc.* 9; 28.4.

61. See *John* 5.56; 6.14; 6.16; 6.31; 10.1; 10.15; 10.17; 10.18; *Matt.* 10.20; 11.2; 11.5; 11.19; 12.15; 12.24; 13.19; 14.13; *Luke* 1.1-2; 28.1; 35.1-2.

point, however, is different than ours. We worry about the text saying things that detract from the dignity of people. Origen's concern is for the dignity of God.[62] When Scripture uses anthropomorphisms, Origen understands that this is language adapted to the needs of the people (*Cels.* 4.71; *Num.* 23.2). But the unsophisticated reader can on the basis of such language think badly of God. Origen faces unflinchingly the scandal posed by many passages when read literally.[63] But he does not give up on Scripture or (like Marcion) conclude to the wickedness of God (*Cels.* 6.61; *Josh.* 12.3). Instead, his spiritual reading seeks to save the nature of God and thereby also save the usefulness of the text (*Cels.* 4.71).

As for history, Origen was hardly unaware of its problems. I have already pointed out how he made vigorous use of the historical information available to him as assistance in understanding scriptural passages. But he clearly differentiates the relative importance of various "historical" reports for contemporary readers (see *Hom. 1 Sam.* 28.2). And he resists trying to verify the historicity of specific narratives. He states with regard to the Gospels, for example, that the present-day reader is not in a position to correct the evangelists on things like the sequence of events that they report (*John* 10.6). He is well aware of the role of bias in interpreting events (*Cels.* 1.52), and the dangers of a selective reading (*Cels.* 1.63). He also knows that historical reconstruction is extraordinarily difficult. His remarks on historiography in *Cels.* 1.42 are particularly illuminating: "With regard to almost any history, however true, [to prove] that it actually occurred and to form an intelligent con-

---

62. See, e.g. *Cels.* 4.13-14; 5.14; 5.24; 6.62; 6.65; 7.12; 7.27; *John* 2.7; *Jer.* 12.1.1; 13.12-17; *Philoc.* 20.1.1; 28.2.3.

63. Because of his convictions concerning the unified character of Scripture, Origen sometimes has trouble acknowledging textual "contradictions," preferring to think of them as "apparent contradictions" or "apparent inconsistencies" (*Cels.* 7.12) that cannot be reconciled at the literal level (*John* 10.15) but may be resolved at a higher level (see *John* 6.14; 6.18; 10.4; 10.5). Sometimes he simply names contradictions and inconsistencies as such (*Luke* 13.4; 33.1; *Josh.* 16.2). He is, in contrast, astonishingly candid about what he considers to be impossibilities in the text (*Exod.* 2.1; 2.2; 6.7; *Josh.* 9.4; 21.1), and about things which, taken literally, are trivial (*Gen.* 7.1), defective (*Gen.* 7.5), or even deceptive (*Jer.* 12.1.1; 13.12-17). And he clearly recognizes and engages those elements in the text that appear as morally problematic (*John* 10.17; *Matt.* 14.24; *Num.* 14.2; *Philoc.* 10; *Gen.* 5.4; *Hom. 1 Kgs.* 28.2).

ception regarding it, is one of the most difficult undertakings that can be attempted, and in some instances an impossibility." Origen gives the example of the Trojan War. Everyone acknowledges that it happened, but because of the fictional elements in Homer, no one can any longer state precisely what happened. He then adds,

> He who wishes to deal candidly with histories, and would wish to keep himself also from being imposed upon by them, will exercise his judgment as to what statements he will give his assent to, and what he will accept figuratively, seeking to discover the meaning of the authors of such inventions, and from what statements he will withhold belief, as having been written for the gratification of certain individuals . . . there is need for candor in those who are to read, and for much investigation, and, so to speak, insight into the meaning of the writers, that the object with which each event has been recorded may be discovered.

He makes these comments when discussing the Gospels. Origen thinks that what they say about Jesus' ministry is broadly true. He particularly insists on the reality of the resurrection event (*Cels.* 3.23). But he does not think it possible (or useful) to seek to go beyond what they tell us.

In this respect, Origen is actually far more critical than modern scholars concerning the irrelevance of history to theology or to spiritual transformation. Events of the past are past (see *Matt.* 12.36). They are, like their actors, dead. But the text is living since it is inspired by the Holy Spirit (*Hom. 1 Sam.* 28.4.2) — the meaning the Spirit wishes to teach is found precisely in the literary shaping, whether figurative or not (*John* 10.4). He says, "If the Scriptures are true, then the Lord speaks not only there, in the congregation of the Jews, but today, too, in this congregation" (*Luke* 32.6). To read the text as a means of recovering the past is to prefer the dead to the living. These things, remember, "were written" (by God's spirit through human authors) for our instruction (1 Cor. 10:11). The historical sense as such, when it becomes the sole object of inquiry, itself turns scandalous, that is, a stumbling block, to a living engagement with the text.

Reading for Transformation

In the midst of a highly technical dialogue with Dionysius about the soul and its relationship to blood, Origen interrupts the discussion to exhort the audience. He quotes Rom. 12:1, "I beseech you, therefore, be transformed," adding, "Resolve to learn that you can be transformed . . . ," and he concludes his exhortation to them with these words, "What is it I really want? To treat the matter in a way that heals the souls of my hearers" (*Dial.* 13.25-15.25). This small moment perfectly captures Origen's entire motivation and goal for interpreting Scripture. As a pre-Augustinian, Hellenistic moralist, Origen was sunnily optimistic about the human person's capacity to be transformed by knowledge. Transforming knowledge, however, is certainly not information, even about mystical things. Nor is it a form of self-realization, as the gnostics would have it. Rather it is coming to know God through Jesus (*Cels.* 6.68) and being transformed into the mind of Christ, since Jesus is a "living pattern to men" (*Cels.* 2.16). Origen emphasizes in his response to Celsus that the healings Jesus worked in the Gospels are continuous with the healing of people's souls in the present (*Cels.* 1.67; 2.48).[64] The good news has the power to transform (*Cels.* 1.63; 8.47). Indeed, the most stunning evidence Origen can offer for Christian claims is the miracle of moral transformation in the pagan world: he can point confidently to churches throughout the empire filled with people who have turned from wickedness to the teaching of Jesus and lives of virtue (*Cels.* 1.67; 3.78; 4.4).

The reading and study of Scripture, then, is a way of advancing in such moral (spiritual) transformation into the image of Christ. Clearly, reading does not accomplish this by itself. Origen emphasizes the need to be transformed in mind and heart in order to read properly. The word can dwell within those who prepare themselves (*John* 6.22). He declares flatly that the Gospel of John cannot be understood unless one puts on the mind of Christ (*John* 1.6-7). And in his *Commentary on Matthew,* he declares with reference to the story of Bartimaeus, "if one wishes to be healed, let him follow Jesus" (14.5). Reading Scripture, then, must take place in the context of the practice of the church (*Lev.* 5.14.1). "I hope to be a man of the church," he says (*Luke* 16.6), and he

---

64. See also *John* 6.17.

calls for prayer as well as study in seeking the wisdom offered by Scripture (*Josh.* 8.3; *Hom. Cant.* 2.11). Jesus must be sought in the church as well as in Scripture (*Luke* 18.2-3).[65]

Being transformed into the mind of Christ is relatively straightforward when reading the New Testament, since it everywhere speaks of Jesus. Even in the New Testament, there is need to be reminded of the real point of study. Origen asks his listeners, "What profit is it to you, if Christ came once in the flesh, unless he also comes into your soul?" (*Luke* 22.3).[66] The real challenge, however, comes in reading the Old Testament. Remember the available options: reading it literally and accepting it literally means to "gather with the Jews" (*Gen.* 6.1); reading literally and rejecting it means to side with Marcion and lose the promises (*Jer.* 9.1.2; 10.5.1; 11.3.1); reading with the simple believers means asserting the spiritual character of the law but with no idea how to actually read the law (*Exod.* 2.2). Origen takes on the task of affirming the inspiration — and therefore the spiritual character — of all of Scripture, and therefore the implication that all of Scripture speaks spiritually — together with the minutest examination of Scripture in all its parts.

Sometimes the task is fairly easy. Preaching on Genesis 1, he can connect creation in the divine image with the restored image of God revealed by Christ, and implore, "let us, therefore, always contemplate that image of God that we might be transformed into his likeness" (*Gen.* 1.15), or ask with reference to Genesis 15, "what will it profit you if God should renew the promises, and you should not be renewed?" (*Gen.* 10.1). There are other parts of the Old Testament that powerfully resist such moral appropriation. In such passages, Origen's search for the mind of Christ is more complex, and it is these places that his anagogic readings sometimes appear to us — as they probably did to his first numbed hearers — as a bit fanciful, a kind of tour de force. It is all the more important, then, to recognize his own distaste for inappropri-

---

65. It is possible to learn a great deal about the practices of the church from Origen's writings (*Cels.* 8.22; 8.29; *John* 1.15; 6.34; 6.36; 10.16; *Matt.* 10.18; 10.23; 11.15; 11.17; 11.18; 12.11; 12.14; 13.7; 14.1; 14.13; 14.23; 14.25; *Num.* 2.1; 5.1; 23.4; *Josh.* 4.1; 5.1; *Comm. Cant.* 3.3; *Jer.* 5.14.1).

66. In illustration of the generic distinction between commentary and homily, whereas Origen's commentaries on Matthew and John rarely move directly to the exhortatory, his homilies on the Gospel of Luke make that turn constantly (*Luke* 1.6; 2.1-6; 3.4; 5.4; 11.6; 12.2; 20.7; 26.5; Frag. 252).

ate allegories (*Gen.* 5.5) or the anagogic for the sake of the anagogic (*Luke* 23.5). Hardest are those texts that are historically unlikely and/or morally reprehensible. Of certain portions of the law, Origen says that if they had to be taken literally, "I would be ashamed to say and confess that God gave such laws" (*Exod.* 7.5.7). But he is never daunted or deterred. And in rising to the challenge posed by the books of Numbers and Joshua, he has left us the finest memorial of his devotion and skill.

Throughout Origen's 28 homilies on Numbers and 26 homilies on Joshua, we can almost see his struggle with the text energizing his mind and expanding his imagination. No need to remind you of the difficulties of those books: the people of Israel are unworthy, Moses is nonheroic, and God's direction leads to conflict, battle, war, conquest, and extermination. Then there are the interminable lists of names, and the dry-as-dust apportionment of the land. Concerning this last topic, Origen cries out, "What are we to do, I say, we, members of the church, who are reading this? If we understand it in the sense of the Jews, it will certainly appear to us useless and vain" (*Num.* 28.1). In other words, the text speaks of things that may have applied to the people in the distant past, but if read at the literal level, cannot have pertinence to the present.

As he moves through the narrative of Numbers in his preaching, however, Origen begins to pick up a powerful theme. He sees analogies between Moses and Paul (*Num.* 2.1), and following that thought, between what the ancient narrative said about the people and the land at the bodily level, and what analogies might be suggested at the spiritual level, for life now and in the future (3.2). By the seventh homily, he has identified the ancient Canaan that was filled with Israel's enemies with the spiritual enemies that Christians must now combat (7.5). By the 12th homily, he begins to see the struggles of the people in the wilderness as an analogy to the stages of growth in the spiritual life of Christians (12.3). He gets massively sidetracked by Balaam (13-20), but in the 21st homily he returns to the connection that was authorized already by the Letter to the Hebrews, namely that between Joshua and Jesus (21.1; see Heb. 3:1–4:16). Moses led the people out of Egypt and through the wilderness, but it was Joshua = Jesus who led them into the promised land.[67] Toward the end of his preaching progress (*Num.* 27.2),

---

67. The Joshua-Jesus typology is worked out also in *John* 6.26.

Origen expounds the entire analogy: at the literal level, the story speaks of the liberation of Israel from Egypt, but at the spiritual level the story speaks of the Gentiles leaving the slavery of paganism for the divine law, and at the eschatological level it speaks of the soul leaving the captivity of the body for life with God. He then reads the 42 stops of the people in the desert as stages in the Christian spiritual life, which is a spiritual combat (27.4-12). This is not only a magnificent act of imagination, it is worked out by the most assiduous attention to every twist in the text.

Origen's reading of Numbers prepares the way for his homiletical exposition of the book of Joshua, an even more difficult text at the literal level. He declares, "They combated the inhabitants of the land; we are engaged in a spiritual battle" (*Josh.* 1.7). The things that happened to the ancient Israelites in the past, "all these things," says Origen, "are accomplished in you spiritually" (4.1). As they passed out of Egypt, so must Christians pass from vice to virtue (1.7). It is not the literal land that is the promise, but our spiritual heritage (2.3). The literal Jericho is a type of this world (7.4). The time after baptism is a time of spiritual combat (5.2). It is not enough to be exterior Christians without interior transformation (10.1). The crucifixion of Christ must be a present reality in Christian lives (8.3). The literal slaughter of the inhabitants of the land, therefore, must be read as our spiritual victory over the powers of evil (8.7). And so forth.

Origen's interpretation may not be to our taste, but it is a coherent and consistent way of reading, and one that has never been equaled as a specifically Christian reading of the Old Testament. Commenting on the love that Moses shows toward his enemies, Origen says,

> Thus we find the gospel powerfully in the law, and the Gospels can only be understood as based on the foundation of the law. I do not call this law the "old" testament if I understand it spiritually. The law is "old" only for those who understand it carnally. Clearly, for such as them it has become "old." It is obsolete because it has not retained its force. For us, in contrast, who comprehend it and explain it spiritually according to the meaning of the gospel, it is always new, and the two testaments are for us one new testament, not because of a temporal date, but because of the newness of sense. (*Num.* 9.4)

Origen's hermeneutic is based on the conviction that the same Holy Spirit that wrote the text of Scripture is at work in the script of human lives (*Matt.* 13.6), and that the point of reading Scripture is to find out how the master-story of Jesus our Lord is to be discovered ever anew in the story of Israel, of Jesus, and of the church.

Learning from Origen

How might the postmodern church be instructed by premodern Origen with respect to the interpretation of Scripture? I think we have much to learn at the level of sensibility rather than at the level of specific method. A contemporary exegetical and hermeneutical stumbling-block can illustrate. In 1 Tim. 2:11-15, the command, "Let women be silent in the assembly" — and indeed the entire passage — is infamous.[68] As part of Paul's so-called "Pastoral Letters," it presents literary and canonical problems. Many today challenge its authorship. Did Paul write this, and if he did not, does it have authority for the church? The passage also appears to create a contradiction in Scripture, since it stands in tension with other Pauline and non-Pauline instructions and the practice of the early churches with regard to women. Above all, the passage is a moral stumbling block, a scandal, for contemporary readers. Simple Christians who put the passage into practice literally bring the good news into disrepute among those seeking the equal dignity of all women, especially when the injunction serves as cover for the degradation of women created in the image of God. More sophisticated Christians read it literally, cannot accept the Paul found in the passage, and deny its authority for the church. Contemporary exegetes and theologians marginalize the passage, ignore it, or deny it. The one thing they refuse to do is engage it as part of the inspired word of God, as part of Scripture. They treat the Pastorals the way Marcion treated Torah. In short, the contemporary church, reading the passage literally, falls into the two camps described by Origen as the simple and the heretics.

---

68. For a full discussion of both exegetical and hermeneutical aspects of the passage, together with contemporary bibliography, see Luke Timothy Johnson, *The First and Second Letters to Timothy* (New York: Doubleday, 2001), 198-211.

What would it mean to learn from Origen in this case? We have no extant reading of his on the passage. Were we to have such a reading, we would undoubtedly find it unsatisfactory, because to him it would not have been morally offensive. Origen is truly Platonist in his steady depreciation of women's ability (see *Num.* 1.1; *Gen.* 4.4; 5.2; *Lev.* 4.7.4). But learning from Origen is not repeating his opinions or imitating his precise methods. It is rather seeking to share his sensibilities and convictions and employ them in our context. What then?

We would begin as Origen always did, with complete intellectual honesty about the difficulties presented by the literal sense. We would expose all levels of difficulty in the passage with passion and precision, knowing that Scripture cannot heal us until we discover also how it wounds. It is not enough to say we do not like Paul's opinion and stop reading the passage — forever. The logic of that approach leads to an anthology of comforting passages that confirm us in our identity rather than a Scripture that challenges us to transformation. We would, then, be ruthlessly analytic in showing how Paul uses his own opinion, misreads Genesis, betrays his own best insights into the nature of the good news in Christ Jesus. In order to see these things, we would need to read the passage not only within the context of 1 Timothy or even Paul, but of the Scripture as a whole, and read it according to the "mind of Christ" (1 Cor. 2:16).[69]

Then we would seek the spiritual sense — not allegory, but a moral understanding that enables us to gain insight into the good news as it is found in this passage. We might begin, as Origen did, by examining all that Scripture has to say about prophetic women and women leaders and women who instruct, drawing from Judith and 2 Maccabees and Esther, and Paul himself, and of course from the story of Jesus.[70] We might ask who taught Jesus if not the Mary who reversed by her faithful obedience the disobedience of Eve?

We might also, drawing on contemporary experience and the wisdom God has taught the church through the Holy Spirit over the ages,

69. See Luke Timothy Johnson, *Scripture and Discernment* (Nashville: Abingdon, 1996).

70. One of the intriguing aspects of the history of interpretation of this passage is that, until the middle ages, most commentaries on 1 Timothy moved in the direction of ameliorating the passage by just the sort of scriptural contextualization I describe; see Johnson, *The First and Second Letters to Timothy,* 26-35.

inquire into the necessity of some distribution of tasks in the church and household, if not necessarily this one. We might ask about the value of silence and quiet in learning for all God's children, and ask how this might be an occasion for both genders to learn from each other. We might ponder the way this passage does point to the importance of child-bearing and child-rearing. Then, we might follow Paul's too casual reading of Genesis with a much more careful one that leads to another sort of conclusion. We might do a number of creative things. But we would read it. By God (and for God) we would together shake this passage until it spoke to us a wisdom that is worthy of the God who shapes our lives and inspired this writing. And then, we would have learned from the teacher who urged his hearers not to stay like children but to grow in wisdom (*Luke* 20.7), and declared, "what is said about Jesus applies to the just. For it was not only for himself that Jesus 'progressed in wisdom and stature and grace with God and men,' but also in each of those who accept progress 'in wisdom and stature and grace,' Jesus progresses in 'wisdom and stature and grace with God and men'" (*Jer.* 14.10.1).

CHAPTER FOUR

Augustine and the Demands of Charity

The point of engaging patristic and medieval interpreters is not to approve of all their readings. They are often as wrong-headed as present-day interpreters, if usually more interesting. Neither is the point to become premodern in our view of the world, even if we could. Much in the premodern outlook — such as its pervasive sexism — is reprehensible. Nor is the point turning our back on the Enlightenment or historical criticism. The Enlightenment represents a fundamental gain for human consciousness, not least in its search for peaceful communication across tribal boundaries. And having learned the benefits of historical criticism — among them a deeper appreciation for the character of the biblical writings themselves as witnesses and interpretations of religious experience and conviction — it would be wrong not to make use of them.

The point of enlarging our hermeneutical conversation to include the distant as well as the recent past is to find a way of recovering the soul of biblical scholarship within the church, not as an exercise in nostalgia, but as a form of creative anamnesis that enables us to move forward.

For such an enlarged conversation to be more than a gesture towards inclusiveness, however, it must move beyond stereotypes, whether positive or negative, toward a serious and critical consideration of specific interpreters and specific readings. Equally unhelpful is the dismissal of all pre-Enlightenment exegesis as "allegorical" and the celebration of all pre-Enlightenment exegesis as "edifying."[1] We need rather to read Origen and Chrysostom and Theodore carefully enough to discern between what we truly should leave behind and what we desperately need to learn. The forays I make in these short chapters do not do the job, but serve only to suggest the value and the possibility of such a critical engagement. The task itself appears all the more complex and daunting when we realize that our conversation partners include figures of considerably more talent and intelligence than our own, such as Augustine of Hippo.[2]

Placing Augustine

St. Augustine was born almost exactly 100 years after the death of Origen (354 C.E.), was a professional rhetorician before his conversion to Christianity in 386, became a priest in 391, and bishop of the North African city of Hippo in 395, where he served until his death in 430.[3] Technically, he is post-Constantinian. Yet neither the place of Christianity nor the stability of the empire was so secure as it might seem to

---

1. Thus, the title of David C. Steinmetz's "The Superiority of Pre-critical Exegesis," *TT* 37 (1980): 27-38, is deliciously shocking to contemporary sensibilities, but the author does not try to show that *in every respect* the precritical is superior to so-called critical scholarship.

2. As in the chapter on Origen, the discussion of Augustine as biblical interpreter is based on my own reading of the primary sources. Augustinian studies is a world unto itself, with at least two separate journals (*L'Année Théologique* and *Revue des Études Augustiniennes*) devoted entirely to writings about Augustine. For basic orientation, see Agostino Trape, "Saint Augustine," in Johannes Quasten, *Patrology* 4: *The Golden Age of Latin Patristic Literature* (Westminster, Md.: Christian Classics, 1986): 342-462. On Augustine's life, see Peter Brown, *Augustine of Hippo: A Biography* (Berkeley: University of California Press, 1967); Frederik van der Meer, *Augustine the Bishop: The Life and Work of a Father of the Church,* trans. Brian Battershaw and G. R. Lamb (London: Sheed and Ward, 1961). On Augustine as exegete, see Bertrand de Margerie, S.J., *An Introduction to the History of Exegesis,* trans. Pierre de Fontnouvelle, 3: *Saint Augustine* (Petersham, Mass.: St. Bede's, 1991); Pamela Bright, ed. and trans., *Augustine and the Bible.* The Bible through the Ages 2 (Notre Dame: University of Notre Dame Press, 1986).

3. The most important sources for Augustine's life include his *Confessions* (= *Conf.*), his *Retractions* (= *Retract.*) — especially for his compositions — and his many letters (= *Epp.*). Shortly after his death, the *Life of St. Augustine* was composed by a companion, Possidius, who also had access to Augustine's library at Hippo.

later observers. Between Augustine's sixth and ninth years (360-363), the emperor Julian aggressively sought to turn the empire back to paganism.[4] And the last 20 years of Augustine's life, beginning with the sacking of Rome under Alaric in 410, saw the crumbling of the western empire under barbarian invasions. Augustine died in the third month of the siege laid against Hippo by the Vandals, and one of his last compositions was a letter of advice concerning the responsibilities of the clergy in the face of these circumstances (*Ep.* 228). Augustine made use of imperial assistance when he could. He is infamous for interpreting the line in Luke 14:23, *compelle intrare,* as legitimation for the forced submission of Donatist separatists (*Ep.* 93). But he always remained uneasy about the state's assistance, knowing how unreliable and corrupting it could be.[5]

Whatever favor or disfavor shown by the empire, Augustine's experience of the church was more that of the diaspora than at first appears, above all because his world was still intellectually and religiously pluralistic. Official paganism was weakened,[6] but Julian had demonstrated its recuperative powers, and Augustine found it necessary at the end of his life to mount a massive intellectual defense of "the City of God Against the Pagans."[7] Pagan philosophers like Porphyry (ca. 232–ca. 303) attacked Christianity more systematically and effectively than had Celsus.[8] Pagan practices and perceptions, furthermore, infiltrated

4. For deeply unflattering accounts of Julian's short reign, see Socrates, *Hist. eccl.* III, 1-23; and Sozomen, *Hist. eccl.* V, 1-VI, 2.

5. See *Epp.* 23; 66; 185. 6-8, 15.

6. Sozomen remarks cryptically in *Hist. eccl.* VI, 35, "As to the pagans, they were nearly all exterminated about the period to which we have been referring" (the late 4th century). For a sense of the respective positions at the beginning of Augustine's time as bishop, see the exchange of letters between the Grammarian Maximus and Augustine (*Epp.* 16, 17), and between the pagan Nectarius and Augustine (*Epp.* 90, 91, 103, 104).

7. The first 10 books (of 24) in *The City of God* (composed between 413 and 426) are written in response to the claims of Greco-Roman religion and philosophy.

8. Unlike the otherwise unknown Celsus, Porphyry is a major figure in the history of philosophy, as an exponent of Neoplatonism. Porphyry wrote a work in 15 books called "Against the Christians," which was ordered destroyed in 448 and survives only in the fragments cited by Christian apologists like Methodius of Olympus, Eusebius of Caesarea, Apollinaris of Laodicea, and Augustine himself. In addition to the frequent references to Porphyry in *The City of God,* see the set of answers for pagan

an increasingly popular Christianity.[9] Judaism was no longer an active disputant in Augustine's world.[10] But the dualistic religion known as Manichaeism was a powerful gnostic rival to orthodox Christianity. It was now entering the second of its six centuries as a great world religion, and was attractive enough to have won the allegiance of Augustine himself from the age of 19 to 29 (373-383).[11] Christianity was also increasingly divided from within: Arianism enjoyed the favor of many bishops and not a few emperors.[12] In Augustine's North Africa, the church was disastrously split between Catholics and Donatists. This separatist movement had existed for 60 years by the time Augustine became bishop and had at least 270 bishops. The schism was deep and bitter, involving cultural and political animosities as much as doctrine, issues of property and power as much as morals, and tinged with acts of violence.[13] Augustine did not work in an enclave of comfortably established catholic orthodoxy. He sometimes preached while pagan rev-

---

questioners in *Ep.* 102, at least one of which has Porphyry as the source. Augustine takes up Porphyry's challenge to the Gospels in *The Harmony of the Gospels* (see the discussion below).

9. One example that taxed him pastorally was the custom of the *refrigerium,* or celebratory meal in honor of the martyrs, which continued the pagan practice of memorial meals for the dead; see esp. *Epp.* 22, 29, and the entire discussion in Van der Meer, 471-526.

10. Augustine includes a *Tractate against the Jews* among his polemical works (PL 42: 51-64), which, on the basis of Rom. 11:22, argues that the Old Testament prophecies have been fulfilled in Christ and urges an attitude of charity toward the Jews. Unlike Origen, however, his biblical interpretation shows no awareness of contemporary Jewish readings.

11. The Persian teacher Mani (ca. 216-276) combined elements of ancient Persian religion, Gnosticism, and Christianity into a powerful amalgam that gained adherents eventually as far west as North Africa and as far east as China. For Augustine's own life as a Manichaean, see *Conf.* IV-V. The power of this dualistic teaching is acknowledged also in his short work, *Against the Epistle of Manichaeus Called the Fundamental,* in which he recognizes how difficult it is to come to a proper sense of the truth: "And, last of all, let those rage against you who have never been led astray in the same way that they see you are" (2). Between 388 and 399, Augustine wrote nine works against the Manichaeans.

12. For an account of the quickly changing fortunes of the Arians and the Orthodox during the 4th century, see Sozomen, *Hist. eccl.* I, 15-25; II, 16-19; II, 21-34; III, 18-24; IV, 2, 14, and 25-26; VI, 7-22.

13. See, e.g., *Epp.* 88, 105, 111, 185.

elers made festival outside, and sometimes held disputations before loudly angry crowds.[14]

Augustine lived in the Latin West in a period of its decline, and so his cultural world was considerably smaller than Origen's. Origen not only knew Greek and Hebrew, but had living contact with the world's greatest library and with Jewish scholars. He learned Greek literature from infancy, together with the Scriptures. Augustine had no Hebrew and little Greek (although he kept slogging at it).[15] His was an entirely Latin world; even his Platonic philosophy was mediated through translation. His primary training was in Latin literature and rhetoric (*Conf.* I, 16-18). His intellectual appetite was, however, voracious, and his genius is recognizable in the way his mind could work powerfully with anything that came into view.[16]

He came to the Scriptures late — having been repulsed by them earlier in his life because of the crudeness of their language (*Conf.* III, 5, 9) and their inconsistency in moral teaching (III, 7, 12) — and when he did, he had to read them in Latin translations that ranged from the competent to the wretched — he saw bits and pieces of Jerome's new Vulgate translation (begun in 382) but did not make it the basis of his liturgical or homiletical practice.[17] Augustine was a prodigy of energy, dedica-

---

14. In *Ep.* 126, Augustine recounts the embarrassing riot in the church caused by those who wished to ordain some of his guests by force. In *Tractates on the Gospel of John* VII, 24, we read that he deliberately extended his sermon so that his congregation would not be tempted to take part in the pagan festival that was occurring outside the church. For the day-to-day pastoral context in which Augustine worked, see Van der Meer, 129-98. For an example of audience participation in doctrinal debates, see the *Disputation against Fortunatus*, 19, and *Ep.* 44; in a sermon, see *Ep.* 29; and in a ceremony, see *Ep.* 213.

15. He found Greek unintelligible as a young man (*Conf.* I, 13-14) and never shows any real mastery of the language beyond the rudiments of vocabulary and basic grammar. Peter Brown (36) comments, "Augustine's failure to learn Greek was a momentous casualty of the Late Roman educational system: he will become the only Latin philosopher in antiquity to be virtually ignorant of Greek."

16. His sermons show many examples of his ability to move with dazzling speed from an exegetical observation through a philosophical disquisition to a stunning spiritual insight; see, e.g., *Serm.* 103 (on Luke 10:42), on "the one thing necessary." The unfinished treatise, *On Music*, written in six books at Tagaste between 388 and 391, shows how wide-ranging his interests were (see *Ep.* 101), as do the many digressions in *The City of God*.

17. One reason why Pope Damasus wanted Jerome to undertake the Latin trans-

tion, and intelligence. He studied the Scripture until he died, and only a fool would dismiss him as an autodidact, or deny that his mind became ever more suffused with a scriptural imagination that was capable of astonishing insights. As an interpreter of Scripture, however, Augustine certainly began with severe disadvantages, and some of them he was never able to overcome.[18]

A final difference between Origen and Augustine is the role each played in the church. Origen was deeply enmeshed in the church's life, but he was never more than a presbyter. His duties consisted mainly in preaching. His time otherwise could entirely be given to a scholarship and writing that was magnificently supported by his friend and patron Ambrose. Augustine had been a Christian only five years when he was ordained a priest (against his will) and then a bishop shortly after. Everything he did by way of scholarship had to be on top of his exhausting labors as the leader of his church (see *Ep.* 73), and increasingly as the intellectual leader of the church in the West. Because he was the prize intellectual, he was besieged immediately to answer every question, address every crisis, answer every heresy, even before he felt prepared.[19] The anxiety that sometimes affects his interpretation of Scrip-

---

lation that has come to be called the Vulgate is the multiplicity and inadequacy of those earlier Latin translations that are usually called "Old Latin" by text-critics. Only in some of his later writings does Augustine appear to make use of Jerome's translation from the Hebrew of the Old Testament, and then only in comparison to the Septuagint; see A.-M. La Bonnardiere, "Did Augustine Use Jerome's Vulgate?" in Bright, *Augustine and the Bible*, 42-51.

18. Shortly after his ordination as a priest, Augustine writes to Valerius, the bishop of Hippo, concerning his lack of preparation to adequately interpret the Scriptures: "I did not do this before, because I did not have time, but, as soon as I was ordained, I planned to use all my leisure time in studying the Sacred Scriptures, and I tried to arrange to have leisure for this duty. Truly, I did not know what I needed for such a task, but now I am tormented and weighed down by it . . . so much is lacking that I could more easily tell what I have than what I lack. . . ." He asks for more time to study before resuming preaching (*Ep.* 21).

19. See, e.g., *Ep.* 36, in which Augustine provides an exhaustive answer to a query from one of his priests concerning fasting, and *Ep.* 47, in which he patiently responds to the 18 (!) questions on a variety of practices posed him by a certain Publicola (*Ep.* 46), the rudeness of whose language matches the humble nature of his concerns. Augustine's ability to take his questions seriously is a model to all authors besieged by equally earnest missives.

ture, I think, has its roots partly in his lack of linguistic skills and scriptural sophistication, and even more in his sense of responsibility to a church that, without his choosing, looked to him for answers.[20]

Augustine as Reader of Scripture

Augustine wrote so much on so many fronts, and has influenced Western thought in such fundamental ways, that a single focus is, almost by definition, distorting. He can be read in terms of his biography as one of history's great conversion stories, as a letter-writer who had a remarkable capacity for friendship, as a philosopher who contributed to Christian Platonism.[21] He can be read as an apologist for orthodoxy, battling Manichaeans, Arians, Donatists, and Pelagians.[22] He can be read theologically as the great teacher of the West on faith, morals, and the monastic life.[23] But whatever of Augustine we might chance to read, we discover Augustine the rhetorician and (apart from a very few letters and philosophical essays) Augustine the interpreter of Scripture.

20. In the Prologue to his *Retractions,* Augustine looks back to his "early manhood" as a time when "I had begun to write and to speak to the people, and so much authority was attributed to me that, whenever it was necessary for someone to speak to the people and I was present, I was seldom allowed to be silent and to listen to others and to be 'swift to hear but slow to speak' (Jas. 1:19)."

21. His *Dialogues* on a variety of philosophical topics (happiness, the immortality of the soul, human liberty) were written between his conversion and his ordination to the priesthood (386-391), and a philosophical interest is exhibited in the Letters of the same period (*Epp.* 1-20). Augustine's distinctive gift is to bring a philosophical turn of mind to every question, seeking the essence of each question before him.

22. In addition to his nine works against the Manichaeans, Augustine wrote over 14 compositions against the Donatists (not counting his letters), 16 compositions against the Pelagians, and 3 against Arians, as well as a single composition each against Priscillianists, Marcionites, and Jews, and an unfinished composition on heresies in general.

23. His most systematic theological treatise is *On the Trinity* (completed by 420); his ecclesiology was forged in controversy with the Donatists (see, e.g., *On Baptism* and *On the Unity of the Church*), as his understanding of grace was sharpened by controversy with the Pelagians (contrast *On Faith and Works* [413] with *On the Grace of Christ and Original Sin* [418]). Among his works devoted to moral issues are two against lying and one each on virginity, a good marriage, widowhood, continence, and patience. He wrote two guides to monastic life.

Once he learned how to read Scripture from Ambrose of Milan, Augustine never ceased engaging this literary world that teased and expanded his imagination, providing him at last a vision of reality in which all that is created is good, all that is evil comes from disordered desire and pride, and all that is broken can be healed through love. He learned allegory from Ambrose (*Conf.* V, 14, 24; VI, 3, 6), and Augustine's love for the figurative is obvious. It was the capacity to read spiritually that enabled this Manichaean dualist to read the Old Testament for the first time and find Christ there. Augustine indulged his love of allegory above all in his sermons, where it appears so abundantly that it sometimes seems pursued for its own sake, as a form of mental playfulness for the man whose mind otherwise found little that was simply fun.[24]

As in the case of Origen, however, it is important to see how allegory is only part of the picture. In all of his polemical and theological writings, Augustine makes vigorous and sustained use of the literal sense. Indeed, his arguments depend on his close readings of the text, whether it is the Gospel of John on the Trinity[25] or the Letters of Paul on grace.[26] We know that Paul was a special love, not least because Augustine's reading of Rom. 13:11-14 in response to the childish chant *tolle lege* ("take and read") represented a turning point in his conversion to Christianity (*Conf.* VIII, 12, 28), a response that had been prepared by his previous intense study of Romans 7 (*Conf.* VII, 21, 27). Augustine read Paul passionately and highly personally. In Paul's language about the flesh and desire (in Latin, *concupiscentia*), Augustine found the clues to disordered human freedom, and in the divided conscience of Rom. 7:15 ("what I want to do I do not do, but what I hate I do") he found the script of his own struggle with passion.

Paul's letters provided Augustine with more than insight into his own story. Like Origen before him, he found in Paul's Corinthian correspondence the invaluable distinction between the Spirit and the Let-

---

24. Not surprisingly, Augustine is particularly tempted to allegory when the Scripture text involves numbers (see, e.g., *Serm.* 51, 83, and 95) or parables (see *Serm.* 87, 90, 93).

25. For readings of the Gospel of John in *On the Trinity,* see I, 6, 9, 12; I, 9, 18-19; I, 12, 25-27; II, 1-5; IV, 9; VII, 6, 12; XIII, 1, 1-4.

26. See the close use of Paul's letters in *On the Grace of Christ and Original Sin* I, 6-16.

ter.[27] In the (unfortunate) Latin translation of *in quo* in Rom. 5:12, Augustine found his teaching that Adam's sin extended to all humans (*Enchir.* 26).[28] In Romans, Galatians, and Ephesians, in particular, Augustine grounded his understanding of grace as the beginning and end of human righteousness, especially against the moralistic optimism of Pelagius.[29] Augustine's strong misreading of Paul in terms of what Krister Stendahl has called "the introspective conscience of the West" — an introspection that, so far as we can tell, Augustine invented[30] — was taken up by Luther[31] and, so reinforced by an interpreter fully as passionate as himself, has shaped an understanding of Paul that has proven hard to shake.[32] But Paul also gave the Augustine who battled the Donatists a vision of the church as a body consisting in both a head (who was Christ) and members (who are in a very real way also Christ), a community that is marked both by diversity and unity.[33] In his polemical and theological compositions, then, when he was using Scripture argumentatively, Augustine could use the literal sense with considerable subtlety. Greater linguistic skill would have helped, but no one can deny the impressiveness of the readings he achieved, even with inferior Latin translations.

---

27. In *Conf.* VI, 4, 6, he recalls how he heard Ambrose quote 2 Cor. 3:6, "the letter kills, but the Spirit gives life." In 412, he devotes an entire treatise, dedicated to Marcellinus, to the topic *On the Spirit and the Letter.*

28. Here is the classic example of the consequences following upon Augustine's weakness in Greek and his dependence on the Latin. The Greek *eph' hō* should be taken in its ordinary sense as "because all men sinned," whereas the Latin *in quo* enabled the rendering "in whom [namely Adam] all men sinned." For examples of how this translation is employed theologically in support of original sin, see *On Forgiveness of Sins and Baptism* III, 1-7, and *On Marriage and Concupiscence* II, 49-50.

29. See, e.g., *On the Forgiveness of Sins and Baptism* (412); *On Nature and Grace; Against Pelagius* (415); *On Rebuke and Grace* (426); *On Grace and Free Will* (427).

30. Krister Stendahl, "The Apostle Paul and the Introspective Conscience of the West," in *Paul Among Jews and Gentiles* (Philadelphia: Fortress, 1976), 78-96.

31. See, e.g., Martin Luther, *The Freedom of a Christian* (1520) and *Lectures on Galatians* (1531).

32. This is wonderfully illustrated by Rudolf Bultmann, *Theology of the New Testament* I (New York: Scribner, 1951), whose reading of Paul is still fundamentally that of Augustine and Luther.

33. See, e.g., *Civ.* XXII, 18; *On Baptism* I, 9, 12, 28; III, 14, 19; *In Answer to the Letters of Petilian* II, 27, 63; II, 71, 158; II, 79, 174; III, 42, 51.

When he set out to expound the scriptural text more directly, the literal sense could cause him difficulty. He was better on texts that lent themselves to straightforward moral exposition.[34] At first blush, for example, his tractate on the Sermon on the Mount in Matthew appears unsophisticated to a present-day reader, but as it unfolds, Augustine's reading becomes increasingly impressive, showing a grasp of the inner logic of the discourse that could result only from prolonged study and has, in fact, rarely been equaled.[35] Similarly, his 10 tractates on the First Letter of John combine a bold argument with clear exposition of the text. The letter has a single theme, he says; it is completely about love.[36] Then he demonstrates that strong thesis with a thoroughly attractive exposition, in the process providing one of the most splendid analyses of charity in Christian literature.[37]

34. Mention should be made here of some extant works that are devoted to the literal level, but which will not be discussed in the chapter. Early in his career, Augustine made a stab at a literal commentary on Romans (PL 35:2087-2106), making it to the third chapter before giving it up as too difficult (*Retract.* I, 24). His short commentary on Galatians, in contrast, was completed (PL 35:2105-2147) and, in proper commentary style, is basically a series of clarifying notes on the text. Three other works are not truly exegetical. Augustine set himself to answer *Questions on the Gospels in Two Books* — dealing with Matthew and Luke — as these were posed to him by others (PL 35:1323-64). A similar work, *Seventeen Questions on the Gospel according to Matthew* (PL 35:1365-76) may or may not be authentic, and in any case shows us Augustine the clarifier of difficulties rather than as interpreter. Finally, the *Speculum de Scriptura Sacra* (PL 34:890-1040), though substantial, is also possibly not by Augustine, and basically collects examples of moral instruction from the Old and New Testaments.

35. Augustine's enthusiasm for numbers makes him seize on the Beatitudes, reading them as seven stages in the life of discipleship, and then correlating them to the seven gifts of the Spirit (I, 3-4) — artificial, yes, but far more nourishing and, in truth, more penetrating of the text — than the dissecting analysis of contemporary commentaries.

36. In the Prologue, Augustine links the First Letter of John to the Fourth Gospel through the theme of charity: ". . . whereas we have for a while intermitted the reading of his Gospel, we may in discoursing upon his Epistle not go from his side: rather, as in this same Epistle, which is very sweet to all who have a healthy taste of the heart to relish the Bread of God, and very meet to be had in remembrance in God's Holy Church, charity is above all commended. He has spoken many words, and nearly all are about charity."

37. Particularly striking is the way in which Augustine develops the notion of fellowship with the Son in terms of living according to the precept of love that shaped Jesus' own life. "Let us hear: for without the fruit of the precept the hearing of the

In contrast, Augustine's six books on *The Literal Meaning of Genesis* caused him no end of trouble. As he tells us in his *Retractions,* he made two earlier efforts before managing finally to work his way through only the first three chapters.[38] He obviously felt the need to deal with the material as a way of rebutting Manichaean speculation about cosmic beginnings,[39] not by recourse to allegorical interpretation, "but according to historical events proper."[40] Everyone knows something about science, Augustine declares, and Christians, supposedly on the basis of Scripture, should not be spouting nonsense and make themselves look ridiculous. "The shame is not so much that an ignorant individual is derided, but that people outside the household of faith think our sacred writers held such opinions, and, to the great loss of those for whose salvation we toil, the writers of our Scripture are criticized and rejected as unlearned men" (*Gen. litt.* 1.19). His treatment contains many fine things, not least the recognition he struggles to reach across many separate chapters, that God continues God's creative activity in the world even now (*Gen. litt.* 5.20-23), or his typically splendid reflection on God's closeness to all creatures (5.16; compare *Conf.* II, 2, 2).

Nevertheless, in several places a note of anxiety enters his discussion. Speaking of the meaning of "day" in the Creation account, he says, "I myself may possibly discover some other meaning more in harmony with the words of Scripture. I certainly do not advance the interpretation given above in such a way as to imply that no better one can ever be found . . ." (*Gen. litt.* 4.28). Augustine's anxiety is understandable, for he has assumed that if the Scripture is read literally, and if it

---

story, how Christ was born, and how Christ suffered, is a mere pastime of the mind, not a strengthening of it" (I, 4). And in commenting how we should walk in the way Christ walked, "He was fixed upon the cross, and yet was walking in this very way: this is the way of charity, 'Father, forgive them, for they know not what they do.' If, therefore, you have learned to pray for your enemy, you walk in the way of the Lord" (I, 9).

38. *Retract.* I, 9; I, 17; II, 50. Augustine had already provided an allegorical reading of the creation account of Genesis in *Conf.* XI-XIII, and will return to the same subject one last time in *Civ.* XI-XII.

39. Augustine's first effort was entitled specifically, *On Genesis, Against the Manichaeans* (*Retract.* I, 19). For examples of Manichaean speculation about origins (according to Augustine), see *On the Morals of the Manichaeans, Reply to Faustus the Manichaean,* II, 3-5; and *On Two Souls, Against the Manichaeans,* 8-9.

40. *Retract.* II, 50.

speaks about the creation of the world, its truthfulness must be measured scientifically. He recognizes, to be sure, that Scripture has been written to nourish souls in ways that humans cannot always grasp (1.20). And when he can't make science and faith mesh, he will always go with "an interpretation in keeping with the context of Scripture and in harmony with our faith" (1.21). There may, in fact, be several interpretations possible that accord with faith, and readers should avoid rushing to one opinion exclusively: "That would be to battle not for the teaching of Holy Scripture but for our own, wishing its teaching to conform to ours, whereas we ought to wish ours to conform to that of Sacred Scripture" (1.18). Putting this principle into practice, he declares about his own interpretation of the creation of humans, "This must conclude what I undertook to say about man. In expressing my views, I have tried to observe moderation so as to show a persevering spirit of inquiry rather than a dogged desire to maintain my opinions in exploring the profound meaning of Scripture" (6.9).[41]

We can appreciate Augustine's difficulty: he knows Scripture is written to teach spiritual truths, and he knows that these can be accessed allegorically. But he is less sure how the literal sense teaches such truths when it takes the form of narrative rather than prescription. If the text speaks referentially (with respect to the visible world) its truth must be verifiable on the basis of science. When science goes one way and Scripture seems to go another, then he has no recourse other than falling back, neither on the literal sense of the text nor on science, but on the truths of faith.

Augustine and the Truth of Scripture

As Garry Wills has recently observed, St. Augustine had a profound commitment to truth-telling.[42] He wrote two separate books against lying, *Deception* (in 395) and *Against Deception* (in 420). There is no sub-

41. Similarly, in *Retract.* II, 50: "In this book many questions have been asked rather than solved, and of those that have been solved, fewer have been answered conclusively. Moreover, others have been proposed in such a way as to require further investigation."

42. See Garry Wills, *Papal Sin: Structures of Deceit* (New York: Doubleday, 2000), 277-312.

ject to which Augustine more frequently or fervently turns on the slightest occasion.[43] His own practice with regard to candor is revealed not only in the *Confessions* and *Retractions* (the most astonishing act of scholarly self-evaluation as examination of conscience in all of history — Augustine corrects even sentences and phrases that might have misled) but also in his *Letters*.[44] Wills has also correctly noted that Augustine's concern with truth-telling was intimately connected to the authority of Scripture.[45]

As God's inspired word, Scripture cannot lie. It is important, therefore, to have a firm philosophical grasp of what lying really is. Lying is not a matter of falling short of the truth out of error. Lying consists in knowing what is true and distorting it in order to deceive another. Augustine's struggle with the text of the first three chapters of Genesis shows how difficult it is to discover, in matters so arcane, just what the truth is, making it safest to rely on the overall trustworthiness of Scripture and of the church's faith. But what about narratives much closer to home?

This is one of the two main issues debated in the tangled and ill-fated correspondence between Augustine and Jerome, the greatest linguist and most learned biblical scholar of the age.[46] In his commentary on Galatians, Jerome had followed the opinion of earlier scholars in asserting that Paul's report of his rebuke of Peter at Antioch was not entirely truthful because both were involved in a "useful dissembling" (Gal. 2:11-14). Jerome wants to avoid the impression that the leaders of the church could ever really disagree, so he softens the entire episode.[47] He avoids one scandal by constructing another. Augustine sees this as a slippery slope. He can deal with human persons not being truthful, even apostles like Peter and Paul. But he can't accept that Paul's *report* of the event was a deliberate falsification, especially when Paul declares in Gal. 1:20 "before God" that he is not lying. Augustine declares,

43. In addition to the two tractates against deception, see *Enchir.* 18-23; *Civ.* XIX, 6; *Ep.* 180.

44. See, e.g., *Epp.* 78 and 209.

45. Wills, *Papal Sin*, 277-92.

46. The correspondence is found in Augustine's letters (*Epp.* 28, 39, 40, 47, 67, 68, 71, 72, 73, 75, 81, 82).

47. Jerome's commentary on Galatians is found in PL 26:310-40, and the passage under dispute is discussed in PL 26:367.

> I think it extremely dangerous to admit that anything in the Sacred Books should be a lie; that is, that the men who have composed and written the Scriptures for us should have lied in their books . . . if we once admit in that supreme authority even one polite lie, there will be nothing left of those books, because, whenever anyone finds something difficult to practice or hard to believe, he will follow this most dangerous precedent and explain it as the idea or practice of a lying author. (*Ep.* 28)

In a follow-up letter, Augustine says, "If the validity of the polite lie be admitted in the Holy Scriptures, how can their authority be maintained?" (*Ep.* 40). And still later he clarifies, "I am not now asking what he did but what he wrote" (*Ep.* 82). Augustine here works with the same distinction that I observed in Origen, between what happened in the past and what the Holy Spirit wrote for our instruction. It is the truthfulness of Scripture that is his concern.

With considerable bluster and defensiveness, Jerome responds by heaping considerable amounts of scorn on Augustine's ignorance. With sure academic instinct, he cites all the authorities in his support (*Epp.* 72, 75). As the conversation (sporadically) proceeds, however, it becomes clear that Jerome is an early but by no means the last example of a man whose learning exceeds his insight. We learn as well from Jerome that a knowledge of Hebrew or conversation with rabbis is not incompatible with a reading of the New Testament that is profoundly anti-Jewish (*Ep.* 75). The more Augustine is pushed on the subject, in contrast, the more we find to admire in his response. His clear and careful reading of all the pertinent New Testament evidence demonstrates what depth of insight can be gained even without technical advantages. Augustine analyzes Paul and Peter in their historical (Jewish) context in a manner far more congenial to present-day readings and based on better supporting historical information (*Ep.* 82). By being a better exegete, the theologian also turns out to be a better historian than Jerome.

Augustine was certainly right to be concerned with the truthfulness of Scripture. His anxiety in this respect can be accounted for at least in part because of the specious plausibility of Christianity's critics. They typically exploited the contradictions in the Gospels as a reason either to reject Christianity's claims altogether (so Porphyry) or to pick and choose among them (so Faustus the Manichee). The problem is that Augustine lacked a theory of language that would enable him to find a place between allegory and literal-as-referential as a mode of truth-telling in Scripture.[48] We see his difficulty in this regard in his *Reply to Faustus the Manichaean* (= *Faust.*).[49] Faustus rejects the Old Testament (*Faust.* IV, 1), but adheres to what he calls "the gospel," namely, the teachings of Jesus (II, 1; V, 1). Only these are reliable because they are from Jesus himself. The Gospel narratives are not reliable.[50] It is child's play to show their inconsistencies and contradictions, such as the fact that Jesus declared the fulfillment of the Law and Prophets in only one (Matthew) of the four Gospels — it can therefore be regarded as spurious (XVII, 1). Faustus's opening gambit, the divergence between Matthew and Luke in their genealogies, is simply the most obvious example (III, 1). He calls Catholics inconsistent because they distinguish between carnal and spiritual in the Old Testament but not in the New Testament (V, 1; VI, 1). Faustus's challenge is not insignificant, as its long afterlife — even to our own day — shows. His is a radical version of *Sachkritik,* or "content criticism": only that is authoritative in Scripture that is consistent with the teachings of Jesus. Inconsistency is eliminated by means of rejecting first the Old Testament and then the Gospel narratives.

Augustine's response to Faustus shows good instincts. He demonstrates the unity between Old and New Testament through the fulfillment of prophecies and types (*Faust.* VI, 2-9; VIII, 2; esp. XII, 2-48). He shows that Catholics keep the moral law while rejecting the carnal ritual laws of the Old Testament (X, 2). And Augustine brings to bear a

---

48. Augustine's struggles with the connection between language and meaning and truth can be seen in *The Teacher* and *On Christian Doctrine* II, 1-6.

49. On the role of Faustus in Augustine's eventual disenchantment with Manichaeism, see *Conf.* V, 3, 3-6; V, 6, 10-V, 7, 13. The *Reply to Faustus* was written ca. 400, in response to Faustus's polemical treatise against the law and prophets (*Retract.* II, 33). Augustine creates the impression of a debate by providing Faustus's quotations and then his responses (*Faust.* I, 1).

50. In this respect, Faustus anticipates that mode of contemporary historical Jesus research that concentrates on the recoverable sayings of Jesus rather than on the narrative framework of the Gospels. See, e.g., Robert W. Funk, Roy Y. Hoover, and the Jesus Seminar, *The Five Gospels: The Search for the Authentic Words of Jesus* (New York: Macmillan, 1993), which stands in a recent tradition that extends from Thomas Jefferson's *Life and Morals of Jesus of Nazareth* through Rudolf Bultmann's *Jesus and the Word,* trans. Louise Pettibone Smith and Erminie Huntress Lantero (New York: Scribner, 1958).

number of important critical criteria of his own. To rebut Faustus's claim that some parts of the New Testament are spurious, he appeals to the evidence of the earliest and best manuscripts (XI, 2). He invokes the authority of the church's Tradition as surety for the reliability of the Gospels (XI, 2). In addition to the rule of faith, he appeals to the canon as a guide to appropriate reading (XI, 5). He states that the context of a passage must determine its sense (XI, 8). The effect of these principles is to place great emphasis on the harmony of Scripture in contrast to his opponents' emphasis on its diversity (and contradictions). And he defends the truthfulness of the Gospels themselves, declaring that the Manichaeans' principles of selection simply enable them to find the Jesus they want:

> You ought to say plainly that you do not believe the Gospel of Christ. For to believe what you please, and not to believe what you please, is to believe yourselves, not the Gospel. (*Faust.* XVII, 3)

Augustine's goal is to defend the narratives of the Gospels as true witnesses of Jesus. He says that the term Gospel refers not simply to the sayings of Jesus, but also to the events of his life: "The name evangelist is properly given to the narrators of the birth, the actions, the words, the sufferings of our Lord Jesus Christ" (*Faust.* II, 2). Again, his instinct is profoundly correct. But as we have seen in the case of Augustine's reading of Genesis according to the letter, he does not have a theory of "narrative truth" that enables him to respond adequately to Faustus; the truth of the Gospel narratives must be referential; they can be allowed to differ in detail, but they must agree in substance or else be open to the charge of error. Augustine therefore tries to harmonize the genealogies of Matthew and Luke through the dubious stratagem of postulating two fathers for Joseph (one natural, one adoptive) (III, 3-4). His goal is to defend the humanity of Jesus and the witness of the Gospels to that humanity, but he is unable to distinguish such witness from historical accuracy even in the matter of the names of ancestors. Trying to prove too much, he falls into danger of the very vice he despises, namely of manipulating the evidence in order to achieve the desired result.

The same tendency is even more obvious in the *Harmony of the Gospels* (*De consensu evangelistarum* = *Cons.*). Augustine says he is writing "against the calumnious charges by certain persons who, in impious vanity or in ignorant temerity, think to rob of their credit as veracious historians those teachers by whose instrumentality the Christian religion has been disseminated all the world over"; and to answer them, he "must prove that the writers in question do not stand in any antagonism to each other. For those adversaries are in the habit of adducing this as the palmary allegation in all their vain objection, namely, that the evangelists are not in harmony with each other" (*Cons.* I, 7). This he proceeds to do in Book II by taking Matthew as the basic narrative structure up to the Last Supper and showing how the versions of Luke, Mark, and John are in harmony with it. Then, in Book III, he shows — an easier task — how the Passion accounts harmonize. Finally, in Book IV he takes up the passages distinctive to Mark, Luke, and John, demonstrating how they fit into the structure already established. As might be imagined, this is a long and involved work, full of ingenuity and careful attention to detail.

Unfortunately, it is also a case when Augustine got so involved with specific battles that he forgot the nature of the war, leaving himself once more open to the charge of obfuscation. Thus, he takes great pains with the precise location of the Sermon on the Mount (or Plain), seeking to reconcile the contradictory locations given by Matthew and Luke (*Cons.* II, 19, 45-47). But he says far too little about the truly critical issue, which is the distinct character of the discourse in the respective accounts (II, 19, 44). He struggles to keep a firm grip on the basic point, which is the truthfulness of the Gospels, and he makes some useful and pertinent observations. The value of witnesses is not their agreement in detail, for example, but their convergence on essentials (II, 27, 60-63). This critical historiographical principle loses its pertinence, however, precisely to the degree that Augustine himself acts as if the agreement on details were important. In this respect, he falls into the same failing as Origen's response to Celsus: seeking to deal with every point exhaustively means weakening rather than strengthening the argument.

Two other failings are more serious. The first is that his entire effort misses the point. Even if Augustine were to demonstrate that the evangelists do not contradict each other, he would not have shown that they are, as he puts it, "veracious historians." They could all agree but still all be in error. Worse, they could all collude in falsehood. Augustine's massive and impressive demonstration fails to respond to the challenge put to the Gospels' historical reliability. Second, Augustine's harmonization of the Gospels detracts from the power of the respective narratives to stand as witnesses to Christ that are all the more valuable precisely because of their varying interpretations of him. By fighting the war on the ground selected by his opponents, Augustine became an unwitting member of that long succession of Christian interpreters from Tatian to the Jesus Seminar who have found the multiplicity of the Gospels a stumbling block to historical truth.[51]

As a preacher, Augustine's practice of implicit harmonization sometimes leads to readings of great power. In trying to explain in John's Gospel how Nathaniel is a "man without guile" (John 1:47), for example, Augustine uses as commentary the story of the sinful woman in Luke 7:36-47, with exquisite appropriateness (*Tractates on the Gospel of John* VII, 1, 16-19). Nor does Augustine shy away from contradictions in Scripture elsewhere that he resolves with careful attention to context and moral reasoning.[52] His anxiety concerning the historicity of the Gospels, however, led him to downplay the very real critical problems presented by their differences. Nevertheless, it is to Augustine's credit that he demands consideration of the truth of Scripture as a question that no authentic interpretation can avoid.

Interpretation for the Church

Writing to Jerome, Augustine is candid about scholarly limitations: "I neither have nor can have as much knowledge of the Divine Scriptures as I see abounds in you, and if I have ability in this field, I must spend it on the people of God. Because of my duties as a bishop, I cannot spend more time and effort in the training of students than on preaching to the people" (*Ep.* 73). The claim that the church made upon Augustine

51. See the critical evaluation of a number of such contemporary efforts in Luke Timothy Johnson, *The Real Jesus* (San Francisco: HarperSanFrancisco, 1996), together with a positive evaluation of the Gospels as discrete witnesses whose "harmony" is found in their convergence on the truth of Jesus' identity and the nature of discipleship, in Johnson, *Living Jesus* (San Francisco: HarperSanFrancisco, 1999).

52. See *Sermon on the Mount* I, 21, 69-72. He repeatedly engages the tension between Paul and James on faith and works; see *On Faith and Good Works* XIV, 23; *On the Trinity* XV, 18; *On Grace and Free Will* VII, 18.

the interpreter is a source of his anxiety but also one of the marks of his greatness, because it elicited from him the fundamental hermeneutical criterion of charity. This central theme in Augustine can be approached from three directions: first, his correspondence with Jerome, second, his tract *On Christian Doctrine,* and finally, some examples of his own interpretation.

Augustine's letters to Jerome raised another important issue in addition to Jerome's interpretation of Paul's truthfulness in Galatians (discussed above). Augustine also has concerns regarding Jerome's translation of the Old Testament directly from Hebrew into Latin. Augustine had appreciated Jerome's earlier translation from the Greek, to which Jerome had appended critical marks (the asterisk and obelisk) to indicate variations from the Hebrew. And he has nothing but gratitude for Jerome's translation from the Greek of the New Testament. But in this new translation of the Old Testament from the Hebrew, Jerome makes no reference to the Greek of the Septuagint, seemingly leaving the authority of that version out of account altogether (*Epp.* 28, 71).[53]

Augustine's anxiety has nothing to do with his personal convenience or a reluctance to change. It is entirely rooted in his care for the church. And although he expresses himself less precisely than we might like, his concerns are real. Translating straight from the Hebrew raises serious questions.

1. What about the authority of the Septuagint? Augustine took its divine inspiration for granted. As a divinely guided translation carried out hundreds of years after the Hebrew, mightn't it be supposed to have insight and meaning lacking to the Hebrew but granted to the 70 inspired translators?[54]
2. This was the version used by the apostles. Augustine makes this point so quickly, we may miss its real bite. The Septuagint, after all, forms the basis of the entire New Testament, and therefore of all Christian claims to the fulfillment of prophecy. Such dependence

53. In *Civ.* XVIII, 43, he revisits the question, arguing for the superiority of the Septuagint in even sharper terms: "Since so clear a sign of divinity has appeared in their work, it is evident that any other accurate translator of these Scriptures from the Hebrew into any other language whatsoever must agree with the Septuagint."

54. Similarly, *Civ.* XVIII, 43.

was made obvious already in Justin's *Dialogue with Trypho:* if Isa. 7:14 said *parthenos,* then Matt. 1:23 is a literal fulfillment, and Scripture speaks truth; if Isaiah says *'almah,* then Matt. 1:23 claims too much.[55] At stake here is the entire issue of a Christian Bible in which Old and New Testaments speak to each other. A translation directly from the Hebrew loses that intricate connection.

3. The Greek churches use the Septuagint (as they do to this day). Won't the Latin church's shifting to a translation based on the Hebrew raise serious questions about the unity of the church catholic? Augustine here anticipates the real if gradual cultural alienation between East and West that led finally to the schism of the 11th century. If the differences in Scripture cannot be blamed for the rift, they were part of the process of gradual estrangement.

4. If the Latin is based on Hebrew and Hebrew is generally unknown (in contrast to Greek in Augustine's world), doesn't this make responsible interpretation depend on the experts who alone know the languages? Again, Augustine is prescient, for as I have pointed out in previous chapters, the church has increasingly been in a kind of "academic captivity" because of the lack of knowledge of scriptural languages.

5. Augustine tells Jerome the story of a disturbance caused in a local church by the reading of Jerome's version, "which was very different from the version enshrined in the memory and hearing of all and sung for so many generations" (*Ep.* 71). At first, this objection sounds suspiciously like obscurantism and willful tradition-for-tradition's sake. But reflection helps us realize that Augustine is really concerned for the unity of the church and the charity owed to the tradition and piety of the simple faithful. Catholics learned this lesson after Vatican Council II when liturgical reform proceeded on a top-down basis without due respect for the ways in which people had experienced God's grace in their accustomed traditions.

Augustine's worries are substantial and deeply insightful. They are the concerns of a theologian who understands the fragile links between testaments (as he had shown in his debate with Faustus) and as a

---

55. See the points made on each side 250 years earlier in Justin Martyr, *Dial.* 66-67.

church leader who has a vision of the entire *oikoumené* and its unity (as he had shown in his disputes with the Donatists). Before moving on, it may be worth noting that Jerome the scholar was completely deaf to these theological and pastoral objections. And it may also be worth observing that Augustine's questions have still not adequately been addressed by a biblical scholarship committed to the life of the church.

Augustine's most extended discussion of biblical interpretation as such is found in *On Christian Instruction* (= *Doctr. chr.*). He wrote the first two books in 396/7, shortly after his becoming a bishop, and the last two books toward the end of his career, some 30 years later (ca. 426).[56] The book is meant to be something of a helpful handbook for students of Scripture. It has a direct and common-sense practicality that still makes it eminently worth reading for those who seek to serve the church through the interpretation of Scripture, whether as preacher or teacher. The most important message Augustine sends his readers about the interpretation of Scripture is communicated implicitly by his compositional arrangement. He encloses the technical study of the Bible (in Books II and III) within a theological framework. In Book I, he discourses on the (spiritual) path humans take back to God through a rightly ordered love. In Book IV, he discusses the art of preaching in the language of Scripture. In short, Augustine sees the goal of biblical study to be the building of the church in charity, and its most natural expression to be teaching within the church.

No surprise that the discussions at both ends of the work focus on the character of the Christian teacher. In Book I, Augustine declares that the virtues of faith, hope, and love do not themselves derive from Scripture, but they are the key to "fearless" interpretation (*Doctr. chr.* I, 40 [44]). Without the proper spiritual disposition, learning in Scripture is useless: "Whoever then appears in his own opinion to have comprehended the Sacred Scriptures, or even some part of them, yet does not build up with that knowledge the twofold love of God and his neighbor, 'has not yet known as he ought to know'" (I, 26 [40]). In Book IV, Augustine insists that the pastor should pray before preaching or teaching (IV, 15, 30), and concludes with the observation that the character of the speaker is more important than the speaker's words: "Let the beauty of his life be, as it were, a powerful sermon" (IV, 29). Every-

---

56. See the discussion in *Retract.* II, 30.

thing else that Augustine says about exegesis must be understood within this ecclesial framework: the best medium of biblical scholarship is preaching and teaching, and the goal of biblical scholarship is building up the church in love.

The second book of *On Christian Instruction* is filled with eminently practical advice for the aspiring exegete. His first three steps are perennially pertinent. The first is "know these books," through multiple readings and even memorization — allowing the language of Scripture to occupy the mind is the basis for everything else (*Doctr. chr.* II, 9 [14]). And it must be said, to our shame, that many contemporary exegetes, even scholars, simply do not know the contents of the Bible. Second, study the clear instructions and commands "governing either life or belief" — have a grasp of the essential before entertaining the debatable (II, 9 [14]). Once more, the present pertinence is fairly obvious. Many present-day seminarians, for example, think of Scripture in terms of a set of insoluble problems, because they are not well-schooled in those basic truths about faith and morals on which Scripture and the Rule of Faith strongly concur. Third, Augustine advises that the interpreter gain some "intimacy with the language of Scripture." With knowledge of the text, with a firm grasp of Scripture's scope, and with a knowledge of languages, one is able to engage specific passages that present problems. Augustine advocates as a fundamental rule that one always move from the more certain to the less certain: "Begin to uncover and examine thoroughly those passages that are obscure, selecting examples from clearer texts to explain such as are more obscure, and allowing some proofs from uncontestable texts to remove the uncertainty from doubtful passages" (II, 9 [14]).

Augustine next discusses various technical aids that can assist interpretation. If one does not know the original languages, for example, then comparing translations is useful for determining the range of possible meaning in the text (*Doctr. chr.* II, 11-15). And there is a variety of fields of knowledge that can be employed in the interpretation of Scripture. Augustine lists the knowledge of numbers (II, 16 [25]), music, and literature (II, 16-17 [26-27]). The knowledge of history — including pagan history — can be particularly helpful in understanding Scripture (II, 28), even though history itself is not normative (II, 28 [44]). The exegete should also cultivate skill in narrative description (II, 29), the arts of medicine, agriculture, and so forth (II, 30 [45]). More than the mere accumulation of knowledge, Augustine stresses the importance of reasoning, of being able to employ logic in analysis (II, 31-35 [48-53]), of being able to apply the principles of rhetoric (II, 36 [45]), and of being able to understand philosophy, especially that of Plato (II, 40 [60]). Finally, the teachings of earlier interpreters can be helpful (II, 40 [61]) — I note that Augustine relegated this most "scholarly" or "academic" of supports to the last position. Too often, for contemporaries, it becomes not only the starting point, but the entire frame of reference. By identifying all these areas of study as legitimate and indeed useful for understanding Scripture, Augustine provided a firm basis for the Christian humanism of the West, governed by his maxim, "Every good and true Christian should understand that wherever he discovers the truth, it is the Lord's" (II, 18 [28]).[57]

Once more, Augustine enfolds the practical advice of Book II within explicit moral exhortation. At the start of this book, he says that the difficulty of interpreting Scripture should encourage humility (*Doctr. chr.* II, 6 [7-8]). All of Scripture teaches the principle of twofold love that he had discussed in his first book (II, 7 [10]), and in order properly to interpret, the teacher must undergo a moral transformation (II, 7 [10-11]). Similarly, he concludes Book II by returning to the primacy of love that builds up others over a knowledge that puffs up the self, demanding of the interpreter a fundamental transformation of life according to the measure of the cross of Christ (II, 41 [62]). Only by being "brought under the yoke of Christ and weighed down by his light burden, grounded, rooted, built up in love, beyond the power of knowledge to puff him up," can the student safely pass on to the more complex aspects of interpretation.

In Book III, Augustine takes up these more daunting difficulties in interpretation. He begins simply enough, by noting that some obscurities can be clarified by checking punctuation and pronunciation, the literary context (see also *Doctr. chr.* III, 25 [37]), the overall sense of Scripture, and the teaching of the church (III, 2-3). The most important way to deal with obscurities and scandalous texts is to be able to distinguish between the literal and the figurative (III, 5). The distinction is not so much literary as it is theological and moral. He instructs the reader to "understand as figurative anything in Scripture which cannot

---

57. Augustine's statement echoes that of Origen in *Cels.* 7.59.

in a literal sense be attributed either to an upright character or to a pure faith," and to discern the overall tendency of a passage toward lust or toward charity (III, 10 [14]). Whatever is wicked or unenlightened must therefore be taken in a figurative sense (III, 12), whereas whatever is virtuous can be read literally (III, 16).

In making this distinction, however, sensitivity to historical context is necessary. Augustine warns against identifying other people's customs as sins (*Doctr. chr.* III, 14 [22]). The scriptural text can therefore have several levels of meaning, with the deeper levels being grounded in the inspiration of the Holy Spirit, though the several senses may have been held consciously by the human author as well (III, 27). In any case, Scripture's meaning is not confined to what the first author intended (III, 28). The process of discernment, however, is neither easy nor automatic. Augustine says, "in figurative expressions, therefore, a rule like this is to be heeded: to reflect with careful consideration for a long time upon what is being read until the interpretation is drawn over to the sway of charity" (III, 15).

The rest of Book III is taken up with the seven hermeneutical rules that Augustine borrows from the Donatist teacher Tyconius (died ca. 390). The rules provide some guidance to figurative meanings (*Doctr. chr.* III, 30). Augustine gives examples of how to apply them, but does not regard them either as adequate or exhaustive (III, 56). Only the first two rules need be mentioned here because of their importance for Augustine's own ecclesial interpretation. The first rule is "About the Lord and His Body," which helps sort out what passages in Scripture should be applied to Jesus and which to the church (III, 31). Note the assumption, however, that Scripture as a whole speaks about both. The second rule is "About the Two Divisions of the Lord's Body," which Augustine prefers to understand as "About the True and Mixed Body of Our Lord," meaning thereby the church as *corpus mixtum,* a place where wheat and weeds grow together, where the good, the bad, and the ugly all persist under the merciful embrace of God (III, 32).

The two principles of interpretation can be seen at work in Augustine's own interpretation of the Psalms. This massive set of reflections in five books was not conceived or written as a single composition, but was cobbled together from written notes and spoken sermons across his long career as a preacher, with some of the Psalms being treated more than once. The *Enarrationes in Psalmos* is the only extant patristic

eloquence (IV, 21), Augustine accomplished two things. First, he provided the Middle Ages with a handbook of rhetoric that was grounded in Scripture rather than in Virgil and Cicero. Second, he helped shape among preachers a scriptural imagination. He showed them not only what Scripture says but how Scripture speaks. Preachers who allowed the rhetoric of Scripture to shape their own speech could be faithful to God's word not only in substance but also in style.

Learning from Augustine

I think present-day interpreters in the postmodern church can learn at least three important lessons from Augustine that are not drawn from his treatment of a single passage but pertain to the entire task of interpretation.

The first is the challenge that interpreters imagine the world that Scripture imagines. Augustine was no more acquainted with the Bible before his conversion than many of us are. His imagination as a young man had been formed and fired by Latin literature, by the philosophy of Plato, and by the mythologies of Manichaeism, just as his practices were those driven by desire for pleasure, possessions, power, and prestige. Through his conversion to Christ, he put on Christ. He adopted a new view of reality and changed all the practices of his life. But he also put on the imaginative world of Scripture. He devoted himself literally day and night to its reading, to its memorization, to its study. He grew in his knowledge of the text, and in his knowledge of the languages, until the end of his life. And he never complained that the world of Scripture was too small. Instead, at the end, it seemed as though he had scarcely made a beginning. If Augustine could learn Scripture so well after the age of 30 that his very speech took on the rhythms of Paul rather than those of Cicero, so can we. If the world imagined by Scripture, that city of God that now fired and formed Augustine's postconversion mind, was large enough for one of the world's true geniuses, it is probably large enough to contain us as well.

The second lesson is that scriptural interpretation needs to engage the issue of truth and not simply the issue of meaning. Intellectual honesty and the need to account for the place that we claim in the world demand that Christians seriously engage the question of how the Bible is true and how the Bible is truly read. A biblical scholarship that evades these questions through research into arcana, or through assembling learned opinions in ever-larger compendia and commentaries, or by playing within the safe boundaries of convention without being willing to take on the truth or falsity of Scripture has relinquished its right to be taken seriously. I have suggested that Augustine's own way of answering the question about Scripture's truthfulness is inadequate, especially in his harmonizing of the Gospels. But his putting that question always into play is something we should imitate.

The third lesson we can learn from Augustine is that the true home of biblical interpretation is the church as the gathering of God's people, the body of Christ, and that the true goal of biblical interpretation is the building up of the church through love. By such a measure, biblical scholarship disqualifies itself when it is content to remain a purely academic enterprise carried out within the university and answerable only to tenure committees and professional peer review, with no contact with the church, no knowledge of the church, no love for the church. By such a measure, biblical scholarship betrays itself when it seeks in the name of science to divide or destroy the faith of the church.

Those who demand a choice between critical intelligence — identified with a single Enlightenment epistemology — and loyalty to the church's faith propose a false dilemma deeply harmful to the body of Christ. Those who would divide the church into the intellectual elite and the blindly loyal are false prophets. By no means am I suggesting that biblical scholarship within the church should be uncritical. Commitment to truth demands critical engagement with Scripture and with Tradition. But such critical engagement, even when it must say no to an accepted reading or no to a popular construal, can and ought to be the expression of the highest loyalty to Scripture and Tradition. We are called to do the truth in love. Loyalty to the tradition and love of the church ought to enable criticism rather than oppose it. Likewise, criticism should seek to enrich the tradition and build the church rather than seek to destroy them.

To be able to dance within such a delicate dialectic, the Scripture scholar must do more than contemplate the church from afar as an interesting object of study, must be a member of the body, grow with it, suffer with it, rejoice with it, pray with it, and seek to build it up into a more perfect expression of the life of its head, our Lord Jesus Christ.

CHAPTER FIVE

Imagining the World That Scripture Imagines

If Scripture is ever again to be a living source for theology, those who practice theology must become less preoccupied with the world that produced the Scripture and learn again to live in the world that Scripture produces. This will require imagination and, no doubt, the willingness to leap. It will require the willingness to leap precisely because embracing imagination means entering truly into a world other than modernity. The Enlightenment banished imagination to the epistemological attic. Championing descriptive forms of knowledge that can be empirically verified, modernity considered the imaginative capacities of the mind as a matter of private fancy. Only slowly are we regaining a sense of imagination as a constructor of worlds. The more we appreciate the constructive power of imagination, the more we can begin to explore the proposition that the truth of Scripture is to be found less in its accuracy in describing the world than in its adequacy in imagining a world.

Imagining Worlds

Scripture as a whole and in all of its parts imagines a world, and by imagining a world, it reveals it to readers. I am not speaking here about ideas. Imagination is always embodied. Images differ from ideas because of the clay that clings to them. The scriptural world is therefore rooted in the physical realm where humans live. By no means, however, is the world conjured by Scripture simply to be identified with the physical realm where humans live and act.

For one thing, the world imagined by Scripture is considerably smaller than the human world we call our own. The spatial world of Scripture is tiny, for example, when compared to the cosmos of Carl Sagan.[1] And the temporal world of Scripture is hardly to be compared to the history of time imagined by Stephen Hawking.[2] The scriptural world seems small also when one thinks of the wide range of possible human activities. Scripture has a narrow focus. It is much concerned with law and morality. It has little interest in romance and affection. It is unconcerned with science and does not pay much attention to visual beauty.

Viewed another way, the world of Scripture appears much larger than that of ordinary empirical human activity. Scripture imagines a world more richly furnished with living and intelligent beings than our own. It has room for angels and demons and assorted spirits of a sort not recognizable to Sagan and Hawking. Most of all, Scripture's world contains — or better, is contained by — God, which makes it the largest of all possible worlds. Carl Sagan imagines, on the basis of evidence largely unavailable or unintelligible to most of us, a universe of immeasurable size, yet he cannot imagine a God related to that great expanse.[3] Stephen Hawking imagines, on the basis of mathematical musings inexplicable to the rest of us, a universe of incomprehensible duration, yet he cannot imagine a God capable of imagining that universe and calling it into being.[4] In contrast, despite its severe spatial and temporal limitations, Scripture imagines — also, by the way, on the basis of experiences and reports not within the normal ken — a world in which every creature is at every moment summoned into being by a Power and a Presence that is at once distant and close, ageless and instant.

No more than Scripture's world are the worlds imagined by Sagan

---

1. Carl Sagan, *Pale Blue Dot: A Vision of the Human Future in Space* (New York: Random House, 1994).

2. Stephen Hawking, *A Brief History of Time: From the Big Bang to Black Holes* (New York: Bantam, 1988).

3. Sagan, 11-57.

4. Or at least, not a God unconstrained by the universe itself; see Hawking, 7-9, 116.

and Hawking (and all the other voices of modernity represented by these two chosen more or less at random) simply "the real world." Like the world imagined by Scripture, they are products of this particular physical space and time humans occupy and act within, but they are both more and less than this physical space and time. The imaginings of Sagan and Hawking open up new perceptions of the here and now inhabited by them and their readers. This place and this time therefore appear different by being placed within a larger space and longer story. It is always the case that our perception of "this" and "now" are shaped by our perspective, and that perspective can be enlarged by imagination, and that enlarged vision can affect our disposition of "this" and "now." We act thus and not so, because we conceive the world to be constructed in this way and not that. To take one example, Sagan's view of earth as a small blue dot in an endless space is in service of ecological sensitivity: the perception of fragility and preciousness carries with it a moral imperative. The world constructed by Scripture also provides enlarged perceptions of the here and now, and provides options for disposing of this and that in ways not otherwise imaginable. By imagining the world as essentially and always related to a God who creates, sustains, judges, saves, and sanctifies, Scripture at the same time reveals that world and reveals this God.

People act on the basis of the imagined world in which they dwell. By acting on what they imagine, they help establish their worlds as real. Those acting on the imaginings of a Sagan or Hawking make the world of Sagan and Hawking less "imaginary" and more "real." Thus, imagination seeks embodiment a second time through enactment. Space travel would have been impossible had not Copernicus and Kepler and Einstein imagined space in a way that no one before them had done. In similar fashion, those who act on the basis of the world Scripture imagines also make it less "imaginary" and more "real." A dream shared is a dream less in danger of disappearance; a dream enacted in ritual attains virtual reality; a ritual extrapolated into the disposition of material possessions shapes the physical space and time in which we live and act.

Living in any of these imaginary worlds as though it were real requires a fundamental acceptance of its premises, an adjustment of vision according to its perceptions, and a decision to act as though these premises and perceptions were not only real but valid. Because Scripture imagines the world in which we live and move as having its source and meaning in an Other who enables us to move and live, we are able to perceive the world this way and decide to live according to this premise. So perceiving and so acting, we incrementally transform the world imagined by Scripture into the physical world in which we live and move.

Theology is the name we give to the effort of our minds and hearts to catch up with the work of the Living God in the world. Or to put it in terms of the conceit of this chapter, theology is the name we give to the effort of our minds and hearts to grasp the world conjured by God and construed by Scripture. Or, even more on the topic, theology is our successfully imagining the world imagined by Scripture, which reveals the world as imagined by God.

Readers who have patiently followed these sentences to this point will surely recognize that my own posture is that we have come to call postmodernism. Nothing is more obvious from my very way of speaking than that I (and the "we" for whom I implicitly speak) do not inhabit the world imagined by Scripture in a full and unself-conscious manner. The world of Scripture is not simply "my" world. If it were, I could not speak of it as one world among others, set beside the imaginative worlds of the Sagans and Hawkings. If we inhabited Scripture's world entirely, we would not know it as Scripture's world, but simply as "the world." But my stance is not that of modernity. I am estranged from the world of Scripture, but I am not contemptuous of it. I do not regard the world as found in Scripture to be erroneous, a matter of bad science and flawed history. In other words, I do not hold Scripture to the epistemological measure of the Enlightenment and declare it untrue. By calling it an imaginative world, and by recognizing that it is capable of generating a "real world" through enactment, I am occupying instead a postmodern perspective. And standing in this position, I can say that the greatest difficulty our generation has in doing theology is our distance from the imaginative world of Scripture, which means, our distance from the God revealed by the world as imagined by Scripture.

Once more then, I return to the theme of these opening chapters, asking from still another angle how our contemporary way of reading the Bible might disable us as theologians, inhibit us from occupying the world imagined by Scripture, and then asking what we as theologians might do to recover that world, and live within a properly scriptural imagination. A way into the questions is through imagination.

Living Cities and Lost Cities

Imagine the world constructed by Scripture as a living city that one might inhabit. This is not so hard to imagine, after all, for Scripture once was such a city for many and still is for some. How do people who have grown up and continue to dwell in a living city know it? Their knowledge is instinctive, connatural, and geared to the practices of the city and its peculiar ways. They understand how things are done here, even if they cannot easily interpret such customs to outsiders. They know how to get from one place to another in the city quickly and with ease, even if they don't necessarily know the names of the streets. They move around their city largely by feel, by means of landmarks and images that inform their every move even when they do not consciously advert to them: here a storefront, there a park bench, a billboard hanging overhead.

Such knowledge is deep, intimate, nonsystematic, comprehensive, practical. Natives of this city know in their bones the accents, nomenclature, handshakes and nods, the intricate timing of speech and silence, the rhythm of everyday exchanges in the market. These are the sort of things that outsiders can spend decades trying to decipher without complete success. They can observe and memorize and imitate, but never get them precisely the way a native would. In a living city, the past is not someplace else, but this place. The city's past continues as part of its present. The past is not memorialized but incorporated. The city's history is not external to its inhabitants, but is part of their biography; indeed, their personal story cannot be told without also telling the story of the city. People know the difference between past and present, but they make no artificial distinction between them: past and present are part of the same stream of life. Where there once were trolley tracks there now run buses, where once there were stop signs now signal lights blink. Where the drugstore stood now stands a boutique. Nevertheless, the speech of children today carries the accents of their parents and grandparents, the feet of little girls skipping rope fall on the steps of their mothers and grandmothers. In this city, there is constant change, yet the change is contained within a deeper continuity, as this city remains, undeniably and indefinably, this and only this place. Are there limits to this sort of knowledge? Yes. Are their dangers to the inhabitants' assumption that they are still living in the same city because they occupy the same place? Of course. But these are the limits and dangers of life itself.

For the first 1600 years of Christianity, the world imagined by Scripture was like such a living city. Patristic and medieval authors — even writers of the Reformation and beyond — act as though the world imagined by Scripture were the real world.[5] For them, there was no great gap between the study of Scripture and the doing of theology. The two activities were virtually one and had the same point: the glorification of God through the transformation of human behavior according to the reality imagined by Scripture.[6] As my chapters on Origen and Augustine have suggested, ancient theologians were not unaware of the existence of other cities and their charms: they lived in a pluralistic culture. And as they engaged Jewish readers and Greek philosophers in serious and public debate, so did medieval theologians also engage Jewish and Arabic philosophers.[7] Nor, as I have also shown, were ancient interpreters ignorant of the difficulties in the text of Scripture; solving these served as a major source of entertainment and the occasion for edification.[8] But in reading them, we nowhere have the

5. See George A. Lindbeck, *The Nature of Doctrine: Religion and Theology in a Postliberal Age* (Philadelphia: Westminster, 1984), 112-24.

6. The essential commonality between Aquinas and the Reformers on this point has been demonstrated by William C. Placher, *The Domestication of Transcendence: How Modern Thinking about God Went Wrong* (Louisville: Westminster John Knox, 1996), 22-68.

7. Origen, *Contra Celsum;* Augustine, *City of God;* Thomas Aquinas, *Summa Contra Gentiles,* I, 60-63; I, 71.

8. Origen says in *Num.* 27.1: "We have begun with this preamble in order to encourage your hearts, because the reading which is in our hands is one of those that present difficulties to understand and seem useless to read. But we can only say that among the writings of the Holy Spirit there is nothing useless or superfluous, even if it appears in certain respects to have obscurities. We must rather turn the eyes of our intelligence toward him who has commanded to write, and to ask of him the meaning. Is there a weakness in our soul? It is he who heals us, 'him who cures all our maladies' (Ps. 103:3). Are we still in the infancy of understanding? May the Lord who guards the little ones assist us, nourish us, and lead us to 'the measure of maturity'

sense that ancient Christian interpreters were visiting Scripture from some other place. The rhythms of Scripture are, for the most part, their rhythms, as Scripture's language is their language.[9] They have no reason to stumble over the different meanings of, say, the word "grace" in Scripture and in their sermons, for it would not occur to them that there would be a difference. They saw the world as one in which grace was not a linguistic puzzle to be solved but an experiential reality to be celebrated. In their city, they could see how their steps fell on the prints made by James and Paul and John.

Cities sometimes die and are covered over with sand. When cities disappear, the worlds of meaning within which so many lives were lived die also. Through archaeological exhumation, some pieces and some sense of those cities can be recovered. In fact, archaeologists can know such cities in ways that none of their inhabitants ever did. The archaeologist can dig through various strata of ruins, exposing to light and to synchronic examination the changes in culture that none of a city's former citizens could ever see so displayed, and perhaps never noticed as they were happening. The archaeologist can date with some precision the stages of the city's former life, can mark the streets and markets and houses with great accuracy, can uncover the system of aqueducts and sewers, can compare this city at each of its stages of existence to other places similarly covered over and now uncovered. The archaeologist might even imagine what the people were like who created and once lived in the city. But the one thing the archaeologist cannot do is actually imagine that city as its inhabitants imagined it when they walked its streets and argued in its halls and made love in its beds. The reason is that for the archaeologist, the past is always past and only past. It has nothing to do with the archaeologist except as a job of research. It makes no claim on the archaeologist's present or future. For the archaeologist, the lost city is just one more city among others.

Since the triumph of the historical-critical paradigm within biblical studies, the relationship of theology to Scripture has resembled

---

(Eph. 4:13). For it is in our power to pass over from sickness to health, from infancy to maturity. It is certainly in our power to ask of God, for God is accustomed to give to those who ask and to open to those who knock."

9. As Lindbeck observes of them, "It is the text, so to speak, which absorbs the world, rather than the world the text" (118).

that of an archaeologist to the site of an ancient and uninhabited city. Without any unfairness, the historical-critical paradigm can be designated a kind of literary archaeology.[10] It has been preoccupied with the exact detection of literary seams — analogous to strata in an archaeological dig — as pointers to sources. The detection of the sequence and age of these sources, in turn, is thought to enable the tracing of the history of ancient Israel or early Christianity. In the best of circumstances, such an exercise would be difficult and hazardous. It can go seriously awry when biblical diggers, like archaeologists who are tempted to extrapolate a lost culture on the basis of a few shards, are overconfident in their capacity to detect layers, assign traditions, and imagine the communities that produced them.[11]

The intellectual curiosity that drives the dissection of ancient cultures is in itself entirely legitimate. When the past culture is the world imagined by Scripture, however, something fundamental is revealed by an approach that so deliberately and decisively divides the world examined from the examiner's own world. The supreme virtue of the exegete within this scientific approach is detachment, which is thought to ensure the "otherness" of the text and enable its "objective" analysis. In contrast, the deadly vice of the exegete is subjectivity, a too passionate interest that can lead to the vice of eisegesis, understood as reading contemporary perspectives anachronistically into an ancient and alien world. The methodologically postulated distance between worlds enables the entire paradigm to work. That distance becomes more than methodological when the Bible is read mainly as an academic concern rather than as a matter of personal and community transformation. When read in the assembly of believers gathered in the name of the resurrected Jesus and in the power of the Holy Spirit, it is impossible to pretend that these texts speaking of the resurrected Jesus and the power of the Holy Spirit belong in a foreign and long-ago land. But when read simply as an exercise in historical research within an acad-

10. The analogy appears, nonironically, with some frequency among practitioners; see, e.g., James A. Sanders, *From Sacred Story to Sacred Text: Canon as Paradigm* (Philadelphia: Fortress, 1987), 79.

11. See Luke T. Johnson, "On Finding the Lukan Community: A Cautious Cautionary Essay," *1979 SBL Seminar Papers*, ed. Paul Achtemeier (Missoula: Scholars, 1979), 1:87-100; and *BRev* 11/6 (1995): 20-25, 44. Most recently, see Philip Jenkins, *Hidden Gospels* (New York: Oxford University Press, 2001).

emy that banishes any explicit confessional stance or speech, the alien character of Scripture is reinforced. The community of readers who might have embodied the imaginative world of Scripture become themselves more and more disembodied — just as the texts of Scripture become more and more fragmented and evaporated into "ideas" — as the analysis of ancient texts is carried out in a context far apart from the practices of piety.

Historical Hegemony

The historical-critical paradigm drives an implacable wedge between the world imagined by Scripture and the worldview of the biblical critic. The approach could not work apart from the premise that the two worlds are, in very truth, different. When Christian theology also bound itself over to the hegemony of the historical paradigm, it found itself to be merely a visitor to the world it once called home. There is no intrinsic reason why historical reconstruction of the past should have any impact on theology. That it did have this impact — that theologians have felt the need not only to consult such reconstructions but even to engage in them[12] — is both remarkable in itself and a sure indicator that the world of Scripture (and Scripture's God) had been collapsed into an Enlightenment sensibility that seemed, at the time, to be larger, even though in retrospect it too seems terribly limited.[13] Christian practitioners within the historical-critical paradigm have managed to carry on by remaining in a state of chronic denial concerning the true state of affairs, which is that the very notion of "approaching" the

---

12. A classic example is Edward Schillebeeckx's effort to use the best of contemporary New Testament scholarship in constructing a systematic christology. The first volume, *Jesus: An Experiment in Christology,* trans. Hubert Hoskins (New York: Crossroad, 1979), was entirely based upon the dissection of sources (Q, etc.) found among American New Testament scholars. The second volume, *Christ, the Experience of Jesus as Lord,* trans. John Bowden (New York: Crossroad, 1980), was likewise indebted to New Testament historians but was stronger to the degree that the theologian could actually work with Paul. The results were so ambiguous and unsatisfactory that Schillebeeckx issued a third volume that attempted to clean up the mess, *Interim Report on the Books* Jesus *and* Christ, trans. John Bowden (New York: Crossroad, 1981).

13. See Placher, 71-107.

Bible as an artifact of a former age is a clear confession that those so approaching come from "somewhere else" and that the scriptural world is no longer their own.

One form of this denial is found in the pretense that studies of early Christianity were simply a form of scientific inquiry, when in fact, as I have pointed out in an earlier chapter, the dominant form of such histories expresses powerful theological convictions that remain either unconscious or implicit. Finding the earliest form of Christianity becomes important because of the conviction that origins define essence. Any development of the church, it follows, is a form of decline. Thus, the expression "early Catholicism," which is standard in New Testament studies, appears as merely descriptive, but bears with it powerfully evocative theological undertones.[14] What claims to be neutral science turns out to be surreptitious theology, as the critical historian secures the "historical essence" of Christianity safe from Catholic influence. The cost of that salvage operation, however, is considerable, since huge amounts of the scriptural world need to be jettisoned in order to save a few pieces intact and usable.[15] The theologian, in turn, rather than being first of all a reader of Scripture who explores its world from within, confident that though much has changed its world remains the theologian's world as well, is now reduced to a client of the biblical guild, dependent on the results of its excavations of a world that, with each dig, became increasingly remote. In truth, the guild did not offer many usable pieces, and lacking the coherent imaginative world from which the pieces had been wrenched in the first place, theology could do little with them.[16]

14. Jonathan Z. Smith uses the phrase "Pagano-Papism," and shows how pervasive it was in Protestant scholarship on Christian origins; see *Drudgery Divine* (Chicago: University of Chicago Press, 1990), 1-35, 114-15.

15. The principle of *Sachkritik* ("content criticism") and its corollary of a "canon within the canon," were suggested by Luther's comments on the Letter of James in his "Preface to the New Testament" of 1522 (*Luther's Works* 35: *Word and Sacrament*, ed. E.T. Bachmann [Philadelphia: Fortress, 1961], 362). Luther could never have imagined the way those principles have been applied by scholars like Robert Funk, *Honest to Jesus* (San Francisco: HarperSanFrancisco, 1996), 103-20.

16. It is painful to observe how little positive content can be drawn from the New Testament by one committed to the paradigm I have sketched; see, e.g., Willi Marxsen, *New Testament Foundations for Christian Ethics*, trans. O. C. Dean, Jr. (Minneapolis: Fortress, 1993).

The odd misalliance between history and theology is even more obviously displayed in the quest for the historical Jesus. Here, the excavation of traditions explicitly sets itself against the world imagined by Scripture and lived in by the church, in order to secure scientifically verifiable information about Jesus as a purely human figure. Stripping away all those perceptions of Jesus within the New Testament as a whole that support the experience of him as resurrected Lord and the perception of him as incarnate word, the enterprise salvages bits of evidence that can be pasted onto a cardboard profile derived from some variation within Judaism. And then this reconstructed figure is proposed to the church as the norm for Christian identity in the present. The quest for the historical Jesus shows the results of a sterile literalism that can neither breathe life into its subject nor engender a genuine Christian existence. It is a search for a usable Jesus by those who can no longer imagine the Jesus imagined by the Gospels.

A second way of trying to close the gap between historical criticism of the Bible and theology is through Biblical Theology.[17] The very name reveals the distance from the imaginative world of Scripture, for it suggests the possibility of a theology that is not biblical, and a study of the Bible that is not theological.[18] The many attempts at constructing a satisfactory biblical theology have succeeded mainly in revealing the contradictions inherent in the enterprise. Efforts to transcend historical criticism by the use of more history simply show how pervasive the historical perspective is.[19] The desire to synthesize diverse literary witnesses leads almost inevitably to the suppression of some of Scrip-

17. For a good orientation, see Steven J. Kraftchick, Charles D. Myers, Jr., and Ben C. Ollenberger, *Biblical Theology: Problems and Prospects* (Nashville: Abingdon, 1995).

18. See Hendrikus Boers, *What Is New Testament Theology? The Rise of Criticism and the Problem of the New Testament* (Philadelphia: Fortress, 1979).

19. See Brevard S. Childs, *Biblical Theology of the Old and New Testaments* (Minneapolis: Fortress, 1993), and my review, "The Crisis in Biblical Scholarship," *Commonweal* 120/21 (3 December 1993): 18-21. Even more startling is the decision to make "the historical Jesus" a key element of New Testament theology in George B. Caird, *New Testament Theology*, comp. and ed. Lincoln D. Hurst (Oxford: Clarendon, 1994), 345-408; and in Richard B. Hays, *The Moral Vision of the New Testament: Community, Cross, New Creation: A Contemporary Introduction to New Testament Ethics* (San Francisco: HarperSanFrancisco, 1996), 158-68.

ture's voices and the privileging of others, while imposing a false harmony by means of some extrinsic category.[20] Biblical theology manages to keep the world of Scripture firmly in the past. The role of mediation assigned to biblical theology only emphasizes the distance between the world imagined by Scripture and the world inhabited by contemporary theologians. Biblical theology fails worst, in fact, when it seems to succeed best. For theologians who actually take up its distilled propositions as "the biblical witness," the living conversation between Scripture and theology is not opened but closed. Biblical theology has remained primarily an academic enterprise, an exercise in the history of ideas, or an ethnography of ancient culture.[21] It derives neither inspiration nor authority from the life of the church, and does not address itself to the transformation of human existence within a community that imagines itself living within the world imagined by Scripture.

The hegemony of the historical paradigm is clear whether scholarship takes the form of theology masquerading as history or history masquerading as theology. And as I have stated in earlier chapters, it is not at all clear that any change can be expected from within an academy that has ever more explicitly distanced itself and the study of the Bible within it from the concerns of believing communities.[22] The development of forms of ideological criticism within the academy only makes more explicit the assumed moral superiority of the contemporary reader to the world imagined by Scripture. When the cross of Jesus Christ becomes a scandal, not because of the way it subverts worldly wisdom, but because it is perceived as a morally dangerous symbol, then theology's relationship with Scripture has become tenuous indeed.[23]

20. See the perceptive comments of Nils A. Dahl, "Rudolf Bultmann's Theology of the New Testament," in *The Crucified Messiah, and Other Essays* (Minneapolis: Augsburg, 1974), 90-128; and my review of Richard Hays's *Moral Vision*, "Why Scripture isn't enough," *Commonweal* 124/11 (6 June 1997): 23-25.

21. This is the approach of Wayne A. Meeks, *The Origins of Christian Morality: The First Two Centuries* (New Haven: Yale University Press, 1993), which remains so chastely descriptive and so nondirective among the varieties of early Christian practice that the few normative statements essayed at the very end cannot altogether avoid seeming capricious.

22. See Jon D. Levenson, *The Hebrew Bible, the Old Testament, and Historical Criticism* (Louisville: Westminster John Knox, 1993).

23. See Dolores S. Williams, *Sisters in the Wilderness: The Challenge of Womanist God-*

Recovering Imagination

Theology will recover a scriptural imagination, not through the efforts of an academic guild committed to historical reconstruction and ideological criticism, but through the scholarship of a faith community, whose practices are ordered to the transformation of humans according to the world imagined by Scripture — a world, faith asserts, that expresses the mind of God. This is the "leap" of which I spoke in my first paragraph. It is a leap of faith because it is a leap that only faith can make. Perhaps it is better expressed in the language of Scripture as a "turning," a conversion demanded by the realization that, whatever its intentions or virtues might once have been, the academic study of the Bible has, for the longest portion of its career, been set against the life and faith of the church as a constant and often hostile critic.

I do not suggest that those (like myself) who are located in academic settings cannot also undertake such a conversion. But their doing so will require almost heroic effort, for they will be going against the grain of the academy's own increasingly distorted criteria and expectations. It is important, therefore, to encourage the development of theologians with scriptural imagination within the community of faith itself. In the paragraphs that follow, I sketch in broad terms four essential elements in recovering a scriptural imagination, elements that do not follow each other in sequence (as stages) but that work together (as components).

1. Scripture as Imaginative World

The most obvious and critical element in this conversion is the appropriate apprehension of Scripture itself. Note that throughout this chapter, I have not distinguished testaments or individual compositions. I have rather adopted the ancient practice of speaking of Scripture as a collection of texts that contain (and create) a world. I have referred to "all of Scripture in all of its parts" as creating this world. We need to ap-

---

Talk (Maryknoll: Orbis, 1993), 143-77. For a more positive feminist view of the cross, see Sally B. Purvis, *The Power of the Cross: Foundations for a Christian Feminist Ethic of Community* (Nashville: Abingdon, 1993).

prehend Scripture as a body of literature that does not primarily describe the world but rather imagines a world, and by imagining it, *reveals* it, and by revealing it, enables it to be brought into being within this physical space that human beings share with one another. When Scripture says that humans are created in the image of God (Gen. 1:26-27; Jas. 3:9), for example, it is not making a descriptive statement based upon empirical evidence. In fact, most of us would agree that empirical evidence would probably argue against the proposition that humans are created in the image of God — unless, like Marcion, we are willing to view the creator God as malevolent and murderous. Scripture is rather imagining humans as thus created in the image of a God who can imagine all things as good, and by so imagining humans also reveals to human readers that possibility of imagining themselves, and even taking that imagination as prescriptive for their behavior toward one another.

I am not calling for a *sacrificium intellectus* by which we as contemporaries living in a world of astrophysics and evolutionary biology retreat out of fear into a biblical cosmology and psychology and pretend that they are adequate to our present-day sense of science. Just the opposite. I propose that we rather expand our minds by entering into the imaginative world of Scripture, for it is only there that we learn of a God who creates us as good, interacts with us at every moment, knows us utterly as we truly are, and saves us by granting us a share in God's own life through the death and resurrection of Jesus.[24]

Despite theories concerning expanding universes and evolving species, it is still possible — and more than ever necessary — to imagine the world as a garden that God has planted for the delight of humans, a garden that humans have, through ignorance and envy, made into a place of deceit and death. It still is possible — and more than ever necessary — to imagine the wood of the cross as the instrument of healing from that mortal wound of disobedience.[25] But such imagining is available only to those who are willing to construe Scripture not as a

24. In *Faith's Freedom: A Classic Spirituality for Contemporary Christians* (Minneapolis: Fortress, 1990), I argue that the peculiar challenge to faith today is to oscillate creatively between worlds constructed by secular analyses and the world constructed by Scripture.

25. I am playing here with Genesis 2-3, Romans 5, and John Wisdom, "The Logic of God," in *Paradox and Discovery* (Oxford: Blackwell, 1965), 1-22.

source of propositions, still less as a cluster of historical sources, but as a vast collection of interconnected and internally coherent images.

To live within the imaginative world of Scripture is not to flee reality but to constitute an alternative reality. This construal of the world does not contradict the worlds of philosophy and science (which themselves scarcely agree!) because it does not compete with them. And like the worlds constructed by philosophy and science, the truthfulness of the world constructed by Scripture must be tested in ways that are appropriate to its scope. Scripture enables me to affirm that the physical universe is expanding and species are evolving and any number of other interesting if not compelling truths, and also to confess that all this random and exciting movement derives from the God who says "Let there be light" (Gen. 1:3). Scripture enables me to confess that in every point pertinent to human religious and moral behavior — that is to say, in every point truly pertinent to being human — calling this universe (expanding or not) a garden planted by God works just fine.[26] Indeed, while the presumed truth of an expanding universe or evolving species translates only abstractly and arduously into a vision of the world with any moral valence, the moral implications of being given a garden to tend are obvious and immediate. Life and all its thoughts are not adequate to spell out what gardening the earth might mean and demand of us.

Once more, the case of Jesus is instructive. Historical questers seek to fix the figure of Jesus in the past, while at the same time proposing that reconstructed Jesus as normative for Christianity.[27] Every such reconstruction, however, represents a narrowing, and therefore a distorting, of the multiple and rich images of Jesus throughout the writings of the New Testament.[28] The life of the faith community is not based on any such reconstruction, and never has been. The church lives by the

26. A fine example of this sort of approach is Sara Maitland, *A Big-Enough God: A Feminist's Search for a Joyful Theology* (New York: Henry Holt, 1995), esp. 25-67.

27. See Luke Timothy Johnson, *The Real Jesus* (San Francisco: HarperSanFrancisco, 1996), 1-56.

28. A reconstruction that has received much favorable response, because it appears on the surface to be much closer to the Gospel presentation of Jesus, is no less narrow and distorting. I refer to N. T. Wright, *Jesus and the Victory of God*, vol. 2 of *Christian Origins and the Question of God* (Minneapolis: Fortress, 1996). See Luke Timothy Johnson, "A Historiographical Response to Wright's Jesus," in *Jesus and the Restoration of Israel*, ed. Carey C. Newman (Downers Grove: InterVarsity, 1999), 206-24, 315-16.

power of the Holy Spirit given by the resurrected Lord Jesus. The faith community, therefore, imagines itself in a world filled with the power of that resurrection life, and in the constant presence of the Living One through word, sacrament, fellowship, prayer, and solidarity with the suffering. It learns Jesus through sacrament, saint, and stranger, as well as through the reading of Scripture. It recognizes the identity of Jesus Christ in and through the multiple narrative portraits of him in the Gospels. The church celebrates this multiplicity of images, even as it celebrates the diversity of its own experience of the risen Jesus.[29] It regards the effort to fix Jesus in history not only as impossible, but also as foolish and beside the point. Or so it should. The remarkable incapacity of the contemporary church to respond with vigor and coherence to this longest and most serious of christological controversies — posed by the quest for the historical Jesus — testifies to the degree to which a truly scriptural imagination has disappeared from Christian theology.

2. Communities of Practice

In order to regain a scriptural imagination, we must cultivate communities of readers in the church whose appropriation of Scripture is grounded in practices of Christian piety. I have suggested that imagination is always embodied. The imaginative world of Scripture must find embodiment in specific disciplines and practices. The most important of these is worship. Not only does worship express and enact the world revealed by Scripture through the praise it offers God, it also shapes a scriptural ethos among believers through the liturgical proclamation of the word in all its forms.[30] The practices of piety include also all of the transformative attitudes and actions associated with the Mind of Christ (1 Cor. 2:16; Phil. 2:5): sharing possessions, healing the sick, caring for the helpless and homeless, visiting the imprisoned, providing hospitality, praying alone and in common.[31] Only in communities

29. See Luke Timothy Johnson, *Living Jesus* (San Francisco: HarperSanFrancisco, 1999).

30. See Don E. Saliers, *Worship as Theology: Foretaste of Glory Divine* (Nashville: Abingdon, 1994), 21-38.

31. See Dorothy C. Bass et al., eds., *Practicing Our Faith: A Way of Life for a Searching People* (San Francisco: Jossey-Bass, 1997).

committed to such a transformed existence can the world imagined by Scripture find authentic hearing and expression.[32]

By a reading community, I mean something specific, namely, groups of people within a parish or school or town who covenant with each other to meet regularly in the name of Jesus and read Scripture as Scripture. Not Bible study, not working through a program, but reading together in faith as a fellowship of disciples. Such groups would be better if pastors shared, not as leaders and teachers, but as fellow learners. Such reading groups, committed to the transformative practices of Christian piety, enable the imaginative reading of Scripture while holding in check the human tendencies toward misguided fantasy and projection. Within such groups, reading a Gospel or an Epistle or a Prophet from end to end, multiple strong readings of the text emerge naturally as a result of the process and the participation of active and strong readers.

In different ways, both the quest for the historical Jesus and biblical theology have sought to suppress the complexities, ambiguities, and contradictions in Scripture by means of a univocal reading. Given a commitment to a single literal sense, and given as well a commitment to the individual interpretation of Scripture, then efforts to discover or create a single univocal understanding of the text are understandable. The text is the only available control. Thus, questers seek a Jesus who is clear and simple and without contradictions. Thus, biblical theologians seek a meaning of the New Testament that is clear and simple and without contradictions. Life itself, however, is not simple or clear, and contains many contradictions. And within a reading community dedicated to the practices of Christian piety, neither the complexities of the biblical text nor the ambiguities of human experience need be feared or suppressed. A community so grounded in practice and so nurtured by Scripture's wisdom can be trusted to read with discrimination and discernment according to the Mind of Christ.[33]

The trust placed in such reading communities is strengthened when theologians within the church direct their efforts to the same process of the transformation of minds and hearts and practices in accord

32. My point is similar to that made by Stanley Hauerwas, *Unleashing the Scripture* (Nashville: Abingdon, 1993).

33. See the fuller discussion in Luke Timothy Johnson, *Scripture and Discernment* (Nashville: Abingdon, 1996), 109-32.

with the world imagined by Scripture. The difference for discourse about Christian morality, for example, can be startling. Scripture can be read, not simply as the source of rules of behavior — these are given already by the scripturally derived norms of the community — but above all as the source of wisdom and the molder of character.[34] Because the ethos of the community is not totally dependent on the literal construal of Scripture, it can embrace all the richness in Scripture. Here as elsewhere, structure is not the opposite of spontaneity but its prerequisite.

There is, therefore, no more urgent task for theology and for the renewal of the church than the creation of reading groups committed to the practices of Christian piety.

3. Learning to Read

One of the most destructive results of the historical-critical paradigm's hegemony over biblical scholarship has been its suppression of imagination in the name of literalism. It was precisely the uses of the imagination in "precritical" scriptural interpretation over the church's first 1600 years that was regarded as dangerous. But if allegory could sin by excess — and no reader of Gregory the Great would deny that it could — the rejection of any voice within Scripture other than the literal and the historical was equally an overreaction, leading to a loss of Scripture's power to speak powerfully and in many ways. Theologians need again to become inhabitants of Scripture as in a familiar and well-loved city, by re-engaging the rich world of image and metaphor within Scripture's compositions.

No one way of reading is instrinsically superior to another. Different modes of reading are better fitted to different purposes. If Scripture is being used to establish the moral norms of the community, then the literal sense (functionally, that meaning most publicly available) is demanded.[35] But if Scripture is being read to enliven the mind and

34. See again my review of Hays's *Moral Vision, Commonweal* 124/11 (6 June 1997): 23-25.

35. See the discussion by Hans W. Frei, "The 'Literal Reading' of Biblical Narrative in the Christian Tradition: Does It Stretch or Will It Break?" in *Theology and Narrative: Selected Essays,* ed. George Hunsinger and William C. Placher (New York: Oxford University Press, 1993), 117-152.

heart, or to expand the imagination, or simply to allow the reader to play contemplatively in the fields of the Lord, then multiple modes of reading are welcome.

As *haggadah* was to *halakah* within classical Judaism, so allegory was to the literal meaning within classical Christianity.[36] For Rabbinic Judaism, *halakah* was a matter of determining community norms from the legal texts of Torah, how people were to "walk" according to the commandments. It was a matter of great seriousness, demanding scholarship, attention to the minutiae of the Hebrew language, and ultimately some sort of authoritative decision *(din)* for a given time and place. It was with respect to *halakah* above all that the various *middoth,* or rules for interpretation, were developed. The same sort of serious attention to the literal sense is required in the process of discernment within the Christian community.[37] Within Judaism, however, the central body of *mitsvoth* is so well and firmly established, so inarguable because of the weight of its antiquity and authority, that such serious determinations are secondary to the reading and debating of Torah for purposes of wisdom and delight. This was the realm of *haggadah,* in which we find equal attention to the text, but also much greater freedom for the imagination. It is no surprise that it is in the realm of *haggadah* that we find the richness of rabbinic theology and ethics (as in the *Pirke Aboth* and the *Aboth de Rabbi Nathan*). Within pre-Reformation, and even some post-Reformation, Christian interpretation, allegory in the broad sense played the same role, enabling Scripture to become an entire world of type and figure, allusion and echo, wisdom and delight. Can anyone who has read Origen's or Bernard of Clairvaux's *Homilies on the Canticle of Canticles* not sense the impoverishment of the Christian imagination that the loss of these homilies would represent?[38]

36. These remarks extend the analogy mentioned in an earlier chapter, and in Luke Timothy Johnson, *The Writings of the New Testament,* 2nd ed. (Minneapolis: Fortress, 1999), 609-13; and *Scripture and Discernment,* 33-44. Compare Stanley Hauerwas, "Stanley Fish, the Pope, and the Bible," in *Unleashing the Scripture,* 19-28.

37. A very useful set of Christian *middoth* for the theological reading of Scripture is provided by Gerald O'Collins and Daniel Kendall, *The Bible for Theology: Ten Principles for the Theological Use of Scripture* (New York: Paulist, 1997).

38. As I showed in an earlier chapter, Origen's flights of imagination were carried out within the strict lines of the community's rule of faith and practice; see *Princ.* I,

It is unlikely that we can recover, or ought to recover, the capacity for such allegorical reading. The challenge is to find ways of reading that lead us into the imaginative world of Scripture in an equivalent fashion. In recent decades, the Biblical Theology movement sought to compensate for the aridity of the historical-critical approach by recognizing some of the intricate intertextual connections within the Bible, and (in a form of literary history) tried to demonstrate the "development" of "biblical themes" and "biblical terms."[39] The effort was subverted by faulty linguistic and cultural assumptions, and became an easy target for scornful attack.[40] The instinct was correct to read the images of Scripture as part of a distinctive world, but was misdirected in seeking that distinctiveness in the difference between "Hebrew" and "Greek" forms of thought.[41] Equally flawed was the assumption that meaning was carried by words rather than through phrases, sentences, and arguments. Members of the Biblical Theology movement assumed that a comparison of all the uses of a particular word could yield its full "theological meaning" that might then be read back into each instance of its use.[42]

Despite legitimate criticism of such premises and procedures, the Biblical Theology movement at least attempted to get to a dimension of the biblical text that historical criticism consistently misses because of its preoccupation with the world that produced the Bible rather

---

Praef. St. Bernard's homilies, likewise, were delivered in the context of a monastic regimen that was highly orthodox and disciplined in practice. Structure gives rise to spontaneity.

39. Some classic examples include Jacques Guillet, *Themes of the Bible,* trans. Albert J. LaMothe, Jr. (Notre Dame: Fides, 1961); Albert Gelin, *The Poor of Yahweh,* trans. Kathryn Sullivan (Collegeville: Liturgical, 1964); Delbert R. Hillers, *Covenant: The History of a Biblical Idea* (Baltimore: Johns Hopkins University Press, 1969).

40. Few works have had such devastating effect as James Barr's dismantling of these premises in *The Semantics of Biblical Language* (Philadelphia: Trinity, 1991).

41. This is also a perfect example of theology being dependent on bad history. One of the most significant advances made by historical study over the past several decades has been to tear down the walls that had been assumed to separate Judaism and Hellenism.

42. Although this was not the intent of *Theological Dictionary of the New Testament,* ed. Gerhard Kittel and Gerhard Friedrich, trans. Geoffrey W. Bromiley. 10 vols. (Grand Rapids: Wm. B. Eerdmans, 1964-1976), this has been the effect on many who have used it, as countless exegesis papers can attest.

than the world that the Bible produces. The world that Scripture produces (imagines) is not simply a haphazard collection of compositions written by various authors speaking from and for diverse communities over a period of centuries, but is also a complex network of literary interconnections established by the use and reuse of symbols that gain depth and richness by means of intricate and subtle allusion. Attention to these interconnections is justified, therefore, because together they create a world of metaphoric structures within which humans can live in a distinctive manner, "worthy of God."[43]

Think, for example, of the pervasive scriptural metaphor of "the way." It has its basis in the physical world of nomadism. For the nomad, moving in the right direction to find water, shelter, or food was literally to walk in the way of life, just as moving away from water or shelter or food was to walk in a way leading to literal death. The combination of movement, direction, goal, and consequence enabled the term "way" to function metaphorically for human behavior itself.[44] As such, we find the metaphor everywhere in Scripture and in the moral literature of Christianity. It can be used to express the simple contrast between patterns of behavior ("the way of light/life" versus "the way of darkness/death"). It also suggests the possibility of "wandering" from a way, and of "turning back" to a right way. Perhaps most elaborately, the metaphor of the way fits within the complex imagery of pilgrimage, so that the (already complex) physical movement from a profane to a sacred place, or from diaspora to homeland, now becomes an image of human life as a whole, which moves from mortal existence in an alien environment to a heavenly homeland.

The metaphor of "the way" is a basic metaphor that organizes a complex system of subsidiary images and metaphors that depend on its maintaining its radical character for their own life and effectiveness.[45] The metaphor also contains an implicit but comprehensive view of reality.[46] Imagining human existence as "being on the way" toward God has the most profound corollaries for every sort of human en-

43. The ideas here resemble those in George Lakoff and Mark Johnson, *Metaphors We Live By* (Chicago: University of Chicago Press, 1980), 14-68.

44. Lakoff and Johnson, 41-45.

45. Lakoff and Johnson, 87-105,

46. See Mark Turner, *The Literary Mind* (New York: Oxford University Press, 1996), 85-115.

deavor: earthly existence is relative, temporary, and preparatory, in comparison with a life with God that is ultimate, eternal, and perfect. Such an understanding encourages a diaspora ethics of itineracy, detachment, dispossession, solidarity, and endurance in suffering, rather than a homeland ethics of stability, engagement, acquisition, and human fulfillment in the present life. It engenders a passover spirituality of "crossing over" from death to life through the bearing of others' burdens on the way; it does not easily support a spirituality of finding or centering the self.

The term "way" does not bear all these connotations by itself. The same metaphor, in fact, might have quite different connotations in another imaginary world, as the expression "The Beauty Way" does within Navaho spirituality. Note as well that the term does not have its full meaning in any single instance of its use, as though the metaphor was always operative for each of the biblical authors. Just the opposite: the term emerges as metaphorical and therefore as world-orienting only for the person who reads Scripture in its entirety, and as directed to the transformation of human identity within communities committed to the practices of Christian piety. Indeed, the analysis of individual sentences, passages, or books will not uncover the force of the metaphor. It exists and exercises its power over the Christian imagination precisely as part of the world imagined by Scripture as a whole.

The metaphor of the way is, as we know, only one of many such basic metaphors in Scripture. I mentioned another early in this chapter, namely, that of the garden. It is apparent at once that these metaphors stand in tension with each other. Living within the imagined world of Scripture does not mean living without tension or even contradiction; it means resolving tensions and contradictions in creative, and equally metaphoric, fashion. For instance, the image of the earth as garden has been incorporated into the metaphor of the way, so that "Paradise Lost" expresses the human sense of exile, while the image of "Paradise Restored" stands at the end of the journey home.

Such metaphors, in turn, are the more powerful when they are embodied by the specific practices of the church. The image of a people on pilgrimage through life is more persuasive when congregations move in liturgical procession through streets and fields on rogation days, chanting the litany of the saints who form the "cloud of witnesses" waiting at the end of their journey toward God, or when they follow the "Light that is Christ" that is the Paschal candle through the darkened nave at the Easter Vigil, or when they visit the sick and elderly to bring eucharistic bread as *viaticum* ("food for the way"), or when they pray in the manner of the *Cloud of Unknowing* or *The Way of the Pilgrim,* or when they walk through city streets seeking out the homeless and providing them with shelter in their church buildings. Such practices of piety make the metaphor of "being on the way" an interpretation of lived human experience and bring the world imagined by Scripture into existence by embodying it in the physical space we humans share with one another.

Connecting with Experience

This brings us to the fourth element in the recovery of a scriptural imagination in theology. If attention to literary interactions is not to become simply another intellectual or aesthetic game, it is necessary to pay equally close and obedient attention to actual human experience in the world. If theology is the effort of our minds and hearts to catch up with the work of the Living God in the world, then attention must be paid to the human stories in which God's work is being enacted. Part of contemporary theology's impoverished sense of God's presence is due to its inattention to the places where that presence is most obvious, namely, in the human drama of idolatry and sin, grace and faith.[47] As that drama is played out in every human story, it can become, if properly heard, revelatory.[48] The same inattention to the human experience of God characterizes the reading of Scripture within the academic guild.[49] Yet the experience of the Living God is the most obvious element in the construction of the imaginary world of Scripture. Morever, the claim to have experienced the *same* Living God through the Lord Jesus Christ was the most compelling reason for joining two disparate sets of compositions into a single anthology called Scripture. And it is

47. For a fuller exposition, see Johnson, *Faith's Freedom.*

48. See Johnson, *Scripture and Discernment,* 135-65.

49. See Luke Timothy Johnson, *Religious Experience in Earliest Christianity* (Minneapolis: Fortress, 1998).

the possibility of experiencing that same Living God in the world today that makes the doing of Christian theology something more than a sterile academic exercise.

Here, then, is the most fundamental turning away from the imaginary worlds of the Sagans and the Hawkings toward the world imagined by Scripture, the most fundamental step toward a theology with scriptual imagination: to live in this world as one created at every moment by an unseen Power who drenches us with grace and transforms us into God's own image, and to regard our own story, and every human story that we hear, as truly revealing the truth of that world.[50] Imagine that.

---

50. Three theological works that possess the sort of scriptural imagination imagined here, and therefore provide hope, are Miroslav Volf, *Exclusion and Embrace: A Theological Exploration of Identity, Otherness, and Reconciliation* (Nashville: Abingdon, 1996); William M. Thompson, *The Struggle for Theology's Soul: Contesting Scripture in Christology* (New York: Crossroad, 1996); and Elizabeth A. Johnson, *She Who Is: The Mystery of God in Feminist Theological Discourse* (New York: Crossroad, 1992).

CHAPTER SIX

Bill Kurz: Response to Luke Johnson

This response to Luke Johnson's chapters appears in the present book before my own five chapters, but my own chapters were finished before I began this reply. In addition, although in fact I had received and quickly perused most of Luke Johnson's five chapters before finalizing all of my own five chapters, both five-chapter sets were nevertheless fundamentally planned and written independently, once we had initially agreed on their basic structure and topics. A few of Luke's especially striking images, such as his contrast between "either/or" and "both/and" exegetical approaches, made it into my own chapters, but for the most part our original chapters were independent.

Thus it was after completing my chapters and then reading Luke's chapters more carefully that I realized that sometimes we each approached similar matters in complementary ways. Sometimes we used different basic metaphors or wrote from diverse outlooks even when our topics and perhaps even conclusions overlapped. Therefore one function of this response will be to point to similarities, differences, and overlaps between our various approaches to similar questions, which are often imagined and described in rather different fashions.

An important function of Luke Johnson's chapters was to set the stage for our entire book, including my chapters. Nevertheless, whatever minor points of clarification or disagreement I might have with those introductory chapters can wait until I respond to Luke's most original work and important insights on premodern exegesis, exemplified in Origen and Augustine. These chapters are clearly grounded in Luke's firsthand readings and research into the primary texts of those patristic authors. I found them especially productive, refreshing, and original as arguing and illustrating how valuable it is to consult again these authors, our great premodern exegetical predecessors. Although my knowledge of Origen and Augustine more closely approximates that of an educated reader than that of a professional historical theologian, I do have some professional expertise in Justin Martyr (especially his *Dialogue with Trypho*) and the Apostolic Fathers. I have also done years of study of the Latin texts of Thomas Aquinas, though my focus was much more his theological than his exegetical works. Especially my research in Justin confirms many of Luke Johnson's insights in his chapters on Origen and Augustine (Chapters Three and Four) concerning their combination of intelligent exegetical insight with vigorous apologetic and pastoral applications of both biblical testaments in service of their faith and church.

I also find many similarities between Aquinas and both Origen and Augustine in their common esteem for and use of contemporary non-Christian writings to enrich their own Christian theologizing and use of Scripture. Like Augustine, Aquinas had limited linguistic expertise and was primarily conversant with Latin sources. Nevertheless, in Latin translations of their works he comprehensively mastered some of the most currently influential non-Christian thinkers (particularly such non-Western Arabic commentators on Aristotle as Averroes). All these premodern Catholic intellectuals boldly enriched their own biblically-based faith and theological thinking with the help of the most prominent thinkers available in their respective cultural milieus. These thinkers, medieval as well as patristic, exemplified the respect for both Scripture and culture, faith and reason that continues to mark the Catholic church today. This respect is illustrated by what many media figures found a surprising defense of reason by Pope John Paul II in his 1998 letter, *Faith and Reason (Fides et ratio),* against widespread contemporary cultural attacks on reason, such as in many varieties of deconstruction.

Although Origen and Augustine were the selected focus of two chapters (Chapters Three and Four), and provided appropriate and fertile examples, other models and exegetical dialogue partners can be found in writers even earlier than Origen. Earlier authors like Justin Martyr similarly combine cultural and Jewish learning and methods, as well as dialogue with Jewish biblical exegesis, interpretation, and applications. In addition, Justin shares some of Origen's ill-fated theological "misfortunes": both writers tried to find explanations and analogies to explain biblical evidence (e.g., about christology) in terms understandable to their own cultures. Both articulated several original, ingenious, and creative insights into Scripture, and made incipient efforts at systematizing theologies and christologies. However, several of their efforts were not destined to be accepted and incorporated into later church Tradition and doctrine. Both Justin and Origen were concerned to interpret Scripture and articulate their theologies in the service of their Christian faith and under the limits imposed by the "rule of faith" (whatever credal statements were then available). Yet despite their desire to remain within the limits of the rule of faith, both of them had some of their personal insights and solutions later rejected as in fact incompatible with that rule of faith, such as aspects of Justin's angel christologies and of Origen's opinions about human souls pre-existing their bodies, or of his *apokatastasis* theories about all fallen men and angels being restored at the end of time.

Nevertheless, despite what a certain dogmatic and historical hindsight might term "wrong turns" in their creative thinking, both gave admirable martyrs' witness of their committed Christian faith before a hostile Roman government — Justin unto death, Origen unto torture. The careers of both thinkers illustrate how sanctity and benefit for the church and even for its theological development do not have to be completely coterminous with the boundaries of what will eventually emerge as Catholic orthodoxy. Even in their shared theological "misfortunes," they actually illustrate the surprising theological range and freedom that has in fact been available over the centuries to Catholic theologians and exegetes, despite the actual later suppression of much of Origen's writings and current wide-spread exaggerations about constant suppression of free theological thinking by Catholic church authorities in Rome.

I also found quite stimulating and fruitful Luke Johnson's comparison and contrast between the linguistically expert Jerome and the less exegetically trained but brilliant and theologically astute Augustine. Though I am no expert in Augustine, my personal reading of his entire *Confessions* in Latin has given me a reasonable feel for the man. Several of Luke's comparisons between Augustine and Jerome also resonate with similarities and differences between some "second-generation" contemporary Catholic exegetes and the "third generation" to which Luke and I belong, especially concerning the balance between scholarship and ministry with respect to ordinary lay Catholics.

My own experience with our great exegetical exemplars of the previous ("second") generation like Raymond Brown (whom alone I will mention because he is no longer living) found similarities between their prodigious learning and output and Jerome's. It also ascertained that contemporary "second-generation" pastoral sensitivities and desire to serve the church might perhaps even be more pronounced than what was mentioned about Jerome's. Of course, Jerome the scholar must also have had an admirable degree of pastoral concern to have produced the Vulgate and have written letters to lay people about how to read Scripture. This seems true even if Jerome happened to be less sensitive than Augustine the bishop about some possibly negative pastoral consequences of such facets of his biblical scholarship as his translating from the Hebrew rather than from the Septuagint, which is so linguistically interrelated with the New Testament and used by the Greek churches. I hope that Raymond Brown would not mind my sharing a conversation he had with me on the occasion of an SNTS meeting in Edinburgh, Scotland. His excitement at having recently finished the manuscript of his *Introduction to the New Testament* was primarily associated with the positive *pastoral* effect he hoped it would have for the church and future Catholic leaders, especially those who do not know Greek. Yet even that book does not fully escape some of the critiques in this book of ours about the need to go beyond primarily historical-critical treatments of the New Testament for the pastoral and theological use of Scripture today.

Luke Johnson's chapters convey several powerful and instructive images, comparisons, and metaphors that demonstrate his skill as a master teacher and apologist. They evidence a writer who is able to demonstrate the reasonableness of minority points of view and of less frequently considered alternatives to virtually unchallenged contemporary "scholarly orthodoxies." Luke's comparison of recent Catholic exegetical history to three generations of immigrants attempts both to show genuine respect to previous generations of Catholic biblicists, on whose scholarly shoulders our current generations stand, but also to point out possible differences of perspectives and even possible blind spots related to the differences in their histories and relationships to the "foreign country" of Protestant-dominated historical-critical endeavors.

Luke's comparison of Catholic biblical worldviews during the premodern, pre-Enlightenment periods to an imagined city in which one lives, in contrast to a city from the past uncovered by archaeological excavation, illustrates powerfully the contrasting perspectives about the world as imagined in Scripture from the world as imagined in Enlightenment, modern, and postmodern theories and methodologies. Premodern interpreters lived in the "biblical city." Their world was the biblical world. It was a world created good by a loving but just God, yet perverted by sinful human behavior, which aroused God's saving compassion in ultimately sending his own Son to rescue humans from the mess they made. In this biblical world, God placed humans at the head of the material universe as images of God responsible for oversight and development of this material world under God's direction.

As belonging to a people who for generations had grown up in this "city," premodern interpreters knew the world of the Scripture in the many ways that natives know their own city, ways that outsiders can never hope to match. By contrast, historical exegetes have functioned toward Scripture more the way archaeologists do when they excavate an ancient city and try to reconstruct what it was like to live there. Such reconstructions cannot hope to approximate the knowledge of the city of someone who actually lived in it. Analogously, historical-critical reconstructions of the bygone and alien world of Scripture cannot come close to the fuller sense of the biblical world which premodern interpreters had, and which to some extent intelligent believers today have who live imaginatively in that world (albeit with necessary adjustments to deal with its obvious differences from the "modern world"). This comparison illuminates why exegesis often seems to ordinary believers so far removed from their own religious and faith concerns.

Other very instructive metaphors in Luke Johnson's chapters include biblical images such as the world as the garden (of Genesis) which is tended by humans under God's supervision. In tension with that image is another biblical image of living in this world as a journey along the way (or the contrasting ways of light and life versus darkness and death), or of the way viewed as pilgrimage to our heavenly promised land. Related to the second cluster of images of the way are Luke

Johnson's many illuminating allusions to rabbinic *halakah* (which is related in Hebrew to walking on the way) and *haggadah*. Although the premodern rabbis established their halakic arguments primarily from the literal meanings of Scripture, they boldly went far beyond those literal meanings in their haggadic search for wisdom.

The very success of many of Luke Johnson's ingenious arguments by analogy paradoxically calls for some caution in evaluating his often very plausible and appealing conclusions. For despite the extent to which arguments by analogies have rhetorical persuasiveness and pedagogic effectiveness, by their nature analogies always include both similarities and differences. As he himself acknowledges, those differences require careful discernment regarding their applicability to any particular contemporary conclusion from such arguments. Some disparities arise between Luke's and my applications and conclusions, for instance, even when we are following similar methodological approaches to the same textual evidence. These differences can be attributed to our divergent histories and perspectives and experiences, which lead us to accentuate diverse aspects of an analogy's dissimilarities.

And although both of us have paid close attention to the life experiences of our students and people to whom we have given counsel, as all good teachers and pastoral workers do, I suspect that our different academic work settings have exposed us to different kinds of wounds and lacks and concerns among those to whom we have listened. For example, my impression is that Luke may have experienced more of people's difficulties and pain which were compounded by church authorities. On the other hand, I may have experienced more of other persons' messed-up lives and confusion resulting from inadequate teaching and harmful advice, and the corresponding need especially of younger generations for clearer pastoral direction and leadership from the church than their parents received (or accepted).

Because of this different set of experienced needs of the faithful, I would tease out another "both/and" set as a further consequence of those emphasized by Luke Johnson: the "both/and" within Catholic scholarship and teaching that incorporates both academic freedom and magisterial authority. I suggest that this "both/and" of academic freedom and magisterial authority seems to be a reasonably logical consequence of what Luke's first chapter discussed as "loyalty to the Tradition and criticism," where he persuasively argues that "[l]oyalty to the church's teaching and practices is no more incompatible to the free exercise of the mind than is loyalty to the norms of the academy" (p. 27). In addition to the acknowledged need for free creativity (as beautifully exemplified by Origen and Justin), I would call attention to the need for church teaching authorities to channel such creativity so as to preserve apostolic faith (as also happened, if not always most happily, in the cases of Origen and Justin, at least after their deaths).

I suggest that rule-of-faith guidelines provide "out-of-bounds" lines, which can paradoxically increase the free creativity of thinkers within those Catholic boundaries. These boundaries help creative thinkers both to preserve and to develop the church's treasures of apostolic witness and beliefs for ongoing Christian living. By way of contrast, experience in academia has made clear to me that when Catholic boundaries are lacking or not in force, an even more intolerant authoritarianism of political correctness can move in to fill the lack. In my experience, political correctness in its respective forms can impose a more stringent uniformity of ideology and consequent marginalization of dissenters from its "scholarly orthodoxies" than Rome does.

Currently I find many of the new generation of graduate students and candidates for priesthood to be much more open to and even desirous of these Catholic faith boundaries than students whom I taught earlier in my teaching career. Some students even see Catholic faith boundaries as helping to preserve their own academic freedom to ask probing fundamental questions of instruction they are given. Catholic dogmatic boundaries can empower them even to challenge their teachers, when some teaching clashes with their own deep sense of Catholic faith or when they experience themselves being manipulated or even bullied by a teacher into accepting some alien ideology. Having clear boundaries can help level the playing field between professors of Bible and religion and simple believers.

From another perspective, Luke Johnson rightly noted how one problem with Catholic exegesis before Pope Pius XII gave official approval to Catholic exegetes using historical-critical methods was the tendency for exegesis to be absorbed into Catholic doctrine (pp. 7-8). In my chapters, when I used the creed and the *Catechism of the Catholic Church (CCC)* to help elucidate and apply biblical passages, I considered it very important to try to avoid even the appearance of such absorption of Scripture into creed or catechism, whether or not I succeeded.

One way I tried to illustrate the difference between actualizing Scripture with the help of creed or catechism and absorbing scriptural exegesis into teachings of the creed or catechism was first to lay some distinctly exegetical foundation before making such applications. One purpose of this foundational exegesis was to point out aspects within the scriptural passage itself which provide justification for the later development, actualization, or application.

Such foundational exegesis will obviously differ when exercised by a linguistically-trained exegete or by an untrained but alert and conscientious layperson. One contribution we professional exegetes can contribute to fellow believers is to demonstrate that there is a continuity, even though it is not identity, between the literal exegeted meanings of biblical passages and the actualizations and applications of those passages in the creeds and teachings of the church in faith and morals. This continuity provides legitimacy for ordinary faith-directed applications and actualizations of Scripture passages by untrained Catholic readers of Scripture, who read those passages in the context of their overall faith perspectives. Although such applications are always subject to correction, so in fact as well as in principle are the exegetical conclusions of professionals.

Ideally, when needed, such correction of biblical interpretations by untrained Catholic readers will come mostly from peers among one's believing community, with help both from exegetes and from church teaching authorities. A similar ideal situation for correction of conclusions by professional exegetes would be correction by their exegetical peers, but with additional input from theologians, saints and mystics (present and past) within the Tradition, and from ordinary believers (who can, for example, challenge the relevancy and appropriateness of exegetes' conclusions for ordinary Catholic living), as well as from church teaching authorities, who have both the burden and the final pastoral responsibility for and oversight of the faith of the entire community. Unfortunately, it seems that for various reasons, perhaps including resentment by exegetes of past mistreatment of their exegetical predecessors at the hands of church authorities, as well as ideological pressure from various forms of political correctness, such peer-correction of erroneous or harmful exegetical conclusions has often failed to materialize. As a result, the most extreme and misleading exegetical conclusions are often published without serious disagreement or correction from scholarly peers. When exegetical conclusions which undermine Catholic faith or morality are then passed on pastorally without correction or warning to the faithful in popular publications or textbooks, or in preaching and teaching on all levels, even into grade school, the confusion among Catholic faithful and ignorance about what the Bible and church actually teach about these issues can be immense.

Two important concerns raised but admittedly not addressed in Luke's chapters are the need for Catholic biblical scholars to direct some of their scholarship to church life and needs, and to provide pedagogy for responsible lay reading of Scripture (p. 33). My chapters try to address at least some aspects of these concerns: my second chapter (Chapter Eight) applies my scholarship to the common and important problem for the church of how to apply Scripture and biblical evidence to the solution of important moral problems. Other chapters suggest uncomplicated ways that lay believers who are not trained exegetes can interpret Scripture responsibly with helps like the Nicene Creed and *CCC*, using them in manners analogous to the ways patristic authors monitored all biblical interpretations by comparison to the creed, which they used as a *regula fidei* for exegesis. Trained exegetes can assure ordinary believers that the basic continuity between these rules of faith and Scripture allows them to use such helps in applying Scripture for their own situations. Of course, such rules of faith and helps do not begin to exhaust the ways that Scripture can be interpreted by Catholics or others. Furthermore, it seems that there will always be serious differences in interpretations among even good-faith Catholic efforts, such as I would not be surprised to find between Luke and myself even in this book.

Luke Johnson's very helpful conception of "imagining the world which Scripture imagines" seems related to the use of a "biblical worldview" in my second chapter (Chapter Eight). In fact, many of his five premises of premodern (especially patristic) biblical interpretation are premises which continue to be maintained in Vatican II's *Dei Verbum (DV)*, *The Catechism of the Catholic Church (CCC)*, and recent encyclicals. In both cases the premises address the aspect of reading Scripture "in the spirit in which it was written" and of actualizing and interpreting Scripture beyond foundational exegesis of the text's original meaning. My chapters will attempt a kind of "second naiveté" in applying Scripture from premises which are similar to those here delineated for premodern interpretation.

I agree with Luke's observations concerning many of the stark divergencies of contemporary secular academic approaches to Scripture from those of the premodern interpreters. My vantage point, however, is slightly different from his. Whereas Luke's teaching experience has been in formerly Christian, Protestant, and/or secular state universities, my experience has been in a university that is still striving to maintain its Catholic identity. Although many of the secularizing phenomena Luke mentioned are present also in my setting, at least some of us professors in this university have for years been concerned about ways to preserve or recapture some of the more Catholic elements of our interpretative inheritance. This has already been foreshadowed by sections of the Vatican II document on revelation which have not received as much notice as other sections which promote historical approaches to exegesis.

> But since Holy Scripture must be read and interpreted in the same spirit in which it was written, no less serious attention must be given to the content and unity of the whole of Scripture if the meaning of the sacred texts is to be correctly worked out. The living Tradition of the whole church must be taken into account along with the harmony which exists between elements of the faith. It is the task of exegetes to work according to these rules toward a better understanding and explanation of the meaning of Sacred Scripture, so that through preparatory study the judgment of the church may mature. For all of what has been said about the way of interpreting Scripture is subject finally to the judgment of the church, which carries out the divine commission and ministry of guarding and interpreting the Word of God. (*DV* §12c)

These Vatican II directives for reading Scripture "in the same spirit in which it was written" coincide very much with the premises of premodern patristic interpretation mentioned by Luke Johnson. The first directive is to attend to "the content and unity of the whole of Scripture." Second is to take account of the "living Tradition of the whole church" and third, of "the harmony which exists between elements of the faith." The first directive of *DV* §12 about the unity of Scripture is the same as the first premise of premodern interpretation.

Luke's second premise, "that Scripture speaks harmoniously," flows from the first premise of the unity of Scripture and is related to it. Although Vatican II does not put as much emphasis as the fathers did on this harmony, its retention of the notion that Scripture is God's word and a unity implies as a corollary that various passages of Scripture will not directly contradict one another. Nor does the quoted passage *DV* §12c explicitly treat the third premise, that Scripture is the word of God and therefore is authoritative; however, *DV* §11 had developed this concept, and the document throughout treats Scripture as God's Word.

Neither is the fourth premise explicitly stated in *DV* §12, namely that Scripture speaks in many ways and on many levels. (This implies that scriptural interpretation must be polyvalent and cannot be limited to one authoritative meaning, as it is according to some historical-critical objectives and claims.) However, that fourth premise too is developed in the catechism and is a reasonable corollary from the unity of Scripture (as in *DV*'s treatment of the Old Testament) and Scripture's harmony with Tradition and the elements of the faith. Moreover, polyvalent interpretation is an insistent claim of postmodern interpretation, especially in the postmodern rejection of historical criticism's objective of a single meaning. The fifth premise, which is said to encompass the others, is a "hermeneutics of generosity or charity." It too is not stated but is implied by the cited Vatican II passage, especially by its thesis statement: "Holy Scripture must be read and interpreted in the same spirit in which it was written" (*DV* §12c).

In short, since recent magisterial documents like *Dei Verbum* and the *Catechism of the Catholic Church* contain many of Luke Johnson's suggestions and ideas, and even tend to implement them in their own ways, I suggest that laypeople can use these documents as one guide to responsible lay interpretation of Scripture. Although Luke and I may disagree in particulars about how to do this, it seems to me that much of what he is advocating as premises of premodern interpretation, which can be usefully interpreted and applied within limits today, is in fact readily available to laypeople in the new catechism and Vatican documents.

Although I believe that Luke Johnson's notion of "imagining the world of the Scriptures" overlaps significantly with my notion of a "biblical worldview" from a Catholic perspective, I see advantages in his expression over mine. A priori it seems more difficult for a person in the 21st century really to have a "biblical worldview" than to "imagine the world of the Scriptures." In my future work I probably will tend to use Luke's expression more frequently.

However, there remains some important content in my expression, "biblical worldview," which may not be fully expressed by the connotations of "imagining the world of the Scriptures." I will want to continue to talk about worldviews, if not necessarily "biblical," then perhaps "Catholic," or "a biblical worldview from a contemporary Catholic perspective," or the like. Therefore, the notion of worldview retains a certain importance for me, especially in comparison and contrast to secular or Enlightenment or modern or postmodern worldviews.

Furthermore, even though presumably both of us as Catholic authors share a "Catholic worldview," from reading Luke's chapters (and many of his other writings), I am sure that we have some significantly different emphases in our respective versions of our common Catholic worldview. One major and important element in my worldview which I see mentioned more often in my own writings than in Luke's is the key centrality which my worldview (as I believe also a "biblical worldview") gives to loving and stable marriage and family, and the conscientious raising of children in Catholic faith and morality, as basic Catholic foundations on which all other elements of practical Catholic living must build. Strong, loving Catholic family seems to me to be the cornerstone for Catholic education, sacramental life, priestly and religious vocations, and for the next generation of knowledgeable, faith-filled, committed and active Catholic laity who contribute to society and culture. My work with people of all ages as priest and teacher continues to underline for me how lack of a loving, stable, believing family in so many people's lives makes receptivity to Christian teaching difficult and undermines most of these other areas, and in fact much of our American culture.

Let the following be my last of these initial responses to Luke's chapters. I have no problem with Luke's apparently principal practical suggestion for promoting such a return to the kind of biblical interpretation which our premodern predecessors evidenced — formation of small biblical faith-sharing groups among Catholic laity. I myself have been asked by Marquette graduate students to host such a group on campus, and I find it very invigorating for the faith (and reason) of us all. However, I think that to re-incorporate such premodern types of faith-driven biblical interpretation today will take much more institutionally based and promoted measures if we are to affect the church at large and not just small pockets of believers. I think that this is one mission that needs our Catholic institutions if it is to be accomplished in a reasonable time among the church at large. This kind of biblical interpretation can be most efficiently promoted in Catholic universities, in both undergraduate and graduate teaching, in Catholic secondary and middle schools, in preparation of future teachers (in universities) and of priests and diocesan and parish ministers (in divinity schools and seminaries). It can also be promoted through parish youth ministers and directors of religious education. It can be taught and encouraged in parish homilies and other parish presentations and continuing education for adults. If we are to return the Scripture to ordinary nonprofessional laity and empower them to read and experience Scripture as God's word to them personally and in community, I suggest that we cast our nets widely and try to bring as many coworkers into this effort as we can.

PART TWO

BILL KURZ

CHAPTER SEVEN

Beyond Historical Criticism: Reading John's Prologue as Catholics

Luke Johnson's chapters raised some questions about just how Catholic is Catholic exegesis, and suggested that postmodern Catholic interpretation can learn from such premodern Catholics as the patristic authors. My chapters that follow will try to address the same problematic of how to make biblical exegesis more responsive to the needs of the Catholic church and its believing members. They will suggest some simple concrete contemporary approaches to actualization and application of Scripture read as a canonical unity. These suggestions will follow the path laid out in Vatican II's *Dei Verbum (DV)* and in the *Catechism of the Catholic Church (CCC)*, especially regarding Vatican II's two mandates to Catholic biblicists (which will be featured in a later chapter).[1] Briefly stated here, the first mandate is the search for the literal meaning of Scripture. This mandate, with the help of historical-critical methods, Catholic exegetes have eagerly been fulfilling. The second mandate is for exegetes themselves, and not only for other categories of theologians or people in pastoral ministry, to actualize and apply Scripture to the church's contemporary needs. The document suggests three approaches to prepare for such actualization: treating the pas-

---

1. See "Dogmatic Constitution on Divine Revelation (Dei Verbum)," in *Vatican Council II: The Conciliar and Post Conciliar Documents,* ed. Austin Flannery (Boston: St. Paul's, 1992), 750-65, esp. 758; and *Catechism of the Catholic Church,* 2nd ed. (Vatican: Libreria Editrice Vaticana, 1997), §109-14.

sage within the faith perspective of the unity of Scripture; reading Scripture from within the church's living Tradition; and utilizing the "analogy of faith," i.e., the coherence of truths of faith among themselves and communality between referents in Scripture and believers' own experiences (cf. *DV* 12 §4, summarized in *CCC* §112-14).

To give my chapters more focus and ground them in particular texts rather than in mere generalities, four of the five chapters (the first, third, fourth, and fifth) will utilize passages from the Gospel of John as their primary examples. One (the second) will address the broader question of different voices in the ecumenical church and correspondingly differing perspectives among readers. Its comparison of approaches from two divergent denominational perspectives, the Protestant approach of Richard Hays and my Catholic approach, will provide a clear-cut example of how differing perspectives can influence how Scripture is interpreted and applied to contemporary questions.[2] Whereas Hays's approach to abortion from Scripture tends to focus directly on the abortion question, searching for historically relevant passages from the kind of "either/or" perspective mentioned by Luke Johnson, my Catholic instincts are to read Scripture more globally from a "both/and" perspective. My approach searches for a biblical Christian worldview about the relationship between God the Creator and human and other creatures (which builds on the creation worldview of Judaism and Genesis), as a broader context for asking what insight the Bible might contribute about a particular issue like abortion, even if that issue is not explicitly treated in Scripture. In addition to delineating differences between Catholic and Protestant instincts about using Scripture as a unified revelation, the second chapter will illustrate how Catholic applications of its discovered biblical worldview on the meaning of human life will also differ from Protestant approaches in terms of when and how to apply extrabiblical and traditional evidence and standards toward formulating a "biblical answer" to a particular issue.

My third chapter will focus on the questions of biblical intertextuality and the unity of Scripture as exemplified in the bread of life discussion in John 6. The fourth will treat spiritual senses and actualiza-

---

2. Richard B. Hays, *The Moral Vision of the New Testament* (San Francisco: Harper-SanFrancisco, 1996).

tion with the example of the feeding of the 5000 in John 6. My fifth and final chapter will provide a test-case for using a simple and readily available authoritative guide to traditional Catholic faith (the CCC) to flesh out contemporary actualizations and applications of the passage in John 20, where Jesus commissions his disciples with "If you forgive the sins of any, they are forgiven; if you retain the sins of any, they are retained" (John 20:23 RSV). The title itself of this first chapter suggests how it sets the contemporary stage: "Beyond Historical Criticism: Reading John's Prologue as Catholics [today]." After briefly reviewing how to get beyond the limits of historical criticism for faith concerns of the church, this chapter will treat the prologue as interpretive key to the Fourth Gospel (FG). Finally, it will also show that there is continuity between the prologue and the insights of the Niceno-Constantinopolitan Creed.

As Luke Johnson pointed out, winning official acceptance in the Catholic church for historical-critical methods was a prolonged struggle for Catholic exegetics. This approval was especially precipitated by Pope Pius XII's *Divino Afflante Spiritu*, but it was even more after Vatican II's 1965 *Dogmatic Constitution on Divine Revelation* that Catholic exegetes finally won virtually universal acceptance, respectability, and even dominance within Catholicism for historical-critical methods.[3] Yet already in the 1980s, grumblings about the limitations of exclusive use of those historical approaches for contemporary personal religious experience and reflection were becoming quite audible, both without and within Catholicism. Dissatisfaction with the alienating effects of historical criticism was being expressed from very disparate quarters and from all shades on the ideological spectrum — by liberationists and feminists, by literary, narrative, and reader-response critics, by Pentecostals and by Protestant and Catholic charismatics, by numerous and diverse historical, systematic, and moral theologians, as well as by many ordinary believers who wanted simply to read and pray from Scripture as God's word to them today, not as some product of the ancient past.[4] Frustrated Catholics were beginning to resonate with the following Matthean Jesus-saying as applied to historical critics: "But

3. See esp. Joseph A. Fitzmyer, "Historical Criticism: Its Role in Biblical Interpretation and Church Life," *TS* 50 (1989): 244-59.

4. Cf. William S. Kurz, *Reading Luke-Acts: Dynamics of Biblical Narrative* (Louisville: Westminster John Knox, 1993), 3-6 and literature cited in the notes.

woe to you . . . because you shut the kingdom of heaven against men; for you neither enter yourselves, nor allow those who would enter to go in" (Matt. 23:13 RSV). Many ordinary believers were coming to feel as if they were being shut out from personal benefit from the Scriptures because the exclusive key to its "valid" interpretation was being jealously guarded by professional exegetes, some of whom seemed little interested in such personal use themselves.

Nevertheless, even in the context of such dissatisfaction Catholics generally continued to acknowledge the value and importance of historical-critical approaches for understanding the original linguistic, cultural, and social meaning and context of disputed texts, words, and expressions, and for guarding against "eisegesis" of alien contemporary or traditional biases into the meaning of the passage. Acknowledgement of the importance of the original significance of the words and cultural context of Scripture for not misinterpreting them, however, did not prevent many nonprofessional believers from the uneasy sense that more and more commands of Paul or even Jesus were being regarded as "culturally conditioned." Ordinary believers felt that such historical judgments were undermining the contemporary relevance of much of what the Scriptures report Jesus and Paul and others as saying, and consequently were undermining the authority of Scripture in general.

Some applications of secular literary criticism to biblical studies in the late 1970s and 1980s provided limited initial relief from a few of the more alienating aspects of historical criticism. Literary, narrative, and reader-response criticisms returned some of the interpretive emphasis to the complete text in its current canonical form and turned away from concentrating too much on sources. They rehabilitated an awareness that the meaning of a written text cannot be limited to "the mind of the author" (increasingly viewed as unascertainable) or to even its "original" meaning for its original readers: rather, a written text takes on a meaning which no longer depends entirely on what its author may have intended to express. Literary approaches brought increased awareness of how different readers bring written texts to life in their own imaginations (or in oral presentation to audiences, as in churches) according to their own backgrounds, experiences, interests, and concerns. They refocused attention on the significance of "interpretive communities" (for Catholics, the church) for ascertaining a text's meaning, and thus on the instinctive differences in the ways diverse denominations or social groups understand the Scriptures.[5]

Further relief from historical-critical constrictions on ordinary believers' access to Scripture's meaning came from increasing attention to the biblical texts as canonical collections (and consequently as parts of new unities and more inclusive writings) held in special reverence and authority by the canonizing church. The very process of canonizing a text for the entire church and for later generations required and provided an actualization and application of each canonized text beyond its original contexts and audiences, which have been the principal focus and objective of historical-critical methods. For example, whatever Paul had been trying to say to the Corinthians within their distinctive cultural and historical context now has to be applied *mutatis mutandis* to different readers from dissimilar times, cultures, backgrounds, and concerns.[6]

The very process of canonization implicitly expects original texts to be applied in new ways and different circumstances from those first envisaged, for the very act of canonization involves a judgment that that book is applicable to other readers and generations and cultures than those for which the document was originally intended. In other words, canonization relativizes the relevance of the original audience and *Sitz im Leben*. Canonizing a book inserts that book into the wider context of the biblical history of all God's saving actions for his people. It declares that the book has meaning for others beyond the original recipients and must be applied to their new and different circumstances. Canonizing a book says that that book is not only a product of the distant past with historical relevance, but that it provides meaning for later believers and readers even to the present day. To paraphrase Luke Johnson's textbook, the canon is the church's working bibliography.[7] In the present context, the canon is the Catholic church's bibliography. Therefore, canonical readers (e.g., 21st-century Catholics in the U.S.) cannot and should not be constricted to just what meaning was communicated between Paul and the original Corinthian readers. Similarly,

---

5. Cf. Kurz, *Reading Luke-Acts, passim.*

6. William S. Kurz, "2 Corinthians: Implied Readers and Canonical Implications," *JSNT* 62 (1996): 43-63.

7. Luke Timothy Johnson, *The Writings of the New Testament* (Minneapolis: Fortress, 1999), 609.

contemporary Catholic readers of the FG prologue can and must read this prologue differently from the FG's original readers and with a 21st-century expanded perspective of time, Tradition, and development of doctrinal awareness and clarity.

As Luke Johnson demonstrated in his chapters, patristic authors provide early models for how Catholics can go beyond original meanings unearthed by the "archaeological" methods of historical criticism in interpreting and applying Scripture. The early Fathers who preached about John's Gospel and prologue provide a venerable example of how very early generations of Christians read, interpreted, preached, and applied the prologue to their own (postbiblical) lives and the lives of their communities. For possible imitation, I would like briefly to draw special attention to three mutually interpenetrating characteristics of patristic reading, preaching, and teaching this Gospel: it was *personal, practical,* and *transparent.*[8]

This effort similarly to read and explain John's prologue in a way that is at once personal, practical, and transparent raises the following preliminary observations. It begins from the presumption that God continues to speak today in Scripture to us believers and readers. In addition, it reads John 1:1-18 with the foundational belief that *Jesus is alive now,* and that I have a personal relationship now with this same Jesus about whom this passage was written. The FG (and New Testament) is not about a dead man whose history we try to recover from the past (a common presupposition in academia), but about the living Jesus to whom we can and do personally relate both individually and as a member of Christ's body, the church. We therefore have to come to know Christ the way we know any living person, primarily through a personal relationship with him or her (especially through faith and love).[9]

Of course, our first step will have to be to make sure we are not *misreading* John 1:1-18, by verifying original meanings of the words and cultural context of the prologue, i.e., through basic groundwork exegesis. Then, as we try to read it personally, practically, and transparently, we ask: What is God saying to me and to us and to the believing commu-

8. William S. Kurz, *Following Jesus: A Disciple's Guide to Luke and Acts* (Ann Arbor: Servant, 1984), 4-6.

9. Cf. Luke Timothy Johnson, *Living Jesus* (San Francisco: HarperSanFrancisco, 1999), ch. 1: "He Is the Living One," and ch. 4: "The Process of Learning Jesus."

nity about Jesus in John 1? Personally, are there sections of the prologue that challenge me? (Most spiritual guides recommend wrestling with God's word the way Jacob wrestled with the angel, until God can overcome my defenses and prejudices, my blocks to what God is trying to reveal to me.)

Since an intrinsic part of Catholics' personal background is our faith and lives as Catholics, we spontaneously and generally will bring to the prologue our awareness of the sweep of Scripture from Genesis to Revelation, the Tradition and history and teaching and organization of the church, our individual and community worship and sacramental life, and our efforts to live God's commandments and ways. However, to focus our example, this chapter will bring particularly the Nicene Creed to bear on our interpretation and actualization of the Johannine prologue. Recently, under the unexamined influence of historical criticism, teachers and preachers of Scripture have often seemed to go out of their way to minimize connections between this biblical prologue which Christians read and the creed which they recite and doctrines which they believe. Consequently, many Catholics seem intimidated into not allowing themselves to recognize their trinitarian and christological beliefs as being expressed in this prologue.

This alleged dichotomy between Scripture and doctrine naturally leads to the question so frequently asked: if this dichotomy exists, how can readers get from the christology of the FG to the Nicene Creed and the Trinity? Without having to relive the ancient history of the church and its overcoming of heresies by conciliar definitions of dogma, how can readers understand the FG prologue in light of the Nicene Creed? My preliminary suggestions will be to read the FG and its prologue in the context of both New Testament and Old Testament (especially creation accounts) and to be alert to theological implications of the FG in its biblical context and as it was reflected on and summarized in the worship, creeds, and dogmas of the church.

Therefore in this chapter I propose to illustrate this individual Catholic's manner of going beyond solely historical-critical exegesis of the Fourth Gospel's prologue to reading John's prologue as a Catholic. Since every reader brings his or her preunderstandings and concerns to a text, Catholics will spontaneously bring their Catholic preunderstandings and concerns to interpret and apply John's prologue to their own lives. Contemporary Catholics reading John's prologue should not be intimidated into having to pretend that they are living in the pre-Nicene 1st century. They can read this prologue as the real readers they are, as Catholic readers today. As Catholics they bring to the text not only what they share with Christians of other denominations (and even that would go considerably beyond the "original sense" of John's Gospel to at least the ecumenical creeds). They can also bring to their reading of the prologue motifs that distinguish them as Catholics, such as their long tradition of doctrinal and theological development, liturgical and sacramental practices, and developed ecclesial structures and diverse spiritualities. Just as multivalent readings of any written text have been endorsed by literary critics, so Catholic readings of John's prologue by Catholics should be desired and valued, not found fault with and shunned.

Reading John's Prologue: Meaning from the Passage

The foundations which the FG's prologue lays are ultimate ones.[10] The prologue grounds the Gospel narrative in cosmic beginnings, in the very origins of the cosmos, even before the world's creation. It begins as does the Bible itself, "in the beginning," in the absolute beginning, in imitation of Greek Genesis to which it unambiguously alludes. For a Catholic reader who also knows about the Septuagint (LXX) or the Vulgate Latin or later Old Testament translations, the theological sweep of the FG prologue is vast, from precreation cosmic beginnings in the heavenly realm to Christian christological and Trinitarian perspectives on the relations of the persons within the Godhead and to the created material universe and its human custodian who is God's image.

Let us begin, however, with the passage itself, first with its actual (Greek) vocabulary and grammar and its intertextual resonances with primarily the Greek versions of the Scriptures originating from the Jewish people. Second, we will consider the prologue's function within the FG narrative to show its relationships to the rest of that Gospel. Finally, we will try to illustrate the validity of reading the prologue in light of and continuity with the Nicene Creed. Most scholars regard

10. Kurz, *JSNT* 62 (1996): 43-63.

John 1:1-18 as a prologue which introduces the main themes of the Gospel to follow, with several scholars comparing these verses to the overture of a musical piece, even though a term as characteristic for the prologue as the personified *Logos* is missing from the rest of the Gospel. The prologue provides the key for interpreting the Gospel narrative to follow, for understanding the much-debated origin and identity of the Gospel's main character, Jesus, and for solving the riddles and understanding the ironies that abound in that narrative.

Close Reading of the Prologue and Its Actualization of Genesis

The FG prologue actualizes the Creation account of Genesis 1 in a manner not wholly dissimilar from 1st-century Jewish midrashic interpretive procedures, but with the startling introduction of the Christian revelation of a mutually distinct Father and Word who are both called God (John 1:1). "In the beginning" recalls and echoes the beginning of the Greek Old Testament (LXX): "In the beginning God created the heavens and the earth" (Gen. 1:1 RSV). To prepare for the statement of causality in Gen. 1:3, "And God *said*, 'Let there be light'; and there was light" (RSV, emphasis added), the FG prologue personifies God's creating word as the Word. This Word was not only "*with* God" in the beginning (John 1:1b), but it "*was* God" (1:1c). All creation came to be through this Word of command from God. Thus the writer recalls how "day" after "day" in Genesis God *said* "let there be" x or y or z, "and it was so" (Gen. 1:7, 9 RSV). Without this creative Word of God "was not anything made that was made" (John 1:3 RSV). Later, verse 10 will repeat that, although "the world was made through him" (RSV), it did not know him.

Clues in Greek Genesis

For additional insight into the prologue's interpretation of the Creation account, let us briefly look further for clues in Greek Genesis that show why the prologue makes some of the interpretive moves that it makes. Some of these interpretations are particularly surprising, given the strong Jewish emphasis on monotheism at the time of the FG. In a religion that so emphasizes the oneness of God, what clues in the Genesis text could have invited this prologue's reference to a personified Word as being with God before and at creation? What would have encouraged its reference both to the personified Word (later called Son) and to the Father as God?

Genesis (LXX) simply begins, "In the beginning God made the heaven and the earth" (Gen. 1:1).[11] Verse 3 narrates the first in the series of acts of creation: "And God said, Let there be light, and there was light." On the face of it, this seems a straightforword and simple account of "the [one] God" *(ho theos)* creating light by a simple command. Since in the Hebrew original of the Greek Bible the word *dabar* is used both for "word" and "command" (as in the Ten Commandments [*debarim*]), it is not surprising that its Greek translation *logos* also carries over that double meaning of either "word" or "command(ment)." When even later biblical writers read Gen. 1:3, "'let there be light' and there was light," it was natural for them to conclude that God made light come to be by a mere command or word (e.g., Ps. 33:6, "By the word of the LORD the heavens were made . . . ; Wis. 9:1, "God . . . who hast made all things by thy word"; Heb. 11:3, "By faith we understand that the world was created by the word of God . . ." RSV). What might have justified the further step of seeing in this command some kind of person or personification (referred to in the FG as the Word) existing along with "the God" and the one through whom all things were made (John 1:1-3)?

If we "fast forward" in the Genesis Creation account to the sixth day of creation, we find a strange expression that puzzled generations of ancient Jewish and Christian exegetes and elicited a good deal of speculation among both groups. On the sixth day, after "the God" commanded that the earth bring forth the various kinds of wild beasts according to their kind (Gen. 1:24-25), this only God made a puzzling reference to "us": "And God said, Let *us* make man according to *our* image and likeness . . ." (v. 26 Brenton, emphasis added). This puzzling plurality in the one God is further reinforced by a similarly unexpected plurality in the singular term "man" *(anthrōpon),* who in this passage

---

11. L. C. L. Brenton, *The Septuagint Version of the Old Testament and Apocrypha* (Grand Rapids: Zondervan, 1972). Unless stated otherwise, all LXX translations are from this edition.

God says is made in "our" image and likeness: "And God made [the] man [*ton anthrōpon*], according to the image of God he made *him,* male and female he made *them.* And God blessed *them* . . . (vv. 27-28a, emphasis mine). The plurality in "the man" who is made in the image of "the God," augments the earlier hints of plurality ("let us make man according to our image," v. 26) in "the God" who creates "the man" in the divine image.

To whom is "the God" speaking when he says "Let us make man according to our image"? Jewish monotheistic interpreters tended to see a reference in "us" to the heavenly court, where God was speaking to his attendant angels. But strictly speaking, the angels were not generally considered to have aided in the creation or making of humans, so the invitation to "us" would seem to have been understood as more rhetorical than factual. God, as it were, would be inviting the heavenly court to watch him create "the man . . . male and female. . . ."[12]

If it is not the angels, then the step to personifying God's word or command of creation (first found in Gen. 1:3) is not surprising. The most common Jewish personification was wisdom *(sophia),* for example in Prov. 8:22, 27, 30, but God's command is even personified as "the Word" *(ho logos)* by Philo. In addition, Wis. 9:1-2 refers to creation by the word; LXX Ps. 32:6 (Heb. 33:6) states, "By the word of the Lord the heavens were made, and all their host by the breath [or Spirit, *pneumati*] of his mouth" (RSV). Philo seems a little closer than the midrashim and targums to the approach in the FG prologue. He suggested that "the God" in Genesis 1 was speaking to the personified *word* or *logos,* to whom Philo refers sometimes as "god" to distinguish the *logos* from "the God" (i.e., as *theos* vs. *ho theos*). Philo explains that whereas "the God" *(ho theos)* refers strictly to the one and only God of monotheistic belief, anarthrous "god" (simply *theos* without the article "the") is used for an extended sense of *divine,* which is applicable to beings like the *logos* or angels who are closer to God than are humans but nevertheless unquestionably inferior to "the God" of Scripture.[13]

12. Cf. Richard J. Clifford and Roland E. Murphy, "Genesis," *NJBC,* 11; Eugene H. Maly, "Genesis," *JBC,* 11.

13. See esp. Thomas H. Tobin, "The Prologue of John and Hellenistic Jewish Speculation," *CBQ* 52 (1990): 252-69, esp. 255-62; "Logos," *ABD* (1992) 4:348-56 and bibliography.

Some Christian exegetes have understood a similar distinction in John 1:1 between "the God" and simply anarthrous "God" *(ho theos* vs. *theos)* for the Word. Although the RSV and many translations translate the clauses "and the Word was with God, and the Word was God" (RSV), the Greek word order and distinction in the two uses of "God," with and without the article "the" *(kai ho logos ēn pros ton theon, kai theos ēn ho logos),* have led some to understand these two clauses in a literalistic rendering as "and the Word was with the God *(ho theos)* and *divine/ godlike (theos)* was the Word." They contend that this verse makes the same kind of distinction between "the God" of Scripture and the Word as merely "god" which the Jewish thinker Philo had made between the one God of the Bible and the word who is "god" in a derivative and secondary sense. They claim that "the God" refers to the one true God in the Septuagint, whereas anarthrous "god" implies that the divinity of the Word has an extended meaning which does not compete with the unique divinity of the one God. In this reading, the Word is not strictly speaking God in the same sense as is "the God" of Scripture.[14]

One problem with this interpretation is that it does not correspond to the normal Greek grammar regarding use or nonuse of definite articles for predicates. It is not uncommon for predicate nouns with linking verbs (as the predicate "God" in "the Word was God") to lack the article "the" — especially when the predicate (God/*theos*) comes before the subject (the Word/*ho logos*) — as in the clause *(theos ēn ho logos,* John 1:1b).[15] Although, therefore, it remains grammatically *possible* to construe this clause as either "the Word was the God" or "the Word was [merely] god [godlike]," most Greek readers would probably have understood the more standard first meaning, that the Word was actually God. This provides respectable grammatical "credentials" within the Gospel text itself for the understanding of John 1:1 which came to dominate later Christian exegesis, that "the Word was God," "true God from true God" (Nicene Creed), as well as being "with the God."

Thus the statements near the beginning of the Johannine pro-

---

14. See the discussion in Raymond E. Brown, *The Gospel According to John (I–XII).* AB 29 (Garden City: Doubleday, 1966), 5; cf. Tobin, *CBQ* 52 (1990): 257.

15. F. Blass, A. Debrunner, and Robert W. Funk, *A Greek Grammar of the New Testament and Other Early Christian Literature,* trans. and ed. Funk (Chicago: University of Chicago Press, 1961), §273.

logue, "and the Word was with the God and the Word was God," reflect Christian meditation on Greek Genesis, in which when "the God" simply said the word or command, the world in its elements came to be. In this manner God created the world by this Word, to whom he spoke when he said, "Let us make man in our image, after our likeness" (Gen. 1:26 RSV). Therefore the prologue goes on to claim, "all things were made through him [the Word], and without him was not anything made that was made" (John 1:3 RSV).

Nor is Christ's role in creation a Christian teaching unique to John's prologue. It seems to have been a relatively early and widespread characteristic of early Christian faith (e.g., "one Lord, Jesus Christ, *through whom* are all things," 1 Cor. 8:6 RSV, emphasis mine; "he has spoken to us by a Son . . . through whom also he created the world," Heb. 1:2 RSV). In other words, reflection on the Genesis Creation account was by no means peculiar to the Johannine prologue's personification of God's creative command, in this case as the Word.

The next major themes in the prologue's actualization of Genesis 1 are those of "the Life" and "the Light" (John 1:4). As the Scriptures of the Jews had constantly emphasized that their God was the "living God," especially in contrast to "dead" idols, so the prologue asserts that in this creative Word was Life, and that this Life was the Light of humans. Mention of Life being in this Word refers to its saving attributes; mention of Light refers to the Word's revelatory functions. Although the prologue changes the topic immediately to the contest between this Light and the darkness that opposes it, the FG itself will continue to put sustained emphasis on Jesus as both Life and Light. Not only does the FG explicitly identify Jesus as Life: "I am the resurrection and the life; he who believes in me, though he die, yet shall he live . . ." (John 11:25 RSV). As himself Life (with perhaps also allusions to the Living God so active throughout Israelite history), Jesus also gives "eternal life," which is one of the most pervasive soteriological strains in both the FG and First Letter of John (1 John).

The complementary emphasis on the Word as Light underscores its function for *revelation:* "and the life was the light of men" (John 1:4 RSV); this "light shines in the darkness" (v. 5 RSV) and was true: "the true light that enlightens every man was coming into the world" (v. 9 RSV). Even though this Light "was in the world, and the world was made through him, yet the world knew him not" (v. 10 RSV). This revelation was offered to humans in a way that left them free either to accept or reject it, for it can be and was rejected, even by "his own" who refused to receive him (v. 11).

The Jesus Event

The prologue next seems to move beyond interpreting Genesis to focusing more explicitly on the Jesus event, beginning (as does the Markan Gospel) with the witness of John the Baptist in verse 6. The prologue characterizes John as witnessing to the Light, with emphasis that he was not himself the Light (vv. 7-8). Immediately after mentioning the Light, the prologue returns its attention to that Light and to its contrasting receptions. "The true light that enlightens every man was coming into the world. He was in the world, and the world was made through him, yet the world knew him not" (vv. 9-10 RSV). Among those who rejected the Light, the prologue "zooms in" on Jesus' own people, the Jews, who did not as a group receive him. (Thus the prologue anticipates how painful a historical trauma for the Johannine community was this Jewish rejection, as it also was for Paul in Romans 9-11.) The prologue's repeated references here to *light* emphasize the Word's role as *revealing* God and his plan to the people.

The prologue contrasts the unreceptive world and "his own" with those who did receive the Light and who believed in his name, who were given power to become children of God, "who were born, not of blood nor of the will of the flesh nor of the will of man, but of God" (John 1:13 RSV). This demonstrates "good news, bad news." The tragic news is that "his own people received him not" (v. 11). But the good news is that all those who did receive him and believe in his name he enabled to become God's children, born "of God." In other words, by belief in Jesus, Christians can become God's children and Jesus' brothers and sisters, even though many of the chosen people, whose lineage God's revealer shared, did not. This will be one of the major points of tension throughout the FG narrative.

The climax of the Word's revelation occurs in verse 14, which relates that the preexistent but purely spiritual and nonmaterial Word now "became flesh and dwelt among us," crossing over from the completely spiritual and divine realms to the realm of human existence.

That is, this revelation took place through the fact that the Word became human (recall the standard Hebrew biblical expression for a human being as "flesh and blood") as a member of the group responsible for the prologue ("and dwelt among us," v. 14 RSV). Thus the group claiming responsibility for the prologue takes on the role even within the prologue of being primary witnesses to the "glory" of the Word become flesh, a glory which identifies the Word as "the only [*monogenēs*] Son from the Father" (v. 14 RSV). Because the Word become flesh "dwelt among us," "we have beheld his glory. . . ." Clarifying the paradox of what this "glory" is will be a major point of emphasis in the FG.

After another brief allusion to the Baptist's witness and his inferiority to the Word or Son (John 1:15), the witnesses behind the prologue claim that "from his fulness have we all received" (v. 16 RSV) *"kai charin anti charitos"* (which I interpret as "even grace succeeding grace" in view of the following verse 17). "For the law was given through Moses; grace and truth [in Biblical Hebrew 'steadfast love and faithfulness'] came through Jesus Christ" (v. 17 RSV). The first "grace" was the law through Moses; the second "grace," (divine) "steadfast love and faithfulness," came through Jesus.

The claim that only the divine one in the bosom of the Father has seen and revealed God is one of the chief contentions of the FG vis-à-vis the Judaism of its time. The prologue is making the challenging claim that no one other than the *monogenēs theos,* the unique God "who is in the bosom of the Father," has ever seen God. Not even Moses has seen God. A fortiori, no one other than the unique God "who is in the bosom of the Father" revealed or explained God or told God's story (*exēgēsato*).

Not only do all these assertions ground the FG account in witnesses who claim to have personally seen the Word become flesh (whom they identify as God's Son and Jesus Christ), and to have gazed on his glory, they also proclaim the primeval origin of the events recounted in the FG to be the preexistent Word with God before creation. These assertions establish the ministry, death, and resurrection of Jesus (with special emphasis on his "glorification" not only in his signs but preeminently in his death-resurrection and ascent back to his Father in heaven) on the foundation of the Word who was the divine instrument of creation and who became flesh. The result of the Word's enfleshment was that the witnesses ("we") could and did see his glory and now identify that glory as the glory of the only one (Son) of the Father.

Thus the prologue explicitly claims that Jesus, the hero of the FG, is in fact the Word or Son of God who was with the Father from before creation. It interprets his becoming man as his being sent down from heaven by the Father to undertake his earthly ministry. It construes Jesus' death as the beginning of his "being lifted up" and "glorified" in a return ascent to the Father in heaven. It makes these claims in direct antithesis to claims of revelation through Moses, and it declares the grace received through Jesus to be superior to that (i.e., the law) which was obtained through Moses. Hence the prologue not only sets the stage for the action of the FG, but it "throws down the gauntlet" of competition and even hostility between Jesus (and those who believe in him) and "the Jews," which will be one of the main plot threads of the FG narrative.

Functions of the Prologue within the Fourth Gospel Narrative

However, to what extent is the claim about the prologue as interpretive key to the Gospel sustained by the Gospel narrative that follows it? Are the controversial pointers to the Son's divinity in the prologue reinforced by the narratives about Jesus in the Gospel, or is the prologue an extrinsic afterthought tacked on to the beginning after the completion of the FG narrative, with little or no follow-through in that narrative? It seems clear enough that the FG's emphases on witness to Jesus and on Jesus' signs and works justify the contention that the claims of the prologue are indeed reinforced by the Gospel narrative.[16] From the beginning, the FG portrays the Baptist exclusively under the aspect of his witness to Jesus (John 1:15, 23, 26-27, 29-36). In Jesus' "credentials" debate with the Jews, he claims even God as his witness (John 8:18). In John 10:37-38, Jesus responds to his opponents' charge of blasphemy for making himself God (v. 33) by pointing to his doing the works of the Father as evidence that "the Father is in me and I am in the Father" (v. 38 RSV; cf. 14:10-11). Sometimes even the crowd is said to bear witness

16. See Brown, *John I–XII,* 18-23.

to Jesus (John 12:17-18). Finally, in the farewell address Jesus foretells that the Holy Spirit and the disciples will bear witness to him (John 15:26-27).

Even more striking FG confirmation of the prologue's claims about Jesus' divinity come from Jesus' signs and works. Although it is true that human figures in the Old Testament like Moses, Elijah, and Elisha were known for their miracles or signs, the cumulative force of the FG emphasis on Jesus' signs, especially on kinds of signs that in the Old Testament were routinely attributed to God himself, reinforces the prologue's claims that "the Word was God." For example, Jesus' first sign at Cana in John 2:1-11 demonstrates the Creator's power to transform water to wine (as God transformed water to blood as a punitive sign to pharaoh at the hands of Moses in Exodus). Moreover, the narrator clearly attributes this first sign to the action of Jesus: "So he came again to Cana in Galilee, *where he had made the water wine*" (John 4:46 RSV, emphasis added).

Jesus' second enumerated sign at Cana, the healing of the official's son in John 4:46-54, is sharply differentiated from those of healers like Elijah and Elisha. First, Jesus is shown complaining: "Unless you [pl.] see signs and wonders you will not believe" (4:48 RSV). Then, instead of coming to heal the boy as the official requests and as Elijah and Elisha had done, Jesus heals the boy *by his word alone* (as God had created the world by his word alone): "Jesus said to him, 'Go; your son will live.' *The man believed the word that Jesus spoke to him* and went his way" (4:50 RSV, emphasis mine).

In John 5, after Jesus cures the sick man at the pool (also by his word alone), and during the resultant controversy over his healing on the sabbath, Jesus claims that *just as the Father continues to work (even on sabbath days) so does he* (5:17), so that the "Jews sought all the more to kill him, because he *not only broke the sabbath but also called God his Father, making himself equal with God*" (5:18 RSV, emphasis added). My later chapters will demonstrate how John 6 portrays Jesus feeding the 5000 in the wilderness (6:1-14), revealing himself to his disciples while walking on water (vv. 16-21) as "I AM" (v. 20, cf. 8:58), and claiming that he himself is the bread from heaven that gives eternal life (6:22-59). All these revelations of Jesus identify Jesus' actions and identity with those which the Old Testament had used exclusively for God. In John 9, Jesus' sign of healing the blind man is explained as revealing "the works of

God" (9:3), as well as revealing that Jesus is the light of the world (v. 5). The climactic sign in John 11, of the raising of Lazarus from death and corruption, is treated as a sign that confirms Jesus' claim to be the resurrection and the life (11:25-27), to which Martha responds by confessing that he is *"the Christ, the Son of God,* he who is *coming into the world"* (v. 27 RSV, emphasis added).

Finally, it is common knowledge that in the FG, Jesus' ultimate sign is his being lifted up on the cross and his consequent resurrection and ascension to be with the Father again. As the epilogue points out, Jesus' signs are used to vindicate his exalted identity and to stimulate belief in him: "Now Jesus did many other signs in the presence of the disciples, which are not written in this book; but these are written that you may believe that Jesus is the Christ, the Son of God, and that believing you may have life in his name" (John 20:30-31 RSV).

Another major way in which the prologue is functionally related to the rest of the FG is in its providing the key for unlocking the many indirect hints and mysteries of the FG narrative. To appreciate how critical the prologue is for interpreting the riddles, parodoxes, and ironies of the FG narrative to follow, one has only to imagine what would be missing if this prologue did not set the stage for the action which follows immediately.[17] That action begins in John 1:19-23 with the testimony of the Baptist, who denied speculation that he might be the Messiah or Christ or the returned Elijah or some other prophet of Jewish end-time speculation. After identifying John with "the voice crying in the wilderness" as in Isa. 40:3 and the Synoptics, the passage compares John with the greater one who comes after him, and recounts John's witness to Jesus as "the Lamb of God, who takes away the sin of the world" (John 1:29 RSV). It further contrasts John's baptizing with water to Jesus' baptizing with the Holy Spirit, climaxed by John's solemn witness "that this is the Son of God" (1:34 RSV).

For first-time readers who had no knowledge of Jesus or his story, all this would be even more enigmatic and abrupt than it already is, if the prologue had not prepared the way by setting the entire Gospel narrative in the cosmic context of God's and the world's mutual relationship and in the creative and revelatory and saving role in the world

17. On the prologue as summary of the FG and explained by it, see Edwyn Clement Hoskins, *The Fourth Gospel,* 2nd ed. (London: Faber and Faber, 1947), 137.

which is played by God's Word and only Son who became flesh and dwelt "among us." By identifying Jesus Christ (John 1:17) with the preexistent Word or Son of God, through whom all things were created and who was the life and light (the salvation and revelation) of humans, the prologue lays the foundation for the narrative's constant riddles and paradoxes about Jesus' origin and "hour" and being "from above" and "sent from the Father." The prologue foreshadows the constant rejection and antagonism of "his own . . . who did not receive him" (v. 11), in contrast to believers in Jesus who became God's children (compare John 1:13 with "born again/from above" in 3:7) and have (eternal) life through this belief (20:31).

The prologue puts solemn emphasis on these believers' witness to the fact that "the Word became flesh and dwelt among us" (1:14) and on their eyewitness testimony to "his glory, glory as of the only Son from the Father" (v. 14 RSV; lit., "glory as of the only one [*monogenēs*] from the Father"). This witness to Jesus' glory sets the stage for the major FG plot line and theme of Jesus' "glorification," from his ironic "being lifted up" and "glorified" in the transition from cross to new life to ascension and return to his Father above, which is the climax of the first 20 chapters.

Finally, the prologue sets the stage for almost constant conflict in the FG narrative by the contrast in John 1:16-17 between the first grace given through Moses, the law, and the second grace through Jesus Christ, "grace and truth," in addition to its concluding denial that anyone but Jesus has ever seen or revealed God. "The only God who was in the bosom of the Father, he has made him known" (v. 18, my literalist translation) sets Jesus high above Moses as not only the sole revealer of the Father, but as "only God *(monogenēs theos)* who is [continuously] in the bosom of the Father."

These almost inconceivable contrasts and claims in the prologue lead directly into the constant misunderstandings, tension, hostility, accusations of blasphemy, and the like, especially between Jewish leaders and Jesus throughout the FG, which propel primary components of its plot. They enable the readers to grasp the plot's multiple levels of irony and paradoxes and to understand Jesus' riddles when the characters within the narrative remain clueless or jump to obviously false conclusions about Jesus, his origins, his identity, or his mission. These conflicting claims between Jesus and "his own . . . who did not receive him" (v. 11) foreshadow the growing hostility to Jesus which eventuates in his arrest, trials, and crucifixion.

Thus in many ways the prologue prepares readers to understand the subtleties and nuances of the subsequent FG narrative. It identifies Jesus with the preexistent Word or Son who was with the Father from before creation. This is the key to later Gospel statements and arguments about his identity and origins, and it makes sense out of expressions of descending from and ascending to heaven above. The prologue foreshadows Jesus' earthly mission of revelation and consequently his contrasting rejection by "his own" and reception by "us" among whom he dwelt and who will be witnesses to his "glory as of an only one [Son] from the Father." This in turn prepares the readers for the later themes of Jesus being lifted up and glorified, beginning with the cross. In short, the prologue clearly does function as the primary interpretive key to understanding the narrative to follow.

Reading the Prologue in Light of the Nicene Creed

Finally, let us test our interpretation by rereading John's prologue in light of the Nicene Creed, which evidently draws more of its distinctive language from the Gospel of John than from the Synoptics. This comparison with the Creed after the exegetical foundation above is meant to manifest that using the Creed to help interpret the FG prologue need not be seen as a return to precritical submersion of Catholic biblical exegesis in Catholic dogma. Not only does the FG itself apply to Jesus the notions of Word, Light, Son revealing the Father, and indicators of divinity, but it alone of the Gospels has the precreation perspective of Jesus as Word before he was made "flesh" in John 1:1-18.[18] It alone of the Gospels draws the climactic conclusion in John 1:18, which denies that anyone (even Moses) has ever seen God, and claims that it is the only God who is in the bosom of the Father who has made him known. The Word or Son reveals the Father, because "if you [oppo-

---

18. The treatment of the Johannine prologue in this chapter draws heavily on my recent contribution to a Festschrift edition of *Perspectives in Religious Studies* honoring Charles H. Talbert: William S. Kurz, "The Johannine Word as Revealing the Father: A Christian Credal Actualization," *PRSt* 28:1 (2001): 67-84, and the literature there cited.

nents] knew me, you would know my Father also" (John 8:19 RSV); "if you [disciples] had known me, you would have known my Father also; henceforth you know him and have seen him" (14:7 RSV). Whoever sees Jesus sees the Father (14:9), for the words and signs of Jesus are works of the Father who is and works in Jesus (14:10-11). Thus the Word of God, who is the Son of God, "enfleshed" or incarnate as Jesus Christ, is distinct from the Father but makes known or reveals the Father and is himself God. Thus, as I interpret this FG prologue in the light of the rest of the Bible, from within the church's credal Tradition, and from my Catholic Christian experience of Scripture, worship, prayer, church, and pastoral practice, the intrinsic resonances of this prologue with the Niceno-Constantinopolitan Creed are pronounced and cannot be dismissed as mere eisegesis. To illustrate this further, let us expound the Creed phrase by phrase as it relates to the Johannine prologue (John 1:1-18).

"We believe in *one God.*"[19] The Word or Son of God is not a second God, but he is with God (John 1:1) and reveals God (1:18). This one God we confess first as **"the Father, the almighty, maker of heaven and earth, of all that is, seen and unseen."** Already in the prologue God is named Father: "glory as of the only Son [lit., only one] from the Father" (John 1:14 RSV); "the only Son [lit., only God], who is in the bosom of the Father, he has made him known" (v. 18 RSV, plus very frequently in the FG). The ultimate source of both divinity and creation is God the Father. Credal clarifications which go beyond what the Johannine prologue mentions, namely that the Father is almighty and maker of heaven and earth and of everything seen and unseen, are spontaneous and natural implications for Christian readers of the prologue's allusion to the Genesis Creation account.

"We believe in one Lord, Jesus Christ, the only Son of God eternally begotten of the Father, God from God, Light from Light, true God from true God, begotten, not made, one in Being with the Father." Although the prologue does not explicitly identify Jesus as Lord, Thomas does so in the climactic FG confession in John 20, "My Lord and my God" (v. 28). The prologue does identify Jesus as only Son. Although it uses neither the word "Son" nor the word "begotten," the fil-

---

19. The version of the Creed here quoted is quite conveniently found in the *CCC*, 49-50, in parallelism with the so-called Apostles' Creed.

ial concept is without doubt implied in John 1:14, "the only one from the Father," and 1:18, "the only God who is in the bosom of the Father." The first Johannine use of the term "Son" for Jesus is in the witness of the Baptist: "And I have seen and have borne witness that this is the Son of God" (John 1:34 RSV). See also 1:49; 3:18; 5:25; 10:36; 11:4, 27; 19:7, and especially the purpose statement of the FG: "but these are written that you may believe that Jesus is the Christ, the Son of God, and that believing you may have life in his name" (20:31 RSV). Hence the notion "begotten" is also implied, even though the term itself does not occur in the FG. The prologue moreover alludes to Gen. 1:1 in stating that this personal being existed "in the beginning" before creation with the Father. The further clarification that his begetting was eternal is already implicit in the prologue as most Christians would naturally actualize it. Since the prologue clearly adds that the Word is God (John 1:1) and also attests (with clarification from the FG) that the Son is from God (the Father), these credal expressions are accepted without hesitation.

Although the prologue uses the term "Light" only for the Word or Son, it is a reasonable step in logic to identify also the Father as Light from which the Son's Light originates. The phrases "true God from true God, begotten not made," are further clarifications which unquestionably result from historical Trinitarian and christological controversies. Nevertheless, Christians actualizing the prologue would naturally accept them as implicit in it, since the prologue certainly portrays the Word or Son from the aspect of God as creating, not from the aspect of creatures as himself created. Since throughout the FG the Son is self-evidently not the Father, but nevertheless like the Father the Son or Word is God (John 1:1; 20:28), the sharing of the divine being by the Son with the Father is a coherent conclusion.

"For us men and for our salvation he came down from heaven ... and became man." Further reference to the power of the Spirit and to being born of the Virgin comes more from the Synoptics than from John, but there is nothing in the FG prologue that would find these claims contradictory or impossible. Reading the prologue within the unity of the biblical revelation leads readily to accepting this aspect of the Creed. The prologue in light of the FG frequently emphasizes that the Son, Jesus, is *from heaven,* and that he (usually under the title Son of Man) descended from heaven. From "the Word was made flesh" in

John 1:14 to "became man" in the Creed is a natural and easy evolution for a Christian who is actualizing the FG prologue, since humanity is already connoted in the biblical term "flesh" (especially as shorthand for the biblical term for a human, "flesh and blood"), with or without the negative further connotations which "flesh" might have. "And the rest, as they say, is history." The further confessions about the Son in the Creed refer to events of saving or faith history, all of which are prominently enough recounted in both the Synoptic Gospels and FG, especially when the FG is read within the unity of Scripture.

Thus contemporary believers' christological interpretations of Scripture are truly in continuity with the emerging beliefs of early generations of Christians who reflected on the composite of their experience. This included their hymns and prayers to Jesus, their baptizing "in the name of the Father, and of the Son, and of the Holy Spirit," along with the meaning of the Johannine prologue, in the historical context of much debate about alternative interpretations of how the Son or Word could be said to be God. In light of such similar interpretations then and now (especially after the Councils of Nicea and Chalcedon), it is not surprising that Christians have come to interpret "In the beginning was the Word, and the Word was with the God" as expressing the eternal existence of the Word who is somehow distinguished from the God mentioned in Genesis, whom Jesus in his ministry referred to as his Father. The Word was with the Father but the Word was not the Father. However, the further statement, "and the Word was God," has for centuries meant to Christians that the Word completely shared the divine nature as God with the God of Genesis whom Jesus called Father. The Word was not the Father, but the Word was God.

Whatever one might theoretically argue about the original senses of the declarations in the FG prologue or about distinctions between functional and ontological christologies, when Catholics actualize the prologue from within their experience of the whole Bible, their ecclesial and interpretive Tradition, and their overall experience of the practices and truths of their faith, the progression in believing readers from what the prologue says to what the Creed confesses is an easy and instinctive one.

CHAPTER EIGHT

Voices in the Church:
Preunderstandings in Applying Scripture

The previous chapter set the stage for going beyond historical-critical reading of Scripture to a more explicitly Catholic reading, using the example of the Fourth Gospel prologue, which was read as interpretive key and overture to the FG narrative that follows. By illustrating the continuity between the two, it challenged the reigning critical prohibitions against "confusing" especially the christology of the Johannine prologue and Gospel with the later dogmatic developments incarnated in the Niceno-Constantinopolitan Creed. It therefore argued that the spontaneous reading and filling of gaps which a contemporary Catholic would do in reading the prologue in light of that creed can be legitimate.

This second chapter will broaden the perspective of the first to a more global search for a worldview based on Scripture, which faith considers a unity as God's word or revelation. It will make explicit the difference in interpretation and application that results from differing preunderstandings which readers (in this example, from different denominations) bring to a biblical passage. Although my other chapters are focused around FG passages as examples, this chapter will investigate the frequently recurring problem of how to apply Scripture to a particular contemporary issue, and what approaches to and resources in Scripture can be used to make this application. The particular example will be the issue of abortion, as approached from Scripture with Protestant preunderstandings by Richard Hays and with Catholic preunderstandings by myself. This interdenominational comparison is done in hopes of providing an especially clear example of how significantly different preunderstandings can predispose readers toward diverse interpretations and applications of the Bible to contemporary concerns. Although even among Catholic exegetes preunderstandings differ markedly, since Hays's book, *The Moral Vision of the New Testament*, is both widely respected and comes from a self-evidently different background than mine, it enables perhaps more clear-cut comparisons than many Catholic examples might do.[1]

Using Luke Johnson's comparison between Protestant "either/or" and Catholic "both/and" interpretive instincts, this chapter will describe Hays's application of Scripture in his abortion chapter as a kind of "either/or" direct focus on the abortion question and on biblical passages that appear historically relevant for making distinctions needed for answering the questions. This may seem surprising in view of the overall focus of Hays's book and his emphasis on the early Christian ethos instead of direct commands and prohibitions as a primary context for dealing with contemporary moral questions. Even though Hays is attempting to arrive at a broader view and context, apparently when dealing with the particular example of abortion he may have unconsciously (perhaps even inconsistently with respect to the primary objective in his book) slipped back into a more historical approach with its "either/or" mentality, as when he gives so much weight to economic and social considerations, which are more closely related to historical and social-scientific than to theological approaches, in an abortion decision.[2]

This chapter will compare Hays's approach in his abortion chapter to the "both/and" approach that corresponds to my instinctive Catholic predilections for reading Scripture more globally. Instead of looking for particular passages in Scripture that seem to provide relevant evidence about abortion, I will search the Bible as a whole for a biblical Christian worldview about the creator-creature relationship — i.e., between God the Creator and human and other creatures (which builds on the creation worldview of Judaism and Genesis). This worldview will provide a

---

1. This chapter relies heavily on my recent article, "Ethical Actualization of Scripture: Approaches toward a Prolife Reading," *Fides Quaerens Intellectum* 1/1 (2001): 67-93. See also the literature there cited.

2. Richard B. Hays, *The Moral Vision of the New Testament* (San Francisco: HarperSanFrancisco, 1996), 449.

broader context within which to ask what insight the Bible might contribute about a particular issue like abortion, even if that issue is not explicitly treated in Scripture. In addition to different interpretive instincts about directly using Scripture, the differing preunderstandings of Catholics and Protestants also result in other disagreements about when and how to apply extrabiblical and traditional evidence and moral standards toward formulating a "biblical answer" to a moral question.

The previous chapter dealt with how ordinary Catholic believers have been intimidated against using the creeds to fill in christological and other gaps in the Johannine prologue. It tried to show a continuity between the prologue and the Creed that legitimizes intelligent comparison between them. Similarly, this chapter deals with ordinary Catholics' intimidation about using Scripture to argue against abortion. It will look at how this intimidation operates by means of their fear of being labelled "fundamentalists" if they dare to quote biblical prohibitions against killing innocent human life as part of their argument against abortion, which is probably not even mentioned in the New Testament, certainly not unambiguously. Admittedly, some Catholics as well as some other Christians, without realizing the implications of what they are doing, simply quote convenient texts from the Bible that seem to support their pro-life argument, without asking whether this was the significance of those texts in their original context. This exemplifies what is meant by prooftexting. However, it is also true that many Catholic and other Christians who have heard sharp criticism of pro-life prooftexting or "fundamentalism" have become thoroughly unnerved about the idea of appealing to Scripture at all in support of their pro-life positions, out of fear of prooftexting or of misusing the Bible in some other way, or of being accused of doing so.

Nevertheless, as a professional biblical scholar myself, I want to assure nonprofessional lay Catholics and other Christians that the Bible does provide a good deal of relevant evidence to which believers can appeal when presenting and defending Christian pro-life positions. I propose an approach to Scripture which does not require every Christian to become a trained professional exegete, but which can be used by anyone who takes the trouble to read the Scriptures with some carefulness and with openness to them as God's revealing word to us in our lives and situations.

First, however, let us look briefly at some of the problems regarding the use of Scripture in contemporary moral arguments, especially regarding life issues. In the context of this book and because I know the Catholic situation best, and also because Catholic moral teachings are reputed to be among the most uncompromising in rejecting abortion and other attacks on human life, my examples in this section will be primarily from and about Catholics.

Use and Abuse of the Bible Regarding Life Issues

A serious scandal for ordinary American Catholics today is the numerous publications by professedly Catholic authors which promote moral opinions which are supposedly based on Scripture but which directly contradict centuries-old Catholic moral positions, especially in sexuality and life concerns. This scandal causes even more confusion among ordinary Catholics when these notions are preached or proposed in confession or pastoral settings or, for example, are espoused by nominally Catholic politicians to justify their promotion of legalized abortion. Nonacademic believers appropriately ask how, after all these centuries, the Bible can only now be saying that it is all right to end one's own or a loved one's life when in misery, or that abortion is a woman's choice.

It is common knowledge how for decades the Bible has been a battleground over sexual and life issues in many denominations, including Catholicism, with both sides claiming biblical support for their mutually contradictory positions. Conclusions have often been decided before Scripture was even consulted. The Bible has frequently been mined for confirmatory evidence and arguments with little attention to the context or original meaning of those passages. Both sides have resorted to prooftexting, although ethical revisionists have also introduced a new twist, a kind of "anti-prooftexting," which is now a fairly common practice of gathering all the biblical passages that seem to prohibit the desired contemporary position and then arguing that none of those passages applies to that contemporary position.[3]

---

3. One well-known representative of such an approach is John Boswell, *Christianity, Social Tolerance, and Homosexuality: Gay People in Western Europe from the Beginning of the Christian Era to the Fourteenth Century* (Chicago: University of Chicago Press, 1980). "Anti-prooftexting" is not uncommon among liberationist approaches to Scripture.

Historical-critical Relativism:
Biblical Norms as "Culturally Conditioned"

One of the most substantial concerns with historical-critical applica-tions of Scripture to ethical judgments relates to typical arguments that this or that statement by Paul or even by Jesus is culturally condi-tioned and therefore not authoritative today. One cannot, of course, deny the importance of being aware of historical contexts and how they influence the content or manner of biblical commands concerning moral or social issues. For example, it is self-evident that some biblical statements about slavery are culturally conditioned and related to a Greco-Roman situation which the tiny minority of Christians were helpless to change. However, this claim for the cultural conditioning and hence the relativity of moral commands and judgments in Old or New Testament continues to be expanded toward ever further revision-ism of biblical and traditional social roles and moral judgments. More and more of what Paul or Jesus said is asserted to be culturally condi-tioned; less and less is treated as authoritative or even applicable to contemporary living. This too is a scandal or stumbling block to the faith of ordinary believers, leading to a widespread notion that social relationships and moral commands in the New Testament are for the most part irrelevant or even inappropriate for modern living.

I will argue that despite the obvious fact that every statement is to some extent culturally conditioned and related to its time and circum-stances of origin, clearly the church has treated Scripture as not just some time-bound relic witnessing to past ideals but as God's authori-tative word to every age and every culture. Much of what is authorita-tive in Scripture is apparent to any reasonably intelligent and literate reader and believer.

Finding a Broader Context for Arguments

The way that I propose using Scripture for pro-life argumentation gets beyond minute specifics, for whose arbitration scholarship might in-deed be seen as necessary. Rather, I will propose situating individual pro-life questions like the morality of abortion within a more inclusive biblical perspective on how God relates to and values both individual humans and the people of God. I would like to refer to a biblical worldview which provides a context within which to decide such particular moral questions.

We have seen that, within a Catholic faith perspective, to seek and find the mind of God in Scripture requires reading the particular passages within the overall context of God's total revelation — i.e., not only within all of Scripture, but also in the church's life and Tradition, and amid the coherence of all the truths of faith among themselves and with God's whole plan of revelation. Thus, to argue about human life issues, especially on matters like abortion which are not explicitly treated in Scripture, we treat the passages which we do use within the entire canonical context. That is, our solution to this question has to be consistent with the overall biblical revelation about God and human beings and the created world. Our answer concerning abortion cannot contradict clear divine teaching on related questions, such as the value that God places on all human lives. We cannot prooftext Scripture out of context to support our contemporary ideologies.

Believing readers also read the Scripture from within the living Tradition of their church. Hence, those of us who are Catholics read and interpret the Bible specifically as Catholics. Unlike some Protestants who tend toward a *Sola Scriptura* insistence that something has to be expressly treated in Scripture to be binding, Catholics read and preach from Scripture within our broader Catholic context of revelation. Thus, even though Scripture says almost nothing explicitly about abortion as such, Scripture says a lot about killing innocent human life, about how human life and children are blessings and gifts from God (which Hays also acknowledges), and about how God has a plan for each human life from before birth, about letting little children come to Jesus, and the like. When the Scriptures are read from within the overall biblical worldview about the relationship between God, humans, and the material created world, all this biblical evidence provides a reasonable biblical foundation for a Catholic to make applications to specific cases like abortion.

Further, when we read the Scripture as Catholics, the church's rich moral Tradition (handily summarized in the *CCC* and Vatican II) and explicit magisterial treatments of abortion (such as *The Gospel of Life [Evangelium Vitae, EV]*)[4] can be used as a "rule of faith" analogously to

---

4. Austin Flannery, ed., *Vatican II: The Conciliar and Post Conciliar Documents*

how the early patristic authors used the creeds as criteria for whether a biblical interpretation was acceptable or heretical. Consequently, a Catholic can read what Scripture says about human life and killing and apply that to abortion with the help of moral absolutes which the church teaches, such as that "one may never do evil to achieve good"; that human life is to be protected upon conception (without getting sidetracked into philosophical questions like when the soul is created); that abortion is an intrinsic evil because it is taking innocent human life. Although one should not claim that all of these are explicitly *biblical* teachings, for Catholics they are legitimate traditional helps in interpreting and applying the evidence which Scripture does provide about the meaning of human life in relation to our creator God.

When consulting Scripture regarding abortion, a very helpful third context which Vatican II (*DV* 12) mentions for interpreting and applying Scripture to contemporary living is the "analogy of faith" — how all truths of faith and our experiences of Catholic living cohere among themselves and within God's overall revealed plan of salvation. This can involve an appeal to personal experience like that of counselling distressed women either beforehand when they are considering having an abortion or afterwards when they are suffering from postabortion aftermath.

Differing Preunderstandings — between Protestants and Catholics

When presenting an argument about human life to those who are not Catholics, it is helpful to keep in mind some of the following differences between Protestant and Catholic argumentation and the role of Scripture in each. As a fine example of such an approach, and one which shares several prolife sympathies, let us look at Richard Hays, *The Moral Vision of the New Testament,* and compare some of his differences with the Catholic procedure noted above.[5]

It is not surprising that some of the substantial differences between

---

(Boston: St. Paul's, 1992); *Catechism of the Catholic Church,* 2nd ed. (Vatican: Libreria Editrice Vaticana, 1997); Pope John Paul II, *The Gospel of Life (Evangelium Vitae)* (Boston: Pauline, 1995).

5. Hays, *Moral Vision.*

Hays's and my approach pertain to the use of extrabiblical warrants, even though he admits their necessity. Let us survey some of the most important, before responding to them as a block. Despite a general reluctance to allow abortion, Hays categorically denies the notions of the sacredness of human life and the biblical relevance of rights language, denying not only "modern rights" like the right to privacy, but even the right to life. Regarding the right to life, Hays argues that life is not a right but a gift from God (which may indeed be true of a creature vis-à-vis the Creator, as well as before the actual existence of a particular individual human person).[6] Hays is also reluctant to draw principles from biblical narratives and laws and to argue to conclusions from them. He is even hesitant to extend the prohibition of murder to abortion as a subspecies of killing innocent human life, because of some Old Testament treatments of accidental miscarriages as pertaining more to property concerns than to a fetus's stated right to life (Exod. 21:22-25). In this kind of comparison to Old Testament laws for (accidental) killing of a child in the womb, he does not appear to take sufficient account of a possible New Testament development beyond Old Testament insights, even though in other moral issues like war and peace he does not hesitate to argue New Testament development beyond the Old Testament much more aggressively. However, he does acknowledge that the Septuagint translation and some rabbis and postbiblical Jewish writers introduced a distinction between a formed and unformed fetus, and applied *jus talionis* and murder laws to the killing of formed fetuses.[7]

In response, to me as a Catholic it does not seem to be eisegesis to argue from the biblical evidence that, once God has freely given the gift of life to a human, that particular human as God's image now has a right to life which other humans must respect. This right to life is revealed or at least implied and protected by the stern biblical commandment against killing innocent human life (murder), which is enforced by the severity of the biblical death penalty for such murder. Without this basic foundational right to life, no other rights can exist among humans, and the weak would always be at the complete mercy of the strong. Therefore the burden of proof would seem to lie with anyone who denies that a right to life vis-à-vis other humans is biblical.

6. Hays, *Moral Vision,* 454.
7. Hays, *Moral Vision,* 447.

Closely related to this fundamental difference over whether the right to life is literally "biblical" is Hays's *refusal to allow any moral absolutes* that may be applicable to the treatment of abortion. He treats the "hard case" scenario of a potential Down Syndrome child of a fortyish couple as a prayerful decision. But a prayful decision would imply a spiritual discernment between two choices which are both allowed (because moral even if "tragic"). He thus avoids the more fundamental question whether or not this option to abort is morally permitted at all. His approach does not sound like a question of discovering what God commands in this case, nor like an application of an absolute divine command or an absolute moral principle to this decision. The fact that abortion is not explicitly and absolutely condemned in Scripture seems to function as a kind of unconscious *Sola Scriptura* justification, in an argument from silence, for treating abortion as something much more contingent upon circumstances, such as the inability of the church to provide for the mother and child.[8] Such an approach seems to presume without question that "hard cases" can warrant exceptions to the general biblical ideals of not killing and of being welcoming to life in the womb.

Let us now look at a proposed alternative approach to Scripture and biblical evidence that might be relevant to the question of abortion, which has been developed on the basis of Catholic preunderstandings.

Biblical Perspectives on Human Beings and Life

Because I am trying to illustrate a more inclusive "both/and" approach to consulting Scripture with respect to a particular issue, my presentation will not follow most of the standard treatments of biblical ethics and morality. Many of these conventional approaches tend to treat standard topics like the Ten Commandments, the love commandment, or what the Bible says about subjects like sexuality or life issues.[9] Some provide overviews of New Testament or Old Testament moral teaching.[10]

---

8. Hays, *Moral Vision,* 457.

9. Raymond F. Collins, *Christian Morality: Biblical Foundations* (Notre Dame: University of Notre Dame Press, 1986).

10. Rudolf Schnackenburg, *The Moral Teaching of the New Testament,* trans. J. Holland-Smith and W. J. O'Hara (1965; repr. New York: Seabury, 1979).

I will instead propose a more inclusive canonical horizon (and yet a more instinctive one that does not presuppose professional biblical training), one grounded more simply in a typical biblical worldview of 1st-century Christians. Instead of focusing narrowly on explicit issues, cases, laws or commands, one can situate particular issues within this biblical and Jewish worldview as lived and further developed by Christians. As is clear from both Jesus' teaching and example in the Gospels and from letters and other New Testament writings, early Christians generally took over the biblical worldview from Judaism, but with a special concentration on how the risen Jesus influenced this perspective. Intelligent reading of Scripture and alertness to the indirect ways Catholics learn Scripture, such as in liturgy and preaching, seem sufficient to arrive at a basic sense of the fundamental worldview presupposed in New Testament writings.

Accordingly, I argue that early Christians viewed the world and life from their (Jewish) biblical perspective. Their world was ruled by the one and only God, who created the universe good (not evil, as for some gnostics), and who created humans "in the image of God" (Gen. 1:27 RSV). To these humans God gave dominion over the rest of material creation, but a dominion subordinate to that of their Creator. This perspective on the goodness of God's original creation, and on a genuine but qualified human authority over other material creatures, is straightaway tempered by an awareness of human sin and consequent skewing of the relationships between humans and God and among themselves and with other creatures. The history and condition of sinful human rebellion from God's ways radically modified the moral universe in which humans found themselves. Some things proper to their original state (e.g., the innocent nakedness of Adam and Eve) were no longer appropriate (hence their clothing themselves out of shame).

This biblical perspective is based on belief not only in creation and sin, but also in how God rescued humans from the consequences of sin, as through the exodus from Egypt, through salvation from foreign oppression by the instrumentality of judges and kings, and through the covenants between God and the chosen people. This biblical worldview delineates God's teaching and disciplining this people throughout the ages and progressively revealing his identity and will, especially through commandments and laws, through positive and negative examples of behavior in the Pentateuch and historical books, and through exhortations of prophets and reflections of wisdom writers.

For Christians, this worldview is further transformed through their understanding of biblical history and revelation from the perspective of Jesus' life, death, and resurrection, through their reception of the Holy Spirit, and through their life within the church. Yet the New Testament view remains more in a basic continuity with the theological and moral horizons of their Jewish Scriptures than in their revocation or replacement. Fundamental biblical moral principles remain in effect, such as the goodness of material creation (and thus of material goods and sexuality), the need to obey one's Creator, and to repent of one's sins. Many biblical laws and directives also retained their force, such as the Ten Commandments and their epitome in the love of God and neighbor. Even when Jesus is portrayed as modifying received moral tradition, as in his rejection of divorce, his changes are often based on how things were "from the beginning" (Mark 10:2-9; Matt. 19:3-6), i.e., on the order of creation in the Torah.[11]

Genesis: Creation of Humans in Dominion over the Earth

Especially as an antidote to prooftexting and special pleading, the enduring authority for biblical ethical judgments of the Genesis (and Pentateuch) account of the creation, fall, and God's plan of salvation through his people needs to be acknowledged. The Genesis portrayal of the place and role of humans in the material universe carefully balances human authority over all other material creatures with unambiguous limits to this authority. Human dominion over the earth is delegated and finite. Humans are stewards, not owners or masters, of the earth and its creatures. Their authority is exercised not in their own name but as representatives of God. They are held accountable by the Creator for how they exercise this God-given authority. Thus, the por-

---

11. The similar phrase "in the beginning" echoes the start and title of Genesis. Cf. John Paul II's series of lectures on Genesis and his emphasis on this very phrase, "from the beginning," in his *The Theology of the Body: Human Love in the Divine Plan* (Boston: Pauline, 1997), 25-27.

trayal of Adam as naming the animals and of the first couple as tend-ing the garden of Eden under the friendship and supervision of God their Creator (Genesis 2) provides a powerful foundational symbol for the biblical principles regarding proper use of animals and material goods, as well as respect for the environment. Later laws of the Israel-ites build on this foundation, such as those that forbid cruelty to ani-mals and enjoin consideration for them (e.g., "You shall not muzzle an ox when it treads out the grain"; Deut. 25:4).[12]

In the Image of God

Especially foundational for biblical ethics, particularly concerning hu-man rights and life issues, is the Genesis portrayal of humans as cre-ated in the image of God. After creating the animals (and declaring them good and therefore worthy of respect and proper treatment) God is depicted as saying, "Let us make man in our image, after our likeness; and let them have dominion" over the other living things in the sea and air and on the earth (Gen. 1:26 RSV). It is as God's image that humans have dominion. "So God created man in his own image, in the image of God he created him; male and female he created them" (Gen. 1:27 RSV). This notion of humans in God's image is vigorously reinforced within the biblical worldview by the popular and frequently quoted Psalm 8:

> What is man that thou art mindful of him, and the son of man that thou dost care for him? Yet thou hast made him little less than God, and dost crown him with glory and honor. Thou hast given him do-minion over the works of thy hands; thou hast put all things under his feet, all sheep and oxen, and also the beasts of the field, the birds of the air, and the fish of the sea, whatever passes along the paths of the sea. (Ps. 8:4-8 RSV)

In Genesis the Creator is then shown blessing these creatures who were newly created in the divine image and likeness: "Be fruitful and

---

12. Two New Testament quotations of this commandment continue to treat it as ethically authoritative (1 Tim. 5:18; 1 Cor. 9:9), although the Corinthian use of the quotation argues that the principle applies more to human laborers than to animals (1 Cor. 9:7-14).

multiply, and fill the earth and subdue it; and have dominion over the fish of the sea and over the birds of the air and over every living thing that moves upon the earth" (Gen. 1:28 RSV). As frequently in the Jewish Scriptures, a blessing by God or by a parent or grandparent can also comprise the person's vocation.[13] Here in the Creation account, God's human images are called first, to propagate the human race throughout the world, and second, to subdue the world and all that is in it. This two-part commission, which is repeated in even more radical form after the flood, forms the basis for many of the later biblical commandments and ethical directives.

As images of God, and as commissioned by God, humans are indisputably placed at the top of the biblical hierarchy of material creatures. To fulfill their mission as God's stewards to manage the material world and all the living creatures in it, the original couple obviously has to extend their presence throughout this world, as is done through propagating their race according to God's command. The biblical worldview has no room for a radical ecology that would advocate killing or even avoiding human offspring for the sake of the ecological environment. On the other hand, the biblical worldview likewise has no room for irresponsible pollution and destruction of the environment out of selfishness and greed, for God had pronounced that environment "good" upon creating it and had commissioned his images to care for that environment as his deputies and stewards. In this symbolic foundation for the rest of the biblical narratives and laws, the owners and principal masters of the world are not humans, who are merely God's stewards and surrogate caretakers over other creatures, but God.

Sanctity of Human Life: Human Rights and Killing

Since this biblical worldview clearly places humans at the pinnacle of God's creation as the only material creatures who are said to be in God's image, and as having dominion over other creatures on earth, it

---

13. E.g., to Sarah (Gen. 17:15-16); Isaac's blessing and charge to Jacob (Gen. 28:1-4); Israel's blessing of Ephraim and Manasseh (48:14-20); and Israel to his 12 sons in 49:1-28, "this is what their father said to them as he blessed them, blessing each with the blessing suitable to him" (v. 28).

accords humans a unique status among this world's creatures. Human dominion over plants and animals and their commission to fill and subdue the earth imply indisputable human prerogatives over other material creatures, including rights that are distinctive to humans alone on the earth. Although life itself is obviously a gift from God, after God has given that gift so that now a human life has begun, that human is protected by God against murder and other forms of abuse and oppression by his or her right to life which results from his or her being an image of God. Thus in Genesis 4, Abel's blood shed in murder cries out for retribution, and Cain is severely punished (though protected from revenge killing by others) for murdering Abel his brother.

Even when the Bible permits the killing of animals (e.g., in Genesis 8–9 for sacrifices or food), murder (the killing of *innocent* human life) in all its variations is and remains forbidden (e.g., Gen. 9:5-6) throughout both testaments of the Bible. For later generations this prohibition is most prominent in the Decalogue's precept, "You shall not kill" (Exod. 20:13 RSV). However, well before the Decalogue was given in the biblical narrative, already in the "second beginning" after the flood, God's renewed prohibition of the shedding of human blood is based on the foundational truth of human creation: "for God made man in his own image" (Gen. 9:6 RSV). The expressed reason why humans may not be killed is that they are in God's image; moreover, they persist in God's image, even after the biblical narration of God's displeasure with most of the sinful human race and their destruction through the flood. The gravity of God's commandment not to shed innocent human blood is accentuated by the severity of the punishment for doing so (i.e., death), ironic though this may sound to contemporary sensitized ears, accustomed to hearing of the evils of capital punishment.

In fact, the fundamental and categorical biblical distinction between killing *innocent* human life and killing the guilty could not be more obviously worded than by this primeval commandment: "For your lifeblood I will surely require a reckoning; of every beast I will require it and of man; of every man's brother I will require the life of man. *Whoever sheds the blood of man, by man shall his blood be shed;* for God made man in his own image" (Gen. 9:5-6 RSV, emphasis added). The way that the Bible underlines the gravity of the commandment not to kill another human is to threaten the penalty of capital punishment for doing so. Although *Evangelium Vitae* and the revised *Catechism of the Catholic Church* now argue against the need or propriety of capital punishment in virtually any contemporary circumstance, the biblical tradition and practice of both Jews and Christians (and, in fact, most nations) from ancient times to almost the present make clear that there remains a radical distinction between killing innocent human life and punishing those who do so with their own death.[14]

Nevertheless, the Catholic magisterium (and facets of Catholic Tradition) prevent Catholics from simply quoting the words of Scripture to settle a question like capital punishment today, even though it is explicitly (and frequently) enjoined by the Bible as punishment for grave offences. Still, the evidence of Scripture and Catholic Tradition through the centuries is overwhelming that one cannot simply equate the evil of capital punishment with the evil of shedding innocent human blood, as in murder or abortion. Thus "seamless garment" arguments cannot cancel out as equally objectionable one candidate's position in favor of capital punishment with the opposing candidate's position in favor of abortion. The shedding of innocent human blood (as in abortion) is *absolutely* prohibited; not so capital punishment, which originally was even *prescribed* to redress the disorder of murder (cf. CCC #2266, and perhaps also as a deterrent to murder), and against which recent arguments are instead relative to the circumstances.

Ethical Consequences of the Word Becoming Flesh

Although Christians build their ethics on the foundation of the Jewish Scriptures, an important dimension is added in the New Testament horizon of the Word having become flesh, the Son of God having become incarnated as man like us in all things but sin. Not only does the Son of God's deigning to enter the human condition and "become flesh" confirm the goodness of material creation and the dignity of the human creature revealed by Genesis and the rest of the Jewish Scriptures. The

---

14. For current magisterial statements against capital punishment, see *EV* §56 and CCC §2267.

New Covenant also delineates a New Adam and a New Creation, an elevation of our human condition and an added power from the indwelling Holy Spirit and within the community of Christ's church to live God's commandments more fully. Matthew's Gospel symbolizes this new level of expectation in the antitheses of the Sermon on the Mount, where Old Testament commandments are said to be reinterpreted and radicalized, not abolished: "Think not that I have come to abolish the law and the prophets; I have come not to abolish them but to fulfil them" (Matt. 5:17 RSV). The very first example of this fulfilling of the old law concerns "You shall not kill": "But I say to you that every one who is angry with his brother shall be liable to judgment" (Matt. 5:22 RSV). Other words of Jesus call for nonretaliation and "turning the other cheek" (Matt. 5:38-39). Not only do the Old Testament commandments, like those against shedding innocent human blood, continue to be observed by Christians, but the sayings of Jesus further radicalize and extend them beyond physical acts of killing even into angry attitudes and into nonretaliation.

At least as important as the sayings of Jesus for Christian ethics is his example. Paul looked to Christ Jesus, Son of God, as a living example of how to live. He counselled his communities to "Be imitators of me, as I am of Christ" (1 Cor. 11:1 RSV). He asked the Philippians to "Have this mind among yourselves, which is yours in Christ Jesus, who, though he was in the form of God, did not count equality with God a thing to be grasped, but emptied himself, taking the form of a servant, being born in the likeness of men. And being found in human form he humbled himself and became obedient unto death, even death on a cross" (Phil. 2:5-8 RSV). Not only do Christians continue to obey the Ten Commandments, but they are to obey them even more radically in imitation of the God made man, the Word made flesh who dwelt among us. This obedience is to extend far beyond the performance of God's commandments into self-sacrificial obedience even "unto death, even death on a cross" (Phil. 2:8).

Thus, whereas Old Testament texts contain many pragmatic directives for an actual nation state (Israel), in which the prohibition against killing humans is not applied to divinely sanctioned wars nor to redressing seriously evil deeds, the New Testament example and words of Jesus lead to a much more radical and complete rejection of killing, at times even of apparently legitimate forms of self-defense. The portrayal of even Jesus' disciples as dismayed by some of Jesus' sayings, such as his absolute prohibition of remarriage after divorce, indicates an awareness even by the New Testament authors and their first readers that following Jesus not only includes a continuing obedience to the Ten Commandments, but asks for sometimes heroic obedience beyond what was commonly envisaged in the Judaism of their time. Followers of Jesus are to avoid anger as well as murder, to turn the other cheek, to avoid not only adultery but even looking with lust, to forgo remarriage after divorce, to sell all and follow Jesus if one wants to be perfect (beyond just keeping the commandments), and other demands that sound "unrealistic."

However, the New Testament does not focus only on the example of Jesus as New Adam and on his sayings which expand the limits of commonly accepted demands of the Jewish Scriptures. To do so might discourage more than promote additional heroic obedience and virtue. In the Gospels Jesus promises to send the Holy Spirit to empower his followers. The Acts of the Apostles and New Testament letters and Revelation presume the current and almost omnipresent *action of the Spirit* within both individual Christians and Christian communities and churches. These books also depict and presume strong communities where Christians assist and correct one another, so that *community support* increases an individual's ability to live the augmented demands of the Gospel. Thus the power of the Spirit and supportive matrix of Christian communities enables Paul and others to endorse not only marriage but committed virginity, not only justice but sharing of goods, not only restricting but completely forgoing retaliation or taking a fellow Christian to court. Other New Testament texts require and even presume that Christians who are helpless, such as widows and orphans, will be provided for.

In brief, there seems no evidence that New Testament Christians expected to have lighter obligations than what the Ten Commandments had required, nor that they would be exempt from keeping any of them. On the contrary, they apparently operated out of a presumption that Christians are to obey the commandments even to a heroic degree, in imitation of Christ's self-sacrificing obedience and empowered by his Spirit and supported by the church. Therefore, it seems legalistic to argue that because certain sins are not explicitly mentioned in the New Testament (sometimes neither in the Old Testament), the

New Testament does not forbid those sins, or at least that one cannot appeal to the New Testament when arguing against such sins.

An especially significant example is abortion. Even though the New Testament probably never unambiguously mentions abortion as an example of the command not to kill innocent human life, explicit extracanonical Christian condemnations of abortion and infanticide, which date back to the very first century, support the presumption that abortion was so alien to the first Christians' worldview and practice and so obviously identified with despised pagan sins (e.g., widespread infanticide) from which non-Jewish Christians had been converted, that the New Testament writers never thought it necessary in their particular contexts to mention it. For example, in their discussion of the Jewish ethical "Two Ways," the very early Christian writings, the *Didache* and *Epistle of Barnabas,* mention abortion as part of the way of death or darkness: "You shall not abort a child nor commit infanticide" (*ou phoneuseis teknon en phthorā oude gennēthen apokteneis; Did.* 2.2; *Ep. Barn.* 19.5 is almost identical).[15]

In short, although on occasion the words of Jesus disallow a practice (like remarriage after divorce) which Jewish religion had permitted, even those instances are generally either grounded "in the beginning," in the unfallen state of original creation revealed in Genesis and the Torah, or on the "new creation" brought about by the Word made flesh and his death, resurrection, and pouring out of the Holy Spirit "upon all flesh" (Acts 2:17). Not only do they not weaken the force of the Old Testament moral teaching, but they even make it more stringent, even to the explicitly mentioned dismay of Jesus' disciples.

Although there are a new focus and some more exacting demands made in the New Testament, the fundamental worldview of these early Christians nevertheless remains that of the Jewish Scriptures, but now seen as fulfilled in the Word made flesh, the New Adam firstborn from the dead, the Son whom God sent not to condemn but to save the world. With regard to issues concerning the sanctity and inviolability

15. Michael J. Gorman, *Abortion and the Early Church: Christian, Jewish and Pagan Attitudes in the Greco-Roman World* (New York: Paulist and Downers Grove: InterVarsity, 1982), 49-50; J. B. Lightfoot and J. R. Harmer, *The Apostolic Fathers: Greek Texts and English Translations of Their Writings,* ed. & rev. Michael W. Holmes (Grand Rapids: Baker, 1992), 252-53, 320-21.

of innocent human life, even issues not explicitly mentioned like abortion, the biblical worldview which the first Christians inherited from their Jewish Scriptures not only perdures into the time of the early church, but in fact can be seen as even strengthened. Thus extrabiblical early Christian uses of the Jewish "Two Ways" ethical theory (like the *Didache* and *Epistle of Barnabas*) are more absolute and insistent in prohibiting abortion than are some of their rabbinical 2nd- and 3rd-century contemporaries.

A Catholic Reading of the Biblical Evidence

Finally, if one reads the Bible as a convinced member of the Catholic church, one will spontaneously fill in biblical silences and gaps such as the nonmention of abortion with fundamental Catholic moral principles and the historical tradition of Catholic practice regarding abortion, which goes back to the earliest centuries. When Catholic readers also reflect on the contemporary magisterium's reaffirmation that there are moral absolutes which must be obeyed in all circumstances without exception, not even for "hard cases," and on the principle that "one may not do evil in order to attain good," they would be very slow to treat biblical silence about abortion or any other significant moral issue as a warrant for discerning whether an exception can be made to an apparently absolute prohibition.[16]

For Catholic readers searching the Scriptures about abortion with such preunderstandings from their moral tradition and practice, texts which do not explicitly address abortion can still be quite relevant for illuminating how the biblical worldview and perspective would respond to an issue like abortion. Although it is true that the commandment "You shall not kill" does not answer the question whether abortion is included in the prohibition of killing, the commandment does clearly set some stringent parameters for the further argument over what is permitted. *Pace* Hays, other texts that provide insights into whether the biblical worldview considers and treats the fetus as human

16. On moral absolutes and the illegitimacy of doing evil to attain good, cf. John Paul II, *The Splendor of Truth (Veritatis Splendor)* (Boston: Pauline, 1995), §51-52 on moral absolutes, and §78-81 on not doing evil to attain good.

can at this point legitimately be adduced to support the inclusion of a fetus under the general prohibition against killing innocent human life.[17]

Thus Ps. 139:13-16, by portraying a symbolic world in which God is active in forming human life in the womb, sheds light on abortion, even though it is a poetic rather than propositional statement. Though such passages as this and Jer. 1:5 encompass God's foreknowledge of us even before conception, they certainly include God's care, knowledge, and calling of us within the womb, to which Paul appeals in his own case (Gal. 1:15). In the further light of the treatment in Luke 1 of the conception of Jesus and of how "the babe [John] in my womb" leapt when "the mother of my Lord" appeared before Elizabeth (Luke 1:43-44), which clearly imply the humanity of both Jesus and John in the womb, it is not tendentious to argue that the biblical worldview by the time of the New Testament treats the fetus as a human person. Admittedly, this goes beyond mere historical exegesis of the passage; nor is it yet an argument against abortion; still it certainly provides significant evidence to make that case.[18] It is hard to deny that by the New Testament period the biblical worldview has developed significantly beyond the treatment of the fetus in the law in Exod. 21:22-25 as pertaining to property law. It seems certain that by the time of the New Testament a fetus is spontaneously and customarily regarded as a "babe in the womb" and as a human person for whom God has love and even a vocational calling and plan. If that is so, the step to including abortion as a species under the genus of killing which is forbidden by the fifth commandment is a rather instinctive one.

Conclusion

Comparing my own Catholic perspective to a Protestant one, I have tried to show how differing preunderstandings lead to different applications of Scripture to moral questions. My recommended approach was neither prooftexting nor slavish use of historical criticism. Rather, from my inclusive "both/and" approach to applying Scripture, I recom-

17. Hays, *Moral Vision*, 446-48.
18. Hays, *Moral Vision*, 447-48.

mended situating particular moral questions within a biblical worldview of how God and humans and the rest of material creation interrelate. By respecting the persistent and consistent biblical viewpoint on human beings as images of God and the consequent absolute biblical prohibition against shedding innocent human blood, we could then without prooftexting discuss the relevance of individual passages that mention God's care and calling of humans from the womb, and examples of life in the womb like the interaction in Luke 1 between the two babes in the womb, Jesus and John. We could actualize and apply such passages to new and different situations, like abortion, which are admittedly beyond those original concerns and situations discovered by historical-critical exegesis. Thus we tried to base our responses to abortion questions more holistically and canonically on God's broader biblical revelation of the meaning of human beings as images and potential daughters and sons of God, on God's creating, welcoming, and blessing of new human life, and on God's protection of innocent human life through absolute prohibitions against shedding innocent human blood. Within such a life-affirming biblical context, it was not unwarranted to apply the Bible to our current situation. Within this context and biblical application, it was not unwarranted to argue from the universally accepted major premise that the Bible forbids killing innocent human life, for the double minor premise that life in the womb is human and innocent and loved by God and that therefore abortion is killing innocent human life, to the conclusion that abortion is prohibited.

CHAPTER NINE

Bread of Life in John 6:
Intertextuality and the Unity of Scripture

No matter which side one takes on the seemingly endless argument over the extent of eucharistic emphasis in John 6, one has to admit that a eucharistic reading is not its primary original emphasis.[1] Therefore this chapter will first investigate in John 6 its more foundational christological motifs, namely, how John 6 replaces the Old Testament manna function, which had come over time to be ascribed to the Law, with the Bread that has come down from heaven, which is "eaten" through belief in the Son of man come down from heaven. As in John 4 the Son of man provides living water in order that the Samaritan woman might never thirst, so in John 6 he provides his flesh for eternal life. This chapter's methodological purpose will be to illustrate the dimension of biblical intertextuality and the unity of Scripture in the same John 6 passages that will also provide the basis for our next chapter's discussion of spiritual senses and Catholic eucharistic actualization: the feeding of the 5000, interpreted by Jesus' walking on the water as I AM and his explanatory bread of life dialogues with the crowds and Jews.

Some scholars criticize as naive the use by exegetes of the postmodern concept of intertextuality for intrabiblical interpretation, pointing to the alien and incompatible ideological origins of that term.[2]

---

1. Cf. Raymond E. Brown, *The Gospel According to John (I–XII)* (Garden City: Doubleday, 1966), 272-74.

2. Thomas R. Hatina, "Intertextuality and Historical Criticism in New Testament Studies: Is There a Relationship?" *BibInt* 7 (1999): 28-43.

My use of *intertextuality* must obviously be distinguished from the utter indeterminacy of some of its postmodern meanings and uses, which undermine the referential faith of the church and believers.[3] Still, Catholic theology can learn from postmodern concepts, without uncritically accepting the ideologies from which many of them sprang. Theology can without fear seek the truth which is to be found in any heresy, as my Catholic and humanistic training has always taught me. (This same training defined heresy as an exaggeration of particular aspects of a more extensive truth to the detriment of other important aspects.) For example, within the understanding of intertextuality as interrelationships of particular texts with other texts, as well as within the broader context of language and culture, lies a genuine insight about how all texts have to use conventional language and are related to other texts. Without accepting the total indeterminacy of a deconstructionist form of intertextuality, which would deny any notion of truth or reference by texts to external reality, textual understanding can be enriched by a more nuanced awareness of a text's polyvalent readings and its relationships with other texts.

Components of intertextuality which I would like to appropriate (admittedly eclectically) are the relationship of every text to cultural systems, which encompass language and also other texts. I would like to base my argument on the necessarily conventional nature of all use of language (e.g., conventional Greek vocabulary, grammar, syntax, and genres, plus relationships to previous texts from the same cultural and religious background). It is reasonable to hold that every text utilizes and is related to other texts in its cultural context, and in turn makes its own contribution to meaning in that context. Michael Fishbane contends that intertextuality is particularly pertinent to canonical texts — that closed canon and intertextuality are in fact functional corollaries. He points out how fixed canonical content freed the rabbis for almost limitless intertextual praxis on this corpus.[4]

My use of intertextuality is not the same as literary influence,

---

3. For an informative survey of the history and practitioners of intertextual approaches, see Thaïs E. Morgan, "Is There an Intertext in This Text? Literary and Interdisciplinary Approaches to Intertextuality," *American Journal of Semiotics* 3/4 (1985): 1-40.

4. Michael Fishbane, "Types of Biblical Intertextuality," *VTSup* 80 (2000): 44; see whole paper, 39-44.

which focuses principally on diachronic causality or priority (such as the influence of Old Testament intertexts on New Testament texts). Intertextuality studies also the synchronic relationship of both Old Testament intertext and New Testament text within a common interpretive matrix and corpus of texts (in this case, the biblical canon). As a result, contemporary readers can mutually interpret both texts by each other, regardless of chronological priority. This seems to me to be also inherent in the patristic and traditional notion of the unity of Scripture (which Vatican II reaffirmed without explaining). Paul Dinter approvingly cites "an ancient hermeneutical insight: the Bible can be read as a self-glossing book."[5] However, intertextuality is not just a clever word game or playing with texts. One also asks, What are the purposes and uses of intertextuality? What points are being made by using earlier or traditional or biblical words, phrases, and texts?[6]

A convenient starting point for this treatment of intertextuality is Daniel Boyarin's three senses for intertextuality: (1) texts comprise mosaics of conscious and unconscious elements from all discourses that the author heard or read; (2) texts are implicit or explicit dialogues with the past; (3) since all texts are composed with cultural codes, reality is always represented by texts that refer to other texts through language, which in turn is understood as "a construction of the historical, ideological, and social system of a people."[7] In other words, all written texts, including biblical texts, are necessarily intertextual in that they are constructed using preestablished language and cultural codes which were used in and influenced by other written texts. Excessive originality by a particular author would involve such an idiosyncratic use of language, including neologisms and "unorthodox" grammar, as to be virtually unreadable.

In this sense, some moderate postmodern perspectives in which all

---

5. Paul E. Dinter, "The Once and Future Text," in *The Quest for Context and Meaning: Studies in Biblical Intertextuality in Honor of James A. Sanders,* ed. Craig A. Evans and Shemaryahu Talmon. Biblical Interpretation 28 (Leiden: Brill, 1997), 385, quoting Gerald L. Bruns, "Midrash and Allegory: The Beginnings of Scriptural Interpretation," in *The Literary Guide to the Bible,* ed. Robert Alter and Frank Kermode (Cambridge: Belknap, 1987), 626.

6. Patricia K. Tull, "The Rhetoric of Recollection," *VTSup* 80 (2000): 71-78.

7. Dinter, "The Once and Future Text," 386, citing Daniel Boyarin, *Intertextuality and the Reading of Midrash* (Bloomington: Indiana University Press, 1990), 12-14.

texts are related to other texts (referred to as intertexts) can apply to biblical texts in relation to other biblical texts. These insights could apply not only to antecedent texts which may have influenced the present texts: biblical scholars commonly understand the New Testament to make heavy use of Old Testament antecedents, models, type scenes and other types, themes, special vocabulary, etc. Intertextuality goes beyond such historical approaches. It might also apply simply to the mutual influence on contemporary readers of all the relevant texts in the corpus or canon of texts. (E.g., in John 6, intertextuality can apply to Exodus 16, Psalm 78, and other Old Testament manna and wisdom texts, in mutual relationship with the feeding of the 5000 and bread of life dialogue in John 6.)

In biblical studies, it seems useful to apply intertextuality in circumstances in which both Old Testament and New Testament (or any earlier and later biblical) texts function as units within a corpus of written texts, as well as contribute to the written language and cultural codes by which we interpret all texts. For example, as my first chapter pointed out, a New Testament text is now part of the same canonical corpus as an Old Testament text, even in the more specialized respect of being part of a unified Christian canon of mutually interpreting biblical texts. Therefore the Christian interpreter can legitimately understand an Old Testament text differently because of a New Testament text. Consequently, Exodus texts concerning manna take on new meaning for Christian readers in light of New Testament intertexts like the sixth chapter of the Gospel of John. Historical approaches primarily focus on plausible influence from earlier texts to later texts, which one might reasonably argue that they might have affected. But the intertextual, intrabiblical interpretive approach which I recommend should also permit influence on one's interpretation of related Old Testament and New Testament passages to flow in both directions, Old Testament passage throwing light on the New Testament text, and New Testament on Old Testament text.

Interpretation of books in light of the canon can also be correlated with different readers of those books. Francis J. Moloney provides a useful explanation: implied readers are an aspect of the text as written, but the text is also written with a view toward intended (original) readers. Once a text is incorporated into the canon, it is then also aimed at subsequent real readers into the indefinite future and in any place or culture.[8] Exodus and the consequent Old Testament traditions about the manna as bread from heaven provide insight into Jesus' feeding of the 5000 in John 6, whereas John 6 shows the deeper meaning (including spiritual sense?) for Christians of the Old Testament passages and traditions.

Many biblical allusions to manna and bread of life traditions (especially in wisdom and legal traditions) support both John 6's Christology and its eucharistic connotations and applications. As we look closely at the hints and signals imbedded in John 6, we will find a striking example of innerbiblical links and allusions which implies and illustrates how the Johannine author presupposed the unity of his Scripture. On the foundations of how biblical texts (in this case, John 6) exploit and utilize previous biblical texts, we can build an argument for similar utilization of the entire Christian canon in the same perspective of the unity of Scripture as at least continuing one trajectory set by the biblical texts themselves.

Clues in John 6: Feeding of the 5000

Let us begin as usual by looking for clues in the text to be interpreted, John 6. The first textual clue to provide our exegetical context is the reference in John 6:2 to the crowd following Jesus "because they saw the signs which he did on those who were diseased" (RSV). Another clue is the narrator's apparently extraneous explanatory aside, "Now the Passover, the feast of the Jews, was at hand" (6:4 RSV). The readers are alerted to evaluate signs that Jesus would do in light of previous biblical signs, especially those belonging to the Passover time and setting. The context is also established as primarily Jewish (e.g., as relating more to Jewish than to docetic controversies).

Jesus' test question, "Where are we to buy breads *(artous)* that these may eat?" (John 6:5), and the eventual response that five barley breads and two small fish are hopelessly inadequate to feed so many, together recall biblical passages of God's people being fed in the wilderness, and Elisha's feeding of 100 men with only 20 small barley loaves (2 Kgs. 4:42-

8. Francis J. Moloney, "The Function of Prolepsis in the Interpretation of John 6," in *Critical Readings of John 6,* ed. R. Alan Culpepper. Biblical Interpretation 22 (Leiden: Brill, 1997), 129-48, esp. 135-36, n. 22.

44). The huge increase in number of people (from Elisha's 100 to 5000) seems to refer more to God's feeding the whole Israelite people in the wilderness after the exodus, which is the event explicitly recalled in the Passover feast of the Jews (John 6:4), than to Elisha.

Jesus' handling of the breads is narrated in language that also recalls the Christian Eucharist. Jesus alone is portrayed as taking the loaves (breads), giving thanks *(eucharistēsas),* and giving them to those reclining to eat, just as in the Synoptic Gospels he is shown doing at the eucharistic Last Supper for his disciples (which is not recounted in the FG), and in contrast to the Synoptic versions of this feeding account, where more plausibly the disciples are shown distributing the breads to the 5000 men. The Johannine narrator goes on to mention that after the people were "filled" (John 6:12), Jesus told his disciples, "Gather up the fragments (*klasmata,* later a technical term for the eucharistic breads broken and distributed) left over, that nothing may be lost" (or "perish"; cf. 3:16, "that those who believe in the only Son may not perish"; 6:27, "labor not for food which perishes"; 6:39, "lose nothing of what [the Father] gave me").

The gathered *klasmata* filled 12 baskets from the five barley "breads" (no mention of the fish) which were left over by those who had eaten (*bebrōkosin,* the same root as food, *brōsis,* which will be emphasized in the bread of life discourse to follow, esp. in John 6:27: "Do not labor for the food which perishes, but for the food which endures to eternal life, which the Son of man will give to you . . ."). The language is filled with eucharistic references and allusions to feeding the entire people of God, symbolized by the 12 tribes and the number of 12 baskets. The narrator ends with a note that the men (generic *anthrōpoi*) saw the sign which Jesus did, which led them to conclude (in comparison to Moses and Elisha), "This is indeed the prophet who is to come into the world" (v. 14 RSV). Their attempt to make Jesus king demonstrates how the observers missed the point of the sign, so that Jesus is forced to withdraw from them.

Jesus' Walk on the Sea

The next section, John 6:16-21, the encounter on the sea, is a transition passage introduced by references to Jesus' disciples going by sea toward

Capernaum, which is where the bread of life discourse will take place. These place references unify the three sections of John 6 — the feeding of the 5000, Jesus and the disciples on the sea, and the bread of life discourse which provides the Johannine explanation of the first two. The Johannine version of the sea crossing is less focused on the struggle of the disciples and more on Jesus' walking on the water than the Synoptic versions. It emphasizes Jesus' calming of their fear with "I AM" when they see him walking on the water, and their miraculous arrival at the land toward which they were headed (v. 21).[9] Whatever might be the extent to which this story is a theophany or epiphany, it plainly utilizes a biblical perspective in which Jesus walks on the sea as only Yahweh is shown to do in the Old Testament (e.g., Ps. 77:19 RSV: "Thy way was through the sea, thy path through the great waters; yet thy footprints were unseen"; cf. Ps. 107:23-30; contrast 2 Macc. 5:21 on the arrogance of Antiochus, "thinking in his arrogance that he could sail on the land and walk on the sea").[10] The fact that in this account Jesus also makes use of the same "I am" as does God at the burning bush (Exodus 3) lends additional plausibility to arguments for theophanous aspects within a biblical intertextual context. The passage also more sharply distinguishes the crowd, who misinterpreted the feeding of the 5000 as a sign that Jesus was a prophet like Moses to be made king, from the disciples in the boat, who gathered the 12 baskets of fragments *(klasmata)* and then witnessed Jesus walking on the sea and identifying himself as "I AM." This difference in experience helps explain the different reactions to the bread of life discussion, first by the crowd, then by a broader group of disciples, and finally by the particularly preeminent Twelve (John 6:66-71).

Bread of Life Discussion

The "bread of life discourse" is actually not a single discourse but a series of several questions and reactions from the crowd (and later the

---

9. Charles H. Giblin, "The Miraculous Crossing of the Sea (John 6.16-21)," *NTS* 29 (1983): 96-103.

10. For arguments that Jesus' walking on the water was a theophany, see Francis J. Moloney, *Signs and Shadows: Reading John 5–12* (Minneapolis: Fortress, 1996), 39-40; and Brown, *John I–XII*, 254-56.

disciples) with responses and discourses by Jesus. Some of the interlocutors' questions are clearly beside the point; others reveal the misunderstanding expected of outsiders. Several times, Jesus' answers are accentuated by the solemn declaration format, "Amen, Amen, I say to you" (John 6:26, 32, 47, 53). This "Amen, Amen" pronouncement as solemn introduction to a declaration appears in the Greek Scriptures only in the FG, and only on the lips of Jesus (25 times, plus one unrelated instance as a prayer response in a Codex Sinaiticus variant on the reply to Tobias's nuptial prayer in Tob. 8:8).

Jesus' first use of "Amen, Amen I say to you" in John 6:26 sharply confronts the crowd's irrelevant question, "Rabbi, when did you come here?" (v. 25), and accuses them of seeking Jesus not because of signs but because "you ate the breads and were filled" (v. 26). When the crowds challenge Jesus about what sign he might do that they might believe in him (v. 30), ironically citing the manna in the desert as an example, Jesus uses a midrashic form ("it was not X . . . but Y") to correct them: "Amen, Amen I say to you, it was not Moses who gave you the bread from heaven, but my Father gives you the true bread from heaven" (v. 32, my literal version). After rebuking the Jewish murmuring in v. 41 (which recalls the desert generation in Exodus), Jesus introduces a new and more challenging level of discourse: Amen, Amen I say to you, "he who believes has eternal life. I am the bread of life" (vv. 47-48 RSV). The last straw for Jewish patience was Jesus' solemn response to their protest, "How can this man give us flesh to eat?" (v. 52): Amen, Amen I say to you, "unless you eat the flesh of the Son of man and drink his blood, you have no life in you . . ." (v. 53).

The vigorous debate about whether, how, and to what extent a second eucharistic section of the interchange supplements an initial focus on wisdom under the biblical categories of manna and bread from heaven has the useful result of highlighting several levels of biblical images and allusions in this dialogue.[11] To the more commonly acknowledged references to both wisdom and Eucharist as bread from heaven to be eaten, Joseph A. Grassi adds an important third biblical referent which solves some of the problems in acknowledging eucharistic allusions here. For all the canonical eucharistic accounts have Jesus invit-

---

11. See the fine history of the debate over wisdom and eucharistic elements in this dialogue in Brown, *John I-XII*, 272-74.

ing his followers to eat his body *(sōma)*, not his flesh *(sarx)*. Grassi focuses on the frequent references to Passover and to the Passover lamb, and on the relationship between this dialogue and the first and ultimate Johannine signs of water-to-wine at Cana and the flow of blood and water on the cross, which have been acknowledged but not incorporated into this controversy over eating Jesus' "flesh" vs. "body."[12]

A possible reason why *flesh* and not *body* is used is the applicability of the former term to eating the flesh of Jesus viewed *as the Passover Lamb* of God. This would help explain why there are so many intrusive Johannine references to Passover. John 2:13 and 23 emphasize a Passover setting for Jesus' cleansing of the temple, which is the next major event after the Cana sign and a direct foreshadowing of Jesus' death and resurrection (2:18-19, 21: "The Jews then said to him, 'What sign have you to show us for doing this?' [cf. 6:30]. Jesus answered them, 'Destroy this temple, and in three days I will raise it up.' . . . But he spoke of the temple of his body" [RSV]).

The next FG reference to Passover is John 6:4, in the narrator's introduction to this entire chapter. The remaining Passover references in the FG provide the immediate setting for Jesus' passion (11:55; 12:1; 13:1) and for dating of particular events in Jesus' passion (18:28, 39). Most important for and related to the Passover is the peculiar Johannine dating of the passion as occurring on "the day of Preparation of the Passover" (19:14 RSV), which was the day when the lambs for the Passover were slaughtered. Recall that the first testimony to Jesus, that by the Baptist, was that Jesus is the "Lamb of God, who takes away the sin of the world" (1:29 RSV; cf. v. 36). This emphasis on Jesus as Lamb of God is combined with the Johannine correlation of Jesus' crucifixion with the day the Passover lambs were slaughtered (19:14), and with the insistent witness at Jesus' crucifixion that blood and water flowed from the crucified and pierced Jesus (19:34-35), whose bones were not broken in accordance with rubrics for the Passover lamb (19:33, esp. v. 36 citing Exod. 12:46; cf. LXX Ps. 34:21 [Heb. 33:20], the Lord protecting the bones of the righteous from being broken).

I suggest that this emphasis on Jesus as Passover Lamb makes sense of the otherwise apparently unmotivated introduction of *flesh* in place

12. Joseph A. Grassi, "Eating Jesus' Flesh and Drinking His Blood: The Centrality and Meaning of John 6:51-58," *BTB* 17/1 (1987): 24-30.

of the eucharistic term *body:* "I am the living bread which came down from heaven . . . *and the bread which I shall give for the life of the world is my flesh*" (John 6:51 RSV, emphasis mine). This mention of *flesh* is often considered the first distinct eucharistic reference in this dialogue, even though we have already noted that *body* would have carried a more overt eucharistic allusion. However, if this allusion involves Jesus' reference to himself as Lamb of God, whose flesh is eaten in a Passover setting, it makes sense of Jesus' identification of the bread which he will give as his flesh. When the Jews further ask how this man can give them his flesh to eat, Jesus only reemphasizes his point: "Amen, Amen, I say to you, unless you eat the flesh of the Son of man and drink his blood, you shall not have life in you" (v. 53). The Son of man who has come down from heaven and will be returning there (v. 62) can give his flesh to eat as the *Passover Lamb* of God who takes away the sin of the world (cf. 1:29).

The parallel reference in John 6:53 to blood can be correlated with the forceful witness in 19:34-35 about the flow of blood and water from the pierced side of the Lamb whose bones were not broken in accordance with rubrics for eating the Passover lamb (19:36). That witness to the flow of blood and water from the side of the crucified Jesus is emphasized as true testimony, "that you also may believe" (19:35 RSV). That testimony is further confirmed in the first letter of John: "There are three witnesses, the Spirit, the water, and the blood; and these three agree" (1 John 5:8 RSV).

However, it seems that the additional expression about drinking Jesus' blood needs the further eucharistic setting to make sense. (For Israelites did not drink the blood of the Passover lamb, although by placing it as a sign on their doorposts they did save their lives.) It is true that Jesus' drinking sour wine on the cross is portrayed as an act of obedience to the Father (cf. John 18:11: "Jesus said to Peter, 'Put your sword into its sheath; shall I not drink the cup which the Father has given me?'" [RSV]) and can be contrasted with drinking the miraculous good wine at Cana. It is also true that wisdom traditions as well as eucharistic accounts emphasize both eating and drinking. Still, the repulsive image of drinking Jesus' blood seems a bit intense for most portrayals of Wisdom inviting disciples to eat and drink at her feast. In the end, only eucharistic references seem to adequately account for this reference to drinking Jesus' blood.

A possible stumbling block to this Passover interpretation of eating the flesh of God's Lamb, Jesus, is the negative use of *flesh* in John 6:63: "It is the spirit that gives life, the flesh is of no avail; the words that I have spoken to you are spirit and life" (RSV). However, that negative contrast between flesh and spirit occurs right after Jesus' challenge to the murmuring disciples for being offended at his insistence on eating him as bread that gives eternal life (v. 58): "Then what if you were to see the Son of man ascending where he was before?" (v. 62 RSV). The words and spiritual teaching of Jesus' ultimate ascension put all preliminary worldly and material matters, even eating Jesus' (Passover Lamb or eucharistic) flesh, in perspective. The spiritual truth of Jesus' ascension as Son of man to where he was before he became flesh (1:1, 14; 17:24) is needed as the context for understanding Passover or eucharistic eating of Jesus' flesh, as well as wisdom connotations of believing in Jesus as bread from heaven.

In other words, eating Jesus' flesh must be understood in its FG context by reference to faith in the glorification (via death and resurrection-ascension) of the Son of man back to the Father from whence he came. The reference to scandal at the Son of man ascending where he was before (John 6:62) and the additional location of this controversy over eating Jesus' flesh in the synagogue at Capernaum (v. 59) both hint that the obstacle to faith more directly relates to Jewish beliefs than to docetism: to their inability to believe that the human Jesus came from heaven and was preexistent Word and Son of God made flesh.[13]

In short, eating Jesus' flesh as Passover Lamb supplies an intermediate exegetical step: first is the interpretation of eating bread from heaven as having faith in Jesus as God's Word (and wisdom) made flesh (1:14) and as Son of man come down from heaven; second is understanding "eating Jesus' flesh" as referring to Jesus as Passover Lamb whose bones are unbroken and whose blood was visibly poured out (for us) at his death; third is consideration of eating bread from heaven as the physical (sacramental) eating and drinking involved in Eucharist.

---

13. Cf. Ludger Schenke, "The Johannine Schism and the 'Twelve' (John 6:60-71)," in Culpepper, *Critical Readings of John 6*, 216, who argues that the issue is Jesus' coming in flesh (John 1:14) and ascending back to where he was before (6:62), both of which offend Jewish presuppositions.

As we have maintained, the primary Catholic exegetical instinct is not to choose among these (either/or) but to incorporate them all (both/and). But such an instinct also implies and relies on a strong sense of intertextual biblical association and of unity among many layers of Scripture, both Old and New Testaments. These intertextual senses of Scripture's unity are not later inventions by Catholics; we have tried to demonstrate their presence already in the FG.

Further Insights from Isaiah 55

Michael Riffaterre provides a helpful model for understanding the complexity of intertextuality beyond the mere influence of an earlier text on a later text: the theorization that a reader gains insight into a text (T) through an intertext (T) with the help of an interpretant (T).[14] To understand the text of John 6 in light of its commonly recognized intertexts, Exodus 16 and Psalm 78 (plus other Old Testament and intertestamental manna traditions), we can use Diana Swancutt's insight into the role of Isaiah 55 in John 6 to apply Riffaterre's model of an interpretant.[15] From her initial insight, let us use Isaiah 55 as an interpretant text to help fill gaps between the "eating Jesus" text and its exodus and manna intertexts. In addition to the influence of Exodus 16 and Psalm 78 and manna traditions, Isaiah 55 provides further insight into how John 6 utilizes and applies Exodus manna types and figures in presenting Jesus' invitation to eat his flesh.

Two facts add plausibility to the possibility that Isaiah 55 actually influenced the composition of John 6: the citation in John 6:45 of the immediately preceding section of Isaiah (Isa. 54:13); and the insights that key elements of this passage (which was so important among early Christians) facilitate the linking of otherwise unrelated components in the bread-from-heaven controversy. The following verses from Isaiah 55 seem particularly apropos: Isa. 55:1, "every one who thirsts, come to the

14. Cited in Morgan, *American Journal of Semiotics* 3/4 (1985): 26.

15. Diana M. Swancutt, "Hungers Assuaged by the Bread from Heaven: 'Eating Jesus' as Isaian Call to Belief: The Confluence of Isaiah 55 and Psalm 78 (77) in John 6.22-71," in *Early Christian Interpretation of the Scriptures of Israel: Investigations and Proposals,* ed. Craig A. Evans and James A. Sanders. JSNTSup 148. SSEJC 5 (Sheffield: Sheffield Academic, 1997), 218-51.

waters"; v. 2, "why do you spend your money for that which is not bread, and your labor for that which does not satisfy?"; v. 6, "Seek the LORD while he may be found, call upon him while he is near . . ."; and vv. 10-11, "For as the rain and the snow come down from heaven, and return not thither but water the earth, making it bring forth and sprout, giving seed to the sower and bread to the eater, so shall my word be that goes forth from my mouth; it shall not return to me empty, but it shall accomplish that which I purpose, and prosper in the thing for which I sent it" (RSV).

The invitation to satisfy one's thirst in Isa. 55:1 recalls the biblical pattern of Wisdom offering to provide food and drink, which in turn is grounded in the desert traditions of manna and water from the rock for God's people in the wilderness. Although the focus in John 6 is more on eating the bread from heaven than on satisfying thirst, the later verse, John 7:37, where Jesus invites any one who thirsts to come to him and drink, is plausibly related to the invitation to drink in Isa. 55:1. The next Isaian verse, 55:2, receives more explicit treatment in John 6. "Why do you spend your money for that which is not bread, and your labor for that which does not satisfy?" (RSV). The LXX Isaian word for labor, *mochthos,* is not from the same "root" for work as is emphasized in John 6 *(ergon),* and emphasizes more than John 6 the strenuousness of the labor; but the main point of comparison is close enough, as is the use of the same root for being filled or satisfied (Isa. 53:2 LXX, *eis plēsmonēn;* John 6:12 *eneplēsthēsan).* Also note a similar statement by Jesus about not working for the right kind of food in John 6:27, "Do not labor [work, *ergazesthe*] for the food which perishes, but for the food which endures to eternal life, which the Son of man will give to you. . . . Then they said to him, 'What must we do, to be doing [working, *ergazōmetha*] the works [*erga*] of God?'" (vv. 27-28 RSV). The invitation in Isaiah 55 relates several components of the bread of life controversy in John 6: Jesus offers food (bread) and drink that endure for eternal life, unlike the manna which perishes. This bread is purely a gift — instead of having to work for food like manna, the Jewish interlocutors are simply offered this enduring bread (John 6:27). In response to the question of what they must do to be working the works of God (6:28), Jesus answers "that you believe in him whom he [God] has sent" (6:29b RSV). Metaphors of eating bread here apply to the act of faith in Jesus as sent by God: working the works of God is to believe in the one whom God sent.

Three other verses from Isaiah 55 also seem particularly relevant to the FG, and also to John 6. The exhortation to "Seek the LORD while he may be found" (Isa. 55:6) may well provide background connotations to what the crowd in fact did before this bread of life conversation (John 6:24), even if they sought him for the wrong reasons (6:26: "Truly, truly, I say to you, you seek me, not because you saw signs, but because you ate your fill of the loaves" RSV). This exchange about their seeking Jesus leads directly into Jesus' invitation to labor not for bread that perishes but that remains unto eternal life (vv. 27-28).

The comparison in Isa. 55:10-11 of God's efficacious word to rain that accomplishes its mission also has clear resonances, both to the overall pattern in the FG of the Word sent from the Father and to the bread-from-heaven controversy in John 6. As the rain comes from heaven and does not return to heaven before watering the earth and giving bread to the eater (LXX *arton eis brōsin*, lit., "bread for eating"), so the word that goes forth from God's mouth will not return to God empty, but accomplish or finish *(telesthēi)* what God intended (Isa. 55:10-11), as Jesus declared God's work accomplished or finished before dying on the cross: "Jesus, knowing that all was now finished *(tetelestai),*" declared his thirst "to fulfill *(teleiōthēi)* the scripture" (John 19:28 RSV); after drinking the vinegar he declared, "It is finished *(tetelestai)*" (v. 30).

As an example of an "interpretant" third text that links with and throws light on a text (John 6) and its intertexts (Exod. 16; Ps. 78; and manna and wisdom traditions), Isaiah 55 has proven quite illuminating. The invitation in Isaiah 55 to all who thirst to come and receive both drink and satisfying food or bread corresponds to the initial dynamics of the Johannine discussion of bread from heaven. The Isaian exhortation not to waste one's labor on what fails to satisfy throws light on Jesus' admonition not to labor for the bread that perishes but for that which remains. The Isaian exhortation to "hear, that your soul may live" (Isa. 55:3 RSV) and references to "seek the LORD while he may be found" (v. 6 RSV), as well as allusions to God's ways and thoughts being incomprehensibly higher than human ways and thoughts (vv. 8-9) all prepare for the Isaian assurance that God's word does unfailingly finish or accomplish that for which God sent it (vv. 10-11). This Isaiah "interpretant" text undergirds and unpacks some of the key dynamics both in the FG as a whole and in this chapter, which begins with Jesus' feeding the 5000 and ends with this interchange about Jesus as the bread from heaven. Although Isaiah 55 more immediately pertains to the wisdom and basic christological senses of "bread from heaven," it also applies to any actualization of this bread from heaven, including a eucharistic one.

Conclusion

The dialogue with Judaism in the controversies over the bread from heaven in John 6, which we have elucidated through intertextual use of biblical texts, types, and images understood as parts of a unified Scripture, continues the pattern which already appears in the Johannine prologue (John 1:16-18). The prologue had already claimed that "from his fullness we have all received, grace upon [succeeding] grace" (*charin anti charitos*, v. 16). It had explained this succession of "graces" (note that both receive positive evaluation, as when Jesus reminds the Samaritan woman in John 4 that salvation comes from the Jews) by the following contrast: "For the law was given through Moses; grace and truth came through Jesus Christ" (6:17 RSV).

This contrast is deepened in the final claim of the prologue: "No one has ever seen God; the only Son, who is in the bosom of the Father, he has made him known" (John 1:18 RSV). Here in John 6 the exodus and manna traditions of eating bread from heaven, which Judaism had applied to the law and its observance, are compared as "food which perishes" to the true bread from heaven. John 6 invites the Jewish interlocutors of Jesus to eat this true bread, which is the flesh of Jesus, and explains this "eating" as believing in the Son of man whom the Father has sent from heaven (6:29, 40). In other words, just as the prologue replaces the law given by Moses with grace and truth through Jesus Christ who alone makes God known, so John 6 replaces the Old Testament function of law as the manna or bread from heaven with believing in Jesus, whom God sent from heaven.

When this basic christological understanding of bread from heaven in John 6 is combined with what most of the audience would perceive as eucharistic language about eating Jesus' flesh and drinking his blood, the primary emphasis on faith in Jesus can be perceived with justification by Catholic readers as experienced also or even preeminently in their eucharistic celebrations. For example, Johannes Beutler even makes the exegetical observation that Eucharist was an important concrete way that faith in Jesus was practiced in the community.[16] To this eucharistic actualization of John 6 the next chapter will now turn.

16. Johannes Beutler, "The Structure of John 6," in Culpepper, *Critical Readings of John 6,* 126 (cf. 119).

CHAPTER TEN

Feeding the 5000 in John 6 and the Eucharist: Spiritual Senses and Actualization

Catholics and Eucharist

The previous chapter continued offering personal suggestions for actualizing and applying Scripture in a Catholic manner, along lines suggested by Vatican II. It focused on John 6 from the perspective of intertextuality and the unity of Scripture. It found in the progression from Jesus' feeding of the 5000, to his walking on the sea as I AM, to the bread from heaven controversies a very strong christological affirmation that Jesus, who as Son of Man was sent down from heaven by his Father, is now the bread from heaven, which replaces the previous bread-from-heaven function of the law. Those who ate the manna in the wilderness (and by implication, those who ate the bread from heaven in the form of the law) continued to die. Those who eat this new bread from heaven which is Jesus' flesh will have eternal life (John 6:27, 40; esp. 47-51).

Although the christological emphasis seems the main point of John 6, the passage also has a fairly universally recognized second motif. That subordinate strain is expressed in incontestable eucharistic allusions and language, if not actual eucharistic teaching. This chapter will look again at John 6, this time asking about spiritual senses of Scripture and actualization of John 6, especially with respect to the Eucharist.

A Catholic eucharistic actualization of John 6 seems particularly applicable in view of an increasing problem for Catholics in North

America and Europe — a growing shortage of priests, which is resulting in priestless parishes without regular eucharistic celebrations, if not in parish closings or mergers. Ordinary Catholic people need and are hungry for the Bread of Life that is Christ. As the very pastoral language suggests, one of the main jobs of pastors is to feed their flock, as Jesus commissioned Peter in John 21 to feed his lambs and sheep. For centuries Catholics have held that one of the main tasks of the church's pastors is to feed their flock with Jesus himself, especially in the Eucharist. They have taken quite seriously, even literally, Jesus' challenge that comes at the climax of his bread of life discourse in John 6, "Truly, truly [Amen, Amen], I say to you, unless you eat the flesh of the Son of man and drink his blood, you have no life in you; he who eats my flesh and drinks my blood has eternal life, and I will raise him up at the last day" (John 6:53-54 RSV). Whatever the original sense of these verses, from very early on the Catholic church has given them a eucharistic interpretation.

Therefore this chapter will first briefly review what is meant by literal and spiritual senses of Scripture and by actualizing it for contemporary believers. It will address some of the distances that have to be overcome in actualizing original meanings of a text for later and different audiences and cultural settings, including hermeneutics of suspicion. Then it will recapitulate the most relevant elements in the text of John 6, before seeking their spiritual senses and actualizing and applying them to the Catholic Eucharist.

Spiritual Senses and Actualization of Scripture

To test the concepts of the spiritual senses and actualization and application of Scripture beyond historical-critical results, therefore, we return especially to the feeding of the 5000 in John 6. In this case, our search for the spiritual sense of that miraculous feeding is made easier by the fact that John 6 is itself our primary guide to its spiritual sense. For John 6 already unpacks the meaning of the feeding sign by narrating the theophany of Jesus as I AM walking on the water and by his bread of life discussion. However, that very discourse has been a battleground between Catholic and Protestant interpreters over whether and to what extent the Eucharist is the focus of the discussion and is implied in the feeding of the 5000.[1] First, I would like to recall some points made earlier from a previous article that clarify what is meant by the literal and spiritual senses of Scripture, as well as the relationship between the spiritual senses of Scripture and the actualization and application of Scripture to one's own life and ministry.[2]

Historical Criticism, "Literal Sense" of Scripture, and "Author's Intention"

As noted in my first chapter, American Catholic biblical scholars not uncommonly identify the traditional term the "literal sense of Scripture" with the results of historical criticism. I raised the question whether this identification is inaccurate and may even have serious negative pastoral consequences. We also considered how perhaps the most serious pastoral consequence of identifying literal sense with historical-critical reading is that it tends to make professional exegetes, not bishops and the church's magisterium, the official "gatekeepers" of the literal sense, which everyone agrees is the most basic and indispensable of the various senses of Scripture.

It is important to remember that even Vatican II documents are more than 35 years old and that, in some areas, scholarly awareness has progressed beyond what was known or at least generally discussed in the mid-1960s. Vatican II's 1965 document on revelation, *Dei Verbum* (§12), relies on an emphasis, which was common at that time, on the human author's intention as a key factor for describing the human as-

---

1. Cf. esp. Maarten J. J. Menken, "John 6:51c-58: Eucharist or Christology?" in R. Alan Culpepper, ed., *Critical Readings of John 6* (Leiden: Brill, 1997), 183-204; Vernon Ruland, "Sign and Sacrament: John's Bread of Life Discourse (Chapter 6)," *Int* 18 (1964): 450-62. See also James D. G. Dunn, "John VI — A Eucharistic Discourse?" *NTS* 17 (1971): 328-38; Heinrich Schlier, *Das Ende der Zeit: Exegetische Aufsätze und Vorträge III* (Freiburg: Herder, 1971), ch. 6: "Zur Christologie des Johannesevangeliums," 85-101; and ch. 7: "Johannes 6 und das johanneische Verständnis der Eucharistie," 102-23; Edward J. Kilmartin, "Liturgical Influence on John 6," *CBQ* 22 (1960): 183-91; Francis J. Moloney, "When Is John Talking about Sacraments?" *ABR* 30 (October 1982): 10-33.

2. Parts of this chapter also use my article in a new journal, "Ethical Actualization of Scripture: Approaches toward a Prolife Reading," *Fides Quaerens Intellectum* 1 (2001): 67-94.

pects of God's biblical revelation. "However, since God speaks in Sacred Scripture through men in human fashion, (6) the interpreter of Sacred Scripture, in order to see clearly what God wanted to communicate to us, should carefully investigate *what meaning the sacred writers really intended,* and what God wanted to manifest by means of their words" (emphasis mine).

As mentioned in my first chapter, since 1965 secular literary critics have found the notion of authorial intention more and more problematic, raising difficulties to which they refer as "the intentional fallacy."[3] Private intentions of an author are not ordinarily detectable by other interpreters. All that is available for examination or scrutiny is what the author actually wrote, regardless of the extent to which those words correspond to what he or she intended to express. For example, when challenged over something which they wrote, living authors might sometimes even apologize, claiming that they did not mean to express themselves as negatively as their words implied.

We also saw that another way to view the relationship between a text and its author is that once texts are written, they take on an existence that no longer depends on the intentions and meanings of their authors. One example is how over time the meaning of the words which are written might change, or how the authors might change their minds. A written text is instinctively interpreted not primarily by trying to ascertain what the author may have meant to express, but by examining what the written words in their cultural context conventionally mean to readers who know the accepted usage of the vocabulary and its grammar. Perhaps with respect to this reservation, *Dei Verbum* balances the writers' intentions with what they actually wrote: "The interpreter must investigate what meaning the sacred writer *intended to express and actually expressed in particular circumstances*" (emphasis mine).[4]

As a way to ascertain "what meaning the sacred writers really intended," *Dei Verbum* §12 advises the interpreter to attend to the literary forms of their time and culture: "due attention must be paid to the *cus-*

3. Cf. esp. E. D. Hirsch, Jr., *Validity in Interpretation* (New Haven: Yale University Press, 1967).

4. *DV* §12; cf. Raymond E. Brown and Sandra M. Schneiders, "Hermeneutics," *NJBC,* 1148.

tomary and characteristic styles of feeling, speaking and narrating which prevailed at the time of the sacred writer and to the patterns men normally employed at that period in their everyday dealings with one another" (emphasis mine). The historical meaning of words, phrases, idioms, genres, etc., in the time and culture of the original writing provides objective criteria for trying to approximate the original meaning of the text.

As was mentioned in my first chapter, because of developments in literary criticism and hermeneutics since 1965, contemporary authors like Marcel Dumais now suggest further qualifying this approach to the notion of a literal sense. Dumais argues against identifying literal meaning with authorial intention or even original meaning. He claims that this notion of literal meaning arose from romantic views going back to Schleiermacher and Dilthey. He refers to critiques of this notion by Hirsch, Heidegger, Gadamer, and Ricoeur, and by literary and reader-response critics.[5]

Dumais challenges the notion of a single literal meaning in the mind of the author as belonging to romantic and modernist Enlightenment perspectives, which more recent and postmodern thinkers no longer embrace. He emphasizes instead what has become a common postmodern notion, that all writing, including even Scripture's literal meaning, incorporates a plurality of meanings or multiplicity of significations. Therefore, Dumais maintains that Scripture's literal meaning incorporates even the "spiritual sense." For similar reasons he also disputes the common distinction (as notably expressed by Raymond Brown) between *what the Bible meant (equated with the literal sense)* and *what it means (actualization).*[6]

Instead, Dumais proposes that the *spiritual sense is the literal sense of Scripture grasped in its depth.* Under the expression "spiritual meaning" he would designate three realities: (1) the Bible as *word about God,* as a religious text with religious meaning; (2) the Bible as *Word of God,*

5. Marcel Dumais, "Sens de l'Écriture. Réexamen à la lumière de l'herméneutique philosophique et des approches littéraires récentes," *NTS* 45 (1999): 310-31, esp. 311-14. Cf. related hermeneutical discussions in Dumais, "L'Actualisation de l'Écriture: Fondements et procédures," *ScEs* 51 (1999): 27-47; François Martin, "Jésus et la vérité des Écritures," *LumVie* 46/231 (1997): 47-57; Mario Botas, "Entre l'Écriture et le dogme: la Parole de Dieu," *LumVie* 46/231 (1997): 59-70.

6. Dumais, *NTS* 45 (1999): 314-16; Raymond E. Brown, *The Critical Meaning of the Bible* (New York: Paulist, 1981), 23-33.

which requires a predisposition of faith and openness to transcendence and to the Spirit who inspired it, and implies an affirmation of the text's truth and its correspondence to the extratextual reality to which it refers; and (3) the *christological* as the ultimate *meaning of the Old Testament* (for a Christian). Dumais cites the witness of Aquinas and many others to the literal sense being the basis or root of the spiritual.[7] Only the first two realities call for further mention here.

The notion of Scripture as "word *about* God" refers to the observation that God is the ultimate referent around which the Bible as a whole is organized. The world of the text relates especially to God and God's plan for humanity. Because of this, even the literal sense of Scripture is spiritual. But Dumais would prefer to refer to this as the "religious sense" of the Bible, in view of the fact that the Bible is a religious text.[8]

The reading of Scripture as the "Word *of* God" is the kind that is done by a believer (Jewish or Christian). For a Christian believer, the Bible expresses God's presence in the history of Israel and in Jesus. Obviously, to understand Scripture as God's word requires the preunderstanding of faith as well as an openness to the Spirit who inspired Scripture. Faith and the Spirit create an existential link with the world of the text understood as God's word. They enable the referent of the text to be grasped as authentic.

To recognize the spiritual sense of the text also implies the truth of the text, i.e., that the text correctly expresses the extratextual reality to which it refers. Previous knowledge by the reader of this extratextual referent (God and his works) obviously makes it easier for that reader to understand this spiritual meaning of Scripture.[9] This insight seems related to the traditional Thomistic notion of connatural knowledge of God which enables further reading about God to be done with deeper insight.

If Scripture is self-evidently a *religious text with religious meaning,* it seems reasonable that at least aspects of its spiritual sense or of its foreseeable and foreseen actualization and application might be incorporated within its primary literal sense. Insofar as Scripture is not merely a self-contained literary artifact but is meant to refer to extratextual re-

7. Dumais, *NTS* 45 (1999): 329-30.
8. Dumais, *NTS* 45 (1999): 329.
9. Dumais, *NTS* 45 (1999): 329-30.

alities which include spiritual realities (such as God, prayer, and sacraments, as well as concrete believers, communities, and historical activities), it seems arbitrary to rule out a priori all spiritual senses from its literal meaning.

Spiritual Senses and Actualization

To the extent to which the literal meaning of the Scriptures is indeed linked to an "original" meaning put into the text by its (human) author, there is an obvious distance between that world of the text and its authors and our contemporary world. To overcome this temporal, geographical, and cultural distance therefore requires a second hermeneutical step of actualization or application to contemporary situations to make the original meaning significant for today.[10] But we have already considered some problems with an unnuanced distinction between what the text "meant" and what it "means." When the interpretive perspectives of readers are included in the hermeneutical equation, there has to be some "fusion of horizons"[11] between the text and readers. Paul Ricoeur adds reference to a certain *autonomy* which a text once written attains with respect to its writer. As writing, which is able to be read on multiple occasions by many prospective readers, the text as text has a certain distance from its original context of composition and a certain "surplus of meaning" beyond that original composition. When it is written down, its original meaning is decontextualized somewhat from its initial context of composition, which permits it to be recontextualized or appropriated in the reader's different context.[12]

But there is also a second distance to be overcome, that between the text and its readers. To overcome this, Dumais cites Ricouer's reference to a circular process of scientific *explanation* (to protect against readers' projection of their own meanings onto the text) and personal *understanding* by the readers, which tries to integrate an objective dimension of methodological rigor with a subjective dimension of per-

10. Dumais, *NTS* 45 (1999): 315.

11. Hans-Georg Gadamer, *Truth and Method*, ed. Joel Weinsheimer and Donald G. Marshall, 2nd ed. (New York : Continuum, 1988), 306-7.

12. Dumais, *NTS* 45 (1999): 318-19.

sonal implication.[13] In addition, the distance between text and readers can be and has been approached either with understanding or suspicion, and which approach a reader takes will seriously affect how he or she interprets, actualizes, or applies a biblical text.

In other words, in addition to the problem of understanding ancient texts by contemporary readers, we also hear of serious problems for some readers today with accepting a biblical text because it is perceived to contain some bias. Let us briefly consider the hermeneutics both of understanding and suspicion, as well as two implications of the spiritual sense, for overcoming the fundamental distance between text and reader.

Hermeneutics of suspicion is used notably by liberationist and feminist interpretation of texts to account for the bias of those texts, which the interpreters are trying to counteract. For example, interpreters may be suspicious that there is economic bias against lower classes or patriarchal bias against women in the writing of many ancient texts, and therefore they try to adjust for that bias as they read the texts. Indeed, for some sociological studies, there seems an obvious place for at least some limited hermeneutics of suspicion to adjust for bias in the only available sources.

It may also be true in many instances that to arrive at a historically accurate reconstruction of events reported in a historical text, the interpreter has to be alert to the presuppositions and even biases inherent in the human author's recounting of them, and perhaps adjust one's judgment of those events with this in mind. Further, it may be analogously true that ethical or religious directives and opinions expressed in a text might be similarly colored by the author's often unconscious presuppositions or biases, necessitating a similar adjustment in judging their relevance for readers in a different time and cultural context. Thus, for purposes of historical-critical exegesis, historical or cultural reconstructions, sociological analyses of a text understood as belonging to the 1st century and to a culture quite different from that of the readers, there seems an important role for a hermeneutics of suspicion to play, as long as it also allows the text to have its legitimate say.

Nevertheless, the very expression "hermeneutics of suspicion" raises certain problematic questions when readers want to approach

13. Dumais, *NTS* 45 (1999): 319.

Scripture as God's word giving direction to their lives. It is hard to deny that to read with suspicion is to read with defensiveness or sometimes even with hostility: it is to look for bias and error in the expressed positions taken in the *text*, with little readiness to acknowledge that the bias or error might instead be in the *reader*. To read with suspicion seems self-evidently the opposite of reading with an openness to having one's own preconceptions challenged or even changed by the text. To read with suspicion seems self-evidently to deny to the biblical text in fact if not in theory any genuine authority over the reader.

How can one read with suspicion what one sincerely believes is God's word, God's revelation to oneself? If my Creator and God is addressing me in this text, how can I read it with suspicion and not rather from a receptive or even obedient attitude? How can I read the Bible with suspicion and yet allow it to be what the Letter to the Hebrews (and the church) claims it to be: "For the word of God is living and active, sharper than any two-edged sword, piercing to the division of soul and spirit, of joints and marrow, and discerning the thoughts and intentions of the heart" (Heb. 4:12 RSV)? How can I allow the biblical text of God's word to judge me, the reader, if I the reader am suspicious of and in fact judging the biblical text?

"All scripture is inspired by God and profitable for teaching, for reproof, for correction, and for training in righteousness, that the man of God may be complete, equipped for every good work" (2 Tim. 3:16-17 RSV). How can Scripture be useful for Christians' training or correction if they read it out of a suspicion that presumes their own preunderstandings and values to be correct when they differ from those of the text? For such reasons, authors like Peter Stuhlmacher have called for a Christian biblical hermeneutics of *consent* or a hermeneutics of *understanding* rather than one of suspicion.[14]

---

14. Peter Stuhlmacher, *Historical Criticism and Theological Interpretation of Scripture: Toward a Hermeneutics of Consent*, trans. Roy A. Harrisville (Philadelphia: Fortress, 1977). Cf. Luke Johnson's expression, "hermeneutics of generosity or charity," in his second chapter above. Cf. also Garrett Green, *Theology, Hermeneutics, and Imagination: The Crisis of Interpretation at the End of Modernity* (Cambridge: Cambridge University Press, 2000), Part II: "Christian imagination in a postmodern world," 141-225 (with bibliog.), esp. ch. 8, "The faithful imagination: suspicion and trust in a postmodern world," 187-206.

What Is God's Message to Me?

If the spiritual sense of Scripture is ascertained by a reader only within a stance of faith and openness to the possibly transcendent and personally transforming message of Scripture, a hermeneutics of suspicion seems counterproductive for discovering this spiritual sense, despite its value in the domain of history and sociology. When believers approach Scripture as God's word to themselves and are seeking Scripture's guidance for their lives, they have to be open to what Scripture tells them about God in relation to his people and to themselves as God's adopted daughters and sons through Christ. As they read Scripture, they listen to it as God's instruction to themselves for living their lives according to God's loving plan for them.

Yet how can believers do this responsibly, without prooftexting or reading their own preconceptions into what the text is trying to express? Let us test and apply these theories with a suggested Catholic reading of John 6, which presents the feeding of the 5000, Jesus' walking on the water, and his bread of life discourse. Let us read these in interchange with the Catholic horizon of eucharistic faith and practice.

Elements in the John 6 Text

Since Vatican II has reaffirmed that all responsible reading and senses of Scripture are grounded in the literal sense,[15] let us begin by another close look at elements and evidence within these Gospel passages. First, we have previously noted that the account of Jesus' feeding of the 5000 already contains Old Testament allusions to God's feeding of the people with manna in the desert in their exodus from Egypt, as well as allusions which foreshadow the Christian Eucharist. Second, the "sandwich" editing of the account of Jesus' *walking on the water,* namely between his feeding of the 5000 and his bread of life discourse which explains that feeding, confirms the authorial expectation that the walking on the water is to be interpreted in light of both the feeding and its explanation and is meant, in turn, to throw light on both of them. Third, the account of Jesus' walking on the water makes explicit

---

15. *DV* §12.

the themes of Jesus' perceived absence, then presence to his followers as they battle a storm on the sea which they are crossing. More than in the Synoptic versions of this story, in John 6 Jesus' walking on the water is presented unmistakably as a *theophany,* an appearance of God. Not only does Jesus do what *only God is portrayed in the Old Testtament as doing,* namely *walking on and mastering water or the sea,* but when Jesus identifies himself to the terrified disciples, he uses the key Old Testament self-designation of God, namely I AM.

Finally, the *bread of life discourse* provides the Johannine interpretation of the accounts both of Jesus' feeding the 5000 and walking on the water as "I AM." It identifies Jesus as the Old Testament bread come down from heaven. In the feeding of the 5000 Jesus is portrayed as *providing* the multitude with bread. In the discourse that interprets the feeding and walking on water, Jesus *is* the bread. (This identification of Jesus with the bread from heaven augments the exodus account as reinterpreted in the psalms and Wisdom literature.)

The previous chapter acknowledged the general exegetical recognition that the bread of life discussion begins with Old Testament allusions to *wisdom* as bread from heaven to be consumed by the wise, but it culminates in allusions to "eating my flesh and drinking my blood." Although "eating my flesh" can still be given a wisdom interpretation, controversy continues over the meaning and relevance of the change of verb to the more physical and corporeal notion of munching on *(trōgōn)* my flesh. What makes the eucharistic allusions hard to deny is the parallel mention of "drinking my blood." Even though Wisdom typically is portrayed as inviting learners both to eat and to drink, the shock value of drinking Jesus' blood seems extreme for wisdom allusions. As we previously described, the parallel mentions of eating Jesus' flesh and drinking his blood can most satisfactorily be explained by recognizing their reference to the sacramental reception of Christian Eucharist.[16]

---

16. Even Menken, who emphasizes christological over eucharistic referents here, acknowledges that Johannine Christians and readers would also think of Eucharist as a special occasion for experiencing their belief in the crucifed Jesus ("John 6:51c-58," 202).

Spiritual Sense/Actualization and Application to Eucharist (esp. as Sacrament)

Because John 6 already treats "spiritual" topics, its literal sense contains much of the spiritual sense which we are investigating. We have seen that the literal sense already incorporates the spiritual topics of Christology, Old Testament allusions to God feeding his people with manna in the desert, Christian Eucharist, the theophany or epiphany of Jesus as I AM walking on the water, and wisdom and Eucharist as bread from heaven which nourishes us toward eternal life. However, from the perspective of Catholic faith and experience I would like to unpack some further spiritual dimensions as they relate to Catholic Eucharist.[17]

Secular literary approaches to texts (including the Bible) use the method of reader-response to explore the meaning that emerges when a real reader (in our case, a Catholic reader of the 21st century) reads the text of John 6. Using the metaphor of "fusion of horizons,"[18] let us engage John 6, which includes in its horizon the Johannine eucharistic practices which the text implies and to which it alludes. In our investigation of spiritual and eucharistic senses of John 6, let us correlate its Johannine horizon with the horizon of contemporary Catholic eucharistic beliefs and practices.

John 6:1-15: Feeding of the Five Thousand

The previous chapter called attention to the narrator's focus on signs as the reason why the crowd gathered (John 6:2). Jesus sits on the mountain in the posture of teacher with disciples: the mountain reference recalls Mount Sinai where God revealed the Law to Moses. Verse 4 explicitly relates this event to Passover, which in turn associates Jesus' feeding the 5000 with God's feeding the Israelites in the wilderness in the original Passover from Egypt toward the promised land.

It also noted that Jesus' leading question about how to feed the

---

17. Cf. David Michael Stanley, "The Bread of Life," *Worship* 32 (1958): 477-88; and Moloney, *ABR* 30 (October 1982): 10-33.

18. Gadamer, *Truth and Method,* 306-7.

multitude and Andrew's answer about having five barley loaves and two fish set the scene. The reference to "barley loaves" alludes to the strikingly parallel situation of the prophet Elisha in 2 Kgs. 4:42-44. When someone offers Elisha 20 barley loaves to feed 100 men, and Elisha instructs his servant to set the bread before the men, the servant protests, "How am I to set this before a hundred men?" Elisha prophesies that "They shall eat and have some left" (2 Kgs. 4:43 RSV), and the narrator reports that they did eat and have some leftovers (v. 44).

The parallel with the prophet Elisha, which extends even to the focus on the leftovers, in turn helps explain the response of the crowd after Jesus fed them: "When the people saw the sign which he had done, they said, 'This is indeed the prophet who is to come into the world!'" (John 6:14 RSV). As previously noted, however, the huge difference in numbers and obvious symbolism of the 12 baskets (for the 12 tribes and 12 apostles) give the feeding of the 5000 a more messianic resonance of care for the whole of God's people than Elisha's mere feeding of some hungry men has, even though both feedings involved a miraculous multiplication of loaves.

We have also commented on how the words used to portray Jesus taking the loaves or breads, giving thanks (Greek *eucharistēsas*), and giving them to those seated echo the words and actions of the Christian Eucharist — especially taking the breads and giving thanks. Also, unlike the Synoptic versions of this feeding where Jesus more realistically gives the loaves to the disciples to distribute to the 5000, John 6 has Jesus himself giving the breads, as happened at the Last Supper in the Synoptics.

Other important eucharistic allusions appear in Jesus' command to gather up the fragments, the *klasmata,* which we noted had already become a Greek technical term for Eucharist in such early documents as the *Didache.* Thus, John 6:13's references to 12 baskets of fragments from the five barley loaves recall the 12 tribes and apostles, the Eucharist, as well as the Elisha account with its similar emphasis on leftovers. The people's reaction to Jesus' sign — proclaiming him "the prophet who is to come into the world" (John 6:14 RSV) and wanting to make him king — demonstrates how they missed the true point of the feeding of the 5000.

John 6:16-21: Walking on the Water

From a eucharistic perspective, the next narrative about Jesus walking on the water deepens certain theological dimensions implied in the feeding of the 5000 narrative. The narrative's climax is when the disciples sight Jesus walking on the sea, express their fear, and receive his reassurance and self-revelation: "I AM, do not be afraid" (John 6:20). In the feeding of the 5000 Jesus had acted in a manner similar to how God had fed the Israelites in the desert with manna. Now Jesus reveals himself to his disciples with the theophanous I AM, in effect, as God. In a manner attributed in the Old Testament only to God, Jesus walks to the disciples on the water. He tells them not to be afraid, using language which all Old Testament theophanies or revelations of God use with respect to their recipients — "Do not be afraid." Jesus reveals who he is — I AM — in a manner which imitates the way in which God revealed himself to Moses at the burning bush. He concurrently underscores his presence to the disciples and communion with them in a stressful situation in which they had just experienced his absence.

In preparation for the third section of John 6, Jesus' bread of life discourse, the narrator in John 6:23 recalls once more the feeding of the 5000 with allusions that emphasize its eucharistic dimensions, by referring to the place "where they ate the bread after the Lord had given thanks" (RSV). This reference ignores the fish and uses the same root for giving thanks as the root behind Eucharist.

Bread of Life Controversy

We have also seen how the bread of life discussion in John 6 provides the biblical and theological explanation of the meaning of Jesus' feeding of the 5000. The explanation begins with Jesus' statement to the crowds, "Truly, truly [Amen, Amen], I say to you, you seek me, not because you saw signs, but because you ate your fill of the loaves. Do not labor for the food which perishes, but for the food which endures to eternal life, which the Son of man will give to you . . ." (John 6:26-27 RSV). When later the crowds challenge Jesus to work a sign like the manna in the desert — a demand filled with irony because that is just what the narrator had shown Jesus doing when he fed the 5000 — Jesus solemnly corrects them: "it was not Moses who gave you the bread from heaven; my Father gives you the true bread from heaven" (v. 32 RSV). The bread from God will give life to the world (v. 33). When the crowd asks for this bread, Jesus claims that he himself is the bread of life: "he who comes to me shall not hunger, and he who believes in me shall never thirst" (vv. 34-35 RSV).

After Jesus then transposes the discussion topic to the necessity that they have faith in him, the narrator shows the Jews murmuring against Jesus in the way their ancestors had murmured and complained against God and Moses in the desert (John 6:41-42). Their rejection of his claim to have come down from heaven because Jesus is son of Joseph and because they know his father and mother is especially ironic for readers who have read the Johannine prologue (John 1:1-18) and know that "the Word became flesh" (1:14). The obvious ironic ignorance of his interlocutors recalls the ironic ignorance of Nicodemus about returning to one's mother's womb to be born again (3:4). It provides the narrator an appropriate occasion to refer to the speakers no longer in neutral fashion as "the crowd" (6:24), but under his more antagonistic title of "the Jews" (v. 41) who murmur against Jesus. The prologue also explains the claim of Jesus in response to their continued murmuring: "Not that any one has seen the Father except him who is from God; he has seen the Father" (6:46 RSV). The prologue's climax is the similar claim: "No one has ever seen God; the only Son, who is in the bosom of the Father, he has made him known" (1:18 RSV). Finally Jesus claims to be the bread of life (6:48), "and the bread which I shall give for the life of the world is my flesh" (v. 51c RSV).

We have suggested that the reference here to Jesus' flesh rather than his body (the term used in eucharistic prayers) is related to the Johannine presentation of Jesus as Lamb of God whose flesh is eaten and blood poured out so that the people may live. But when Jesus goes on to insist on his flesh as food and his blood as drink which when eaten and drunk bring eternal life and cause the believer to abide in Jesus and he in the believer (John 6:55-56), the eucharistic overtones are dramatically enhanced, not only regarding the reception of Jesus' body and blood, but also in regard to the mutual "abiding" (or communion) between Jesus and the recipient. Thus as Catholic readers come to the latter parts of the bread of life controversies, they spontaneously (and appropriately) understand the Eucharist as a major way in which they believe in Jesus and therefore eat the bread come down from heaven to give them eternal life.

Catholics searching for a spiritual sense of this Johannine chapter understand the bread of life as preeminently present to them in the Eucharist. This is a spiritual sense or dimension of the feeding of the 5000 account as deepened by Jesus' revelation of presence to his disciples when they thought him absent. It is deepened by Jesus' remarks about himself as bread from heaven, which would bring eternal life to those who ate it, so that Jesus would resurrect them on the last day. Catholics have a strong sense that they need the bread of life which is Jesus in order not to die in the wilderness, and that their communion with Jesus in the Eucharist is the primary way that Jesus is their bread of life enabling them to live forever. They understand as actualized especially in Communion Jesus' promise: "He who eats my flesh and drinks my blood abides in me, and I in him" (John 6:56 RSV). Further, because Communion unites them with Jesus so that they live in him and he in them, Catholics see themselves as having Jesus' eternal life (6:57-58).

In the event when Jesus fed the multitude, he gave them not only bread but fish. But in the explanatory discussions about the bread from heaven, the Johannine Jesus refers only to the bread and how the bread is his flesh. Instead of mentioning the fish, Jesus refers to his blood being true drink, which for Catholic readers will instinctively be regarded as a clear reference to the Eucharist. In light of the feeding of the 5000 and Jesus' revealing himself to his disciples as I AM walking on the sea, the bread of life discourse focuses on Jesus himself as the bread come down from heaven. Jesus himself is the bread of life. Early in this discussion this claim applies primarily to having faith in Jesus. Whereas in the Old Testament one had accepted wisdom, especially as wisdom was incorporated in the Law, the later clear references to physical eating of Jesus' flesh and drinking of his blood justify Catholics' eucharistic interpretation and actualization of these verses. For Catholics today, God's word in John 6 is stressing that for eternal life Catholics need to eat the body and drink the blood of Christ in the Eucharist, which the clergy have a grave obligation to provide for them; they must also catechize them into the importance and proper reception of the sacrament of the Eucharist.

I would like to end this eucharistic actualization and application of the feeding of the 5000 by a brief comparison with the words of the canon or Eucharistic Prayer which the Catholic priest recites at the consecration of the Mass. Many of the same key words occur both in the account of the feeding of the 5000 and in the Eucharistic Prayer, so that Catholic readers can recognize the feeding of the 5000 as a kind of action symbolic of what they experience in the Eucharist. Both the feeding account as interpreted by the bread of life discourse and the Roman Eucharistic Prayer emphasize the words and expressions *take, eat my body, drink my blood.* In addition, the Eastern liturgy emphasizes that Jesus' body is *broken,* the same term used for the leftover *broken fragments* collected into 12 baskets in the feeding narrative.

The heart of all the versions of the contemporary Catholic Eucharistic Prayer is the following: "*Take* this all of you and *eat* it: *this is my body* which will be *given up* for you." "*Take* this, all of you and *drink* from it: *this is the cup of my blood, the blood of the new and everlasting covenant.* It will be *shed* for you and for all so that sins may be forgiven. *Do this in memory of me.*"[19]

As Jesus did in the Johannine version of the feeding of the 5000, the Eucharistic Prayer instructs believers to take the bread and eat it. As the Eucharistic Prayer equates the bread with Jesus' body, the Johannine explanations after the feeding equate bread from heaven with Jesus' flesh to be eaten. The Eucharistic Prayer's symbolic balance of presenting the bread as Jesus' body and the wine as Jesus' blood is of course not found in an account of feeding 5000 with bread and fish. But the bread of life discussions eventually include the necessity to drink Jesus' blood as well as to eat his flesh.

More than the Catholic Roman rite, the Eastern Liturgy of St. John Chrysostom emphasizes how Jesus' body which is to be eaten is "broken for you." The Greek term common to both Eastern liturgy and New Testament recalls the early Christian expression for Eucharist, the broken fragments. "*Take, eat, this is My Body* which is *broken for you* for the remission of sins. . . . Amen. . . . *Drink* ye all of this, *this is My Blood of the new Testament,* which is *shed* for you, and for many for the remission of sins. . . . Amen."[20]

---

19. *The Sacramentary,* ICEL trans. (New York: Catholic, 1985), 542-60, the four main Eucharistic Prayers.

20. *The Divine Liturgy of St. John Chrysostom,* trans. C. C. Canellopoulos (Chicago: Syndicate, 1928), 62-65.

When Catholics who regularly participate in the Eucharist read about the feeding of the 5000 and the explanatory discourses in John 6, the Johannine use of language and expressions, which echo expressions which they frequently hear at eucharistic celebrations, leads them spontaneously to interpret John 6 in a eucharistic spiritual sense, as well as in relation to the original event and the christological meanings given it in the FG. At least for Catholic readers, an important spiritual sense and actualization of the feeding of the 5000 and bread from heaven discussions in John 6 is receiving Jesus in the Eucharist.

CHAPTER ELEVEN

Test Case: "Whose Sins You Shall Forgive" in John 20: Applying Scripture with the Catechism

One of the three approaches to actualizing Scripture mentioned in Vatican II's *Dei Verbum* involves the "harmony which exists between elements of the faith" (§12) or the "analogy of faith" (*CCC* 114), in which to understand and apply a biblical text readers can appeal to their own experience of the referent of the text, i.e., the extratextual relationship, person, sacrament, or the like to which the text is referring. Since forgiveness of sins is the same or at least a very similar experience both as it is described in Scripture and as it is experienced personally by believers today, they can legitimately interpret and apply biblical treatments of forgiveness with help and guidance from their own experience of forgiveness. For this writer, the power of God's forgiveness, healing, and guidance in the sacrament of Reconciliation have been my most powerful experience of priestly ministry. One especially powerful personal setting for this sacrament has been in Catholic retreats for women and men who are suffering after abortions: these retreats are centered around the gospel truth that God is compassionate and forgiving Love for whom no sin is too great to forgive.

However, for advocating a method of actualizing Scripture, it seems important to incorporate contemporary experience of forgiveness of sins in a way that transcends the subjectivism of individual writers or readers. One way to do this would be to utilize a standard and authoritative compendium of church teaching on forgiveness, such as the functional and readily available 1994 *Catechism of the Catholic*

Church (CCC).[1] Since the forgiveness of sins is an extratextual reality which receives serious treatment in both the Scripture and the *CCC*, by the analogy of faith it is possible to use the Catechism as an aid toward actualizing biblical passages and applying them to contemporary Catholic concerns. In addition, since the *CCC* incorporates many carefully selected quotations from patristic authors on this and most other topics, it can provide a feasible way for believers who are not professional scholars to follow some of Luke Johnson's proposals about learning from the Fathers how to read the Scriptures as Catholics.

In this chapter, I would like to recommend that Catholic teachers, preachers, and readers not be afraid to use the *CCC* to apply to Catholics' lives such biblical passages as John 20:19-23, where the risen Jesus tells his disciples, "whose sins you forgive are forgiven; whose sins you retain are retained." Previous chapters have argued for the need to go beyond historical criticism in interpreting Scripture, to recognize different readers and their correspondingly varying approaches to biblical interpretation, to take account of biblical intertextuality and a genuine unity of Scripture, and to seek Scripture's "spiritual senses," e.g., by actualizing Scripture in eucharistic ways. Finally, this chapter will propose a test case of using the *CCC* as a handy compendium of traditional Catholic teaching in applying another biblical text to the Catholic sacrament of Reconciliation. As a matter of fact, the *CCC* itself begins its treatment of sin and the sacrament of Reconciliation from this biblical passage and related biblical evidence, as the church (including patristic authors) has reflected on it, preached it, and applied it through the centuries.

However, it must be acknowledged that when the *CCC* first appeared in English, it was greeted with significant hostility from academics, who criticized, among many things, the Catechism's use of Scripture. Kevin Miller and I responded with an article defending the *CCC*'s use of Scripture as exactly what one would expect in a compendium of traditional church teaching.[2] Other reasons for academic hostility remain, but for the limited purposes of this proposal concerning Catholic biblical interpretation and application, the objection about

---

1. 2nd ed. (Vatican: Libreria Editrice Vaticana, 1997).

2. William S. Kurz and Kevin E. Miller, "The Use of Scripture in the Catechism of the Catholic Church," *Communio International Catholic Review* 23 (1996): 480-507.

the *CCC*'s use of Scripture would have been the most serious obstacle to this proposed use of it. As a matter of fact, I have used the *CCC* as a college-level introductory textbook every year since 1994. It has been extremely popular with and useful for not only Catholic students, but also those of other denominations and even non-Christians. This has convinced me of its pastoral, catechetical, and instructional value as it stands, with whatever limitations it has, and despite the dislike of some academics.

Applying Scripture with the Catechism

To set the stage for applying John 20:19-23 with teachings and practices described in the *CCC*, let us briefly recall some of the Catechism's primary treatments of the forgiveness of sins and the sacrament of Reconciliation. The *CCC* is organized according to the articles of the Apostles' Creed. Article 10 is "I believe in the forgiveness of sins." *CCC* 976 (numbers reflect paragraphs, not pages, which differ in various editions of the *CCC*) points out that the Creed associates belief in the forgiveness of sins with belief in the church and communion of saints. "It was when he gave the Holy Spirit to his apostles that the risen Christ conferred on them his own divine power to forgive sins: 'Receive the Holy Spirit. If you forgive the sins of any, they are forgiven; if you retain the sins of any, they are retained.'" In an aside, the editors explain that the second, sacramental, section of the *CCC* will explicitly treat forgiveness of sins through the sacraments (Baptism, Penance, Eucharist and others).

Later, in the "In Brief" statements summarizing the sacrament of Reconciliation, *CCC* 1485 again quotes John 20:19, 22-23, in which Jesus reveals himself on Easter evening to his "apostles" (an actualization of "disciples" as they are called in the FG): "He breathed on them, and said to them: 'Receive the Holy Spirit. If you forgive the sins of any, they are forgiven; if you retain the sins of any, they are retained.'"

We have seen how every reader brings his or her set of preunderstandings when reading any text, including a biblical text. As readers read and actualize the text in their own imaginations, they incorporate the contents of that text into the context of their own horizon of understanding or worldview. When they actualize a biblical passage, the contents of that passage might either fit readily and easily into their preestablished religious context, or it might clash with their context and challenge them to alter their broader perspective to account for it.

For example, as clarified in the chapter on preunderstandings, if "Bible Christians" who do not believe in confession to a human minister read John 20:19-23 with a genuine openness to what it is saying, they might be challenged to reconcile the risen Jesus' commission to his disciples with their own conviction about confessing only to God. If Christians need confess only to God and not to any human instrument, then why would Jesus send out his disciples with this statement: "Receive the Holy Spirit. If you forgive the sins of any, they are forgiven; if you retain the sins of any, they are retained" (John 20:22b-23 RSV)? Why would Jesus give his disciples authority either to forgive or to retain (that is, decline to forgive) sins, if he were not in fact giving them authority to judge the repentance of a sinner when the latter confessed his sins? Since it is indeed true that only God can forgive sins as "Bible Christians" claim, it is important to note that, according to the FG, Jesus provides to his disciples the Holy Spirit, who also is God, to empower such forgiveness.

Helpful instruments for reading the Bible as Catholics and actualizing it for our own lives and applying it to our own situations would logically seem to be authoritative statements of the church's beliefs and practices regarding the subject at hand. We already used the authoritative Nicene Creed to help us interpret and apply the prologue of John's Gospel. Let us see what happens when we use the treatment of sin and the sacrament of Reconciliation in the *CCC* to interpret and apply the passage on Jesus' commissioning his disciples to forgive sins in John 20. As usual, we begin by grounding our interpretation on a careful reading of the Johannine passage.

Evidence from the Text Itself of John 20:19-23

The setting for this passage is the first appearance of Jesus to the frightened disciples on the evening of the same day that Mary Magdalene had told them that she had seen the risen Lord. The primary reason for Jesus' appearance is to bring peace to his disciples, which he achieved by his greeting of peace and his reassuring them of his identity by showing them his wounds. Peace is therefore also the context in which he gives them the Holy Spirit and commissions them to forgive sins. Not only is peace the context, but peace is a primary result of divine forgiveness and reconciliation (cf. Psalm 32).

As both Jews and Christians believe, it is true that "only God can forgive sins," because sins are offenses against God. But in the FG Jesus has already been clearly shown to have God's power of judgment in John 5:22-30. This divine power of judgment includes the power to forgive or retain sins, because to Jesus the Father has given the final eschatological judgment: "For as the Father has life in himself, so he has granted the Son also to have life in himself, and has given him authority to execute judgment, because he is the Son of man. Do not marvel at this; for the hour is coming when all who are in the tombs will hear his voice and come forth, those who have done good, to the resurrection of life, and those who have done evil, to the resurrection of judgment" (John 5:26-29 RSV).

Apparently for confessional reasons, some Protestant exegetes appear uncomfortable with the notion of Jesus giving to humans authority to forgive sins. This different set of preunderstandings which they bring to the text may contribute to their emphasis that the preeminent notion of sin in the FG is unbelief, which is "cured" more through preaching the word than by absolution of the individual's sins.[3]

Although such an emphasis on sin as unbelief is indeed a predominant theme in the Gospel of John, the evidence about judgment in John 5:22-30 just cited makes it clear that unbelief is not the only definition of sin for this Gospel. Jesus' eschatological judgment and the consequent reward or punishment in John 5:29 is to be based on the distinction between "those who have done good" and "those who have done evil." Complementary and confirming evidence is found in the First Letter of John, which most exegetes attribute at least to the same school as produced the FG or some of its later redactions and additions. I John often refers to confession or expiation of sins in ways that go beyond the cardinal FG notion of sin as unbelief and include individual sinful acts (e.g., I John 1:8-9, "If we say we have no sin, we deceive ourselves. . . . If we confess our sins, he is faithful and just, and will for-

---

3. See the discussion in Steven E. Hanson, "Forgiving and Retaining Sin: A Study of the Text and Context of John 20:23," *HBT* 19 (1997): 24-32.

give our sins and cleanse us from all unrighteousness" RSV; 2:2, "He [Jesus] is the expiation for our sins, and not for ours only but also for the sins of the whole world" RSV). In all of these passages, 1 John refers to sins in the plural, i.e., multiple acts of sinning, not just to the sin of unbelief.

Further, from his first appearance in John's Gospel, Jesus is identified by John the Baptist as the "Lamb of God, who takes away the sin of the world" (John 1:29, 36). As the Passover lamb was an instrument of salvation for the Israelites through his shed blood, so the Lamb of God, slain on the day when the Passover lambs were slaughtered, will take away the world's sin through shedding of his blood (cf. 19:34-37). Now after his resurrection Jesus tells his disciples that as the Father sent him, so he now sends them. He gives them the Holy Spirit which empowers them, and he commissions them to continue his own judging and forgiving function to forgive or retain sins. It is clearly on behalf of the church as its leaders after Jesus' ascension to his Father in heaven that the disciples are to exercise the power and authority which they now receive.

In Scripture, to judge innocence or guilt and to administer punishment or forgiveness and mercy were functions of those who held official authority over the people, not of private citizens. For example, judgment pertained to the authority of Moses, of the king, and now of the leaders of Jesus' church. Similarly in John 20, the recipients of Jesus' commission to judge sins are undoubtedly the group of "official" disciples who would later be the church leaders. The recipients of this authority did not even include as important a friend of Jesus and witness to his resurrection as Mary Magdalene, even though she was the first witness to alert Jesus' "brothers" (20:17), who in the next verse (v. 18) are identified as "the disciples," to the fact that Jesus was risen and alive again (vv. 17-18).

Let us therefore summarize the Johannine evidence about the meaning of Jesus' commission to forgive or retain sins. This authority to forgive sins is transmitted in the context of the resurrected Jesus' mission of bringing peace to his disciples. Reconciliation with God is the most fundamental form of peace to be sought in Scripture. The setting of this transfer of authority is after Jesus' resurrection, and it is meant to prepare his disciples to continue Jesus' saving and forgiving mission from the Father after his return to the Father. (During his physical presence and ministry on earth, only Jesus forgave sins — he did not delegate this to any disciples.) To do this work in his absence and exclusively on his behalf, Jesus empowers his disciples and future leaders of his church by breathing on them the Holy Spirit and giving them the power and authority either to forgive sins or to hold them bound, that is, to decide not to forgive certain sins. This commission clearly does not limit the authority merely to unquestioningly forgiving all sins of all penitents who ask them for forgiveness, nor merely to giving "general absolution" to an entire group of people without hearing individuals' particular sins (as was legitimately done by World War II chaplains before battle but is now being resisted as an abuse of the sacrament in some dioceses). It also gives the authority to make a judgment which will result either in forgiveness or nonforgiveness of the sins confessed. This kind of judgment can obviously not be entrusted to every individual believer or private member of the church but necessarily only to its leaders, whose authority to judge sins of Catholics furthers their mission to lead and direct the Catholic church.

Unity of Scripture in the Unity of God's Saving Plan

As our previous chapters have shown for other passages, contemporary Catholics instinctively and appropriately situate this John 20 passage in the context of their own experience. In this case they refer to their experience of the sacrament of Reconciliation, especially when they read this passage and reflect on the biblical evidence in the context of the entire biblical canon (especially the reception of the "keys of the kingdom" by Peter [Matt. 16:19] and the authority to "bind and loose" first by Peter in Matt. 16:19 and then by the disciples in Matt. 18:18). They recognize the power of judgment which the confessor exercises when he listens to sins which are confessed to him. Obviously, we priests who have heard many confessions almost always make the judgment that the penitent is sorry and so we absolve his or her sins. Nevertheless, one can imagine situations, like a penitent's refusal to break off a sinful adulterous relationship or to make a good-faith effort to stop some pattern of sinning, which could force a confessor to decline to give that person absolution. In other words, the experience of those of us who are priests confirms the fact that confessors who are authorized to forgive sins in Christ's name in fact do act as judges determining whether to forgive or to retain the sins which are confessed to them. In light of this biblical evidence, let us return to the CCC for further actualization and application of this passage to contemporary Catholics' lives and priestly ministry.

The CCC and Sacrament of Reconciliation Resumed

The CCC's summary of the sacrament of Reconciliation acknowledges that the initial and foundational sacramental forgiveness of sins is a function proper to baptism. This accords with principal New Testament patterns of evangelization, such as when preachers in Acts are shown telling potential converts that they must repent and be baptized (e.g., Acts 2:38). The sacrament of Reconciliation is rather a supplemental sacrament to address sins which are committed after baptism (CCC 1486). Despite theories of some denominations about Christians being "saved" once for all and definitively, centuries of experience have convinced the Catholic church that even after the most sincere conversions, believers retain their free will and proclivity to sin. In fact they very frequently do sin, often in serious ways, after their conversion and baptism. Since baptism can be received only once, another sacrament has been determined to be needed for postbaptismal sins. In light of these Catholic preunderstandings, New Testament passages already discussed (such as those in 1 John, Matthew 16 and 18), as well as the most straightforward reading of this passage in John 20, seem most naturally to apply to postbaptismal sins of people who are already members of the church. The New Testament evidence seems to incline more toward church evangelists and leaders having not only a ministry of preaching and baptizing for forgiveness of sins, but also one of forgiving sins committed by Christians after baptism.

CCC 1493 specifies that the manner for receiving reconciliation with God and with the church is to confess to an authorized church minister (e.g., a priest) all the postbaptismal grave sins which have not previously been confessed and which the penitent can remember after careful examination of conscience. One reason why confession of serious sins is necessary is that without explicit and honest confession of particular serious sins, the confessor would not have the information necessary to make his anticipated judgment whether to forgive or to retain the penitent's sins. Furthermore, although there is no church requirement to confess less serious ("venial") sins or faults, for pastoral reasons frequent confession of even lesser sins is strongly recommended, and has been the actual practice of even the pope and exemplary Catholics like Mother Teresa.

CCC 1495 specifies that only priests who have received the authorization ("faculty") of absolving from sin (from church authorities — their bishop or major religious superior who has authority to delegate this faculty) can forgive sins in the name of Christ. Since it is the authority and power of Christ that the church is exercising in its ministry of reconciling sinners, only duly authorized and ordained ministers of the church (priests or bishops) have been delegated by the church in the name of Christ to perform this ministry. This delegation seems a natural extension of the authority given in John 20 to the gathered disciples who were to exercise leadership after Jesus' return to the Father. It is another important application of the Catholic notion of apostolic succession to ensure the continuation and expansion through space and time of various ministries that Jesus entrusted to his disciples.

The spiritual effects of the sacrament of Reconciliation are delineated next in CCC 1496. Obviously, the first effect is reconciliation with God and recovery of God's life of grace, which directly result from the Johannine commission, "whose sins you shall forgive are forgiven them." A consequent second result of reconciliation with God in this sacrament is reconciliation with the church, since sins not only offend God but harm the health and well-being of the church as Body of Christ. This function of the sacrament of Reconciliation demonstrates even more obviously than reconciliation with God why the involvement of those delegated and authorized by the church to hear confessions is required. This was even more apparent in the earliest centuries of church life, when major sins like adultery or murder publicly separated Christians from communion with the rest of the church until the sinners were readmitted to full participation in church life and sacraments (especially Eucharist) through the public administration of the sacrament of Reconciliation. This aspect of reconciliation with the church remains a current practice for reconciling penitents who have been excommunicated from the church for certain sins such as abortion. An important aspect of my own postabortion ministry involves absolving penitents from excommunication, which forbids them from receiving the church's Eucharist, in addition to pronouncing forgiveness of the sins and reconciliation with God.

CCC 1496 adds the following spiritual effects of the sacrament of Reconciliation, several of which are its obvious consequences: remission of the eternal punishment which unforgiven mortal sins would deserve; remission, at least in part, of temporal punishments resulting from sin (this Catholic teaching goes beyond any evidence in John 20); peace and serenity of conscience, and spiritual consolation (this is implied in the original John 20 context of "peace be with you"); and an increase of spiritual strength for the Christian battle (e.g., forgiveness gives new motivation for change in the future).

CCC 1497 further specifies: "Individual and integral confession of grave sins followed by absolution remains the only ordinary means of reconciliation with God and with the church." This is a direct consequence of the dynamics implied by John 20. Such full disclosure is required for judgment regarding absolution from sin by the confessor (who is believed to have received the power of absolution from God's Holy Spirit as well as the authority to determine whether to forgive or retain the sin, i.e., to absolve it or not).

An earlier section of the CCC summarizes other important New Testament teachings about forgiveness of sins in and through the church. First, under the heading, "The Power of the Keys," it applies technical doctrinal language to the New Testament metaphors of Jesus bestowing the "keys of the kingdom of heaven" on Peter (Matt. 16:19) and confirming in heaven whatever Peter and the disciples "bind and loose" on earth (Matt. 16:19; 18:18). CCC 981 quotes the postresurrection mission to the apostles "that repentance and forgiveness of sins should be preached in his name to all nations" (Luke 24:47). This mission is fulfilled not only by preaching God's forgiveness in Christ and calling to conversion and faith, "but also by communicating to them the forgiveness of sins in Baptism, and reconciling them with God and with the church through the power of the keys, received from Christ." As a further aid to its interpretation, the CCC quotes several patristic authors, beginning with St. Augustine, "[The Church] has received the keys of the Kingdom of heaven so that, in her, sins may be forgiven through Christ's blood and the Holy Spirit's action. In this church, the soul dead through sin comes back to life in order to live with Christ, whose grace has saved us" (*Serm.* 214, 11: PL 38, 1071-72). CCC 983 further quotes St. Ambrose (*Paen.* 1, 34: PL 16, 477A) concerning the tremendous power the Lord willed his disciples to have, "that his lowly servants accomplish in his name all that he did when he was on earth"; and St. John Chrysostom (*Sac.* 3, 5: PG 48, 643A): "Priests have received from God a power that he has given neither to angels nor to archangels. . . . God above confirms what priests do here below."

Not only is the Catechism section title of "Power of the Keys" an evident allusion to the Matthew passages where Jesus confers the keys of the kingdom on Peter and the authority to bind and loose first on Peter (Matthew 16) and then on the disciples (Matthew 18). Its quotations of various patristic authors parallels our suggested actualizations of John 20 in light of the sacrament of Reconciliation as well as baptism for the forgiveness of sins. For centuries, the Matthean passages have been assimilated to the commission in John 20 under the principle of the unity of Scripture and of interpretation of Scripture by other comparable parts of Scripture.

The CCC "In Brief" summary statements regarding article 10 of the Apostles' Creed, "I believe in the forgiveness of sins," provide a broader biblical and doctrinal context of interpretation for John 20. CCC 984 links forgiveness of sins with the Creed's faith in the Holy Spirit, using an allusion to John 20: "for the risen Christ entrusted to the apostles the power to forgive sins when he gave them the Holy Spirit." Paragraph 985 clarifies that "the first and chief sacrament of the forgiveness of sins" is not the sacrament of Reconciliation but Baptism, which unites Christians to the risen Christ and imparts the Holy Spirit. Paragraph 986 then clarifies, with implied reference primarily to postbaptismal sins, that "by Christ's will, the Church possesses the power to forgive the sins of the baptized and exercises it through bishops and priests normally in the sacrament of Penance." Lastly CCC 987 repeats the teaching of the Roman Catechism: "In the forgiveness of sins, both priests and sacraments are instruments which our Lord Jesus Christ, the only author and liberal giver of salvation, wills to use in order to efface our sins and give us the grace of justification" (Roman Catechism, I, 11, 6)." The combined teaching of this section is a broad biblically-based perspective on forgiveness of sins, grounded in Christ's salvation and the power of the Holy Spirit, exercised in the church first through the sacrament of Baptism and also that of Penance or Reconciliation, in which both priests and sacraments function as instruments of forgiveness from our sins for our one and only savior Jesus Christ.

Finally, a section of the CCC is devoted to the question that is especially pressing in the light of Scripture and for ecumenical and apologetic discussions: "Why a sacrament of Reconciliation after Baptism?" to which paragraphs 1425-26 provide its answer. CCC 1425 recalls the magnitude of God's gift of sanctification in the sacraments to help Catholics realize how much sin is excluded for the person who has "put on Christ." Yet it reminds readers of 1 John 1:8, "If we say we have no sin, we deceive ourselves, and the truth is not in us," and of the Lord's Prayer, "Forgive us our trespasses" (Luke 11:4; Matt. 6:12). CCC 1426 further recalls that Christians' holiness "without blemish" is given them by conversion to Christ, Baptism, and the reception of the Holy Spirit and of the eucharistic Body and Blood of Christ as food. But it balances this with the teaching of Trent: "Nevertheless the new life received in Christian initiation has not abolished the frailty and weakness of human nature, nor the inclination to sin that Tradition calls concupiscence, which remains in the baptized such that with the help of the grace of Christ they may prove themselves in the struggle of Christian life" (Council of Trent [1546]: DS 1515). Because of this remaining proclivity to sin, a further sacrament is needed for forgiveness of postbaptismal sins.

Conclusion

This chapter has experimented with the use of the CCC to help apply the commission by the risen Jesus to his disciples in John 20 to forgive or retain sins. It first demonstrated that the patterns and evidence of the biblical text do support the centuries-old tradition of interpreting this passage in light of the church's evolving practice of the sacrament of Reconciliation. Investigation of the treatment of John 20 within the broader topic of forgiveness of sins showed how the CCC situates this passage and exercise of the sacrament of Reconciliation within the broader creedal context of how God forgives sins, as well as of the church's "power of the keys" and the meaning and practice of the sacrament itself. The chapter has also tried to illustrate the reasonableness of using the CCC to help interpret, actualize, and apply John 20 to contemporary Catholic practice of the sacrament of Reconciliation.

CHAPTER TWELVE

Luke Johnson: Response to Bill Kurz

The chapters of this book written by Father Kurz are quite different from the ones I have written. Rather than speak in broad programmatic terms, he deals with specific texts and issues. Rather than engage the voices of past interpreters, he places his reading of John's Gospel in the context of contemporary voices. Rather than talk about what should be done by Catholic scholarship, he has tried through example to offer some samples of what a Catholic scholar might actually do. In this response, I want to begin by celebrating these differences in perspective and approach, and suggest that they serve as an opening for still others to join what we want to be a constructive conversation concerning the future of Catholic biblical scholarship. Father Kurz and I agree that there is no single right answer to the situation we face, nor is there any single scholar's view that can or should determine the way forward. What is most important is that we agree on the need for such a conversation, and bring to it our best efforts.

Perhaps the best way to further the conversation between Father Kurz and myself is to respond to certain elements in each of his chapters, noting some ways in which his interpretive practice is in continuity with the tradition of premodern interpretation and some ways in which it represents an improvement on the practices of our ancestors. I will also raise a few questions that occur to me as I read his chapters.

In his first chapter (Chapter Seven), "Beyond Historical Criticism: Reading John's Prologue as Catholics," Father Kurz joins a large number of contemporary scholars who see the literary criticism of the Gospels as a positive development within the biblical guild. In this approach, the final, canonical form of the text is read in its literary integrity. The narrative is not chopped up into disparate sources or quarried for the "authentic" bits that might go back to Jesus, but is read precisely as a narrative, with close attention given to the development of plot, characters, and themes. To borrow the helpful language of Sandra Schneiders in *The Revelatory Text: Interpreting the New Testament as Sacred Scripture,* literary analysis deals with the world within the text rather than the world "behind the text." By the very nature of composition, narratives possess meaning beyond the "original intention" of their authors, and open themselves to the interpretation of readers beyond the ones originally envisaged by the authors. Since the Gospels are also part of the church's canon, they therefore present themselves to readers within the church in every age as stories that create an imaginative world into which others can enter and even dwell.

This new approach — and it truly is new — bears some resemblance to patristic interpretation in its conviction that texts about the past are significant not only for what they report about past events (accurately or inaccurately) but for their potential to reveal God's wisdom through the human construction of the story. Origen would add to this only the conviction that God's Holy Spirit was also at work both in the shaping of the narrative and in guiding the reader to the deeper wisdom to be found in the narrative. But patristic and medieval interpreters rarely if ever saw compositions whole. The premise of contemporary literary criticism, that narratives bear meaning immanently in and through the composition as such and as a whole, is only rarely spotted in antiquity. Patristic and medieval interpreters had much more of an atomistic approach to narratives, seeing them more in oracular terms. Among ancient interpreters, the desire to have the Gospels speak to the world of the readers sometimes by-passed a full immersion in the world within the text.

The development of literary criticism within biblical scholarship is also to be applauded because it enables us to ask the question about the truth of narratives in ways that are more creative and flexible than were available, for example, to Augustine. We can think of the Gospels as rendering the figure of Jesus truly even if they disagree in their telling and cannot be harmonized as historical sources. They speak truth precisely as witnesses and interpretations, in and through the form of narrative.

As positive as the development of literary criticism is, it is not without problems for the theological use of the Bible. Theological engagement does not necessarily, or even naturally, move from the level of narrative analysis to the level of a particular theological issue. More often, theologians approach the text more tangentially. The classic example is preaching from the lectionary. In Catholicism, the preacher deals with at least four readings from Scripture. None of them is found in its original narrative context. How then should the sort of meaning that comes from literary analysis — a meaning that arises from the composition as a whole — affect the way in which a part of that narrative (for example, a parable) is put into conversation with other fragmentary texts from all over the Bible? At the moment, I think that literary analysis of the Bible has an important role to play, but that it is an indirect role. I think that the close reading of narratives (and of epistles) as a whole prepares readers for the more disjointed and fragmentary conversation among biblical texts demanded by theology and preaching. It does this by providing readers with a deep and intuitive sense of the theological voice of each composition, thus enabling them to hear expression of that voice (even in short utterances) more responsibly.

Another way in which Father Kurz's reading of John's prologue reminded me of patristic interpretation was in seeking a fit between Scripture and the Rule of Faith, or the Creed. I pointed out in my chapter on Origen (Chapter Three) that he begins his theological work, *On First Principles,* by asserting the Rule of Faith as the fundamental framework for all reading of Scripture and all theological speculation. As Father Kurz notes, this fit is most evident in the case of the Fourth Gospel, because the language of the Creed was in part shaped by the reading of this Gospel. His point is that for contemporary Catholics, "seeing" in John's prologue the Jesus whom they confess in the Creed is not a fundamental misunderstanding of the Creed or a fundamental misreading of John. And this is an important point. Both Creed and Gospel are reflections on the identity and work of Jesus in light of his resurrection and continuing power and presence in the Christian community, both during the era when Gospel and Creed were formed and today.

There is another aspect to the relation between Scripture and

Creed, however, that should also be brought out, and that is the way in which they do not stand in a simple equation. If that were the case, then one could read the Creed right off the page of John, and one could fully engage the Jesus of John when reciting the Creed. Christian experience tells us otherwise. Creed and Scripture stand instead in a dialectical relationship. The Creed lives out of Scripture and expresses the truth of Scripture in propositional form, but it does not come close to capturing the rich ambiguity of the person of Jesus as presented by John's Gospel. Conversely, the language of the Creed, even though richly scriptural, is also very much affected by the philosophical idioms and the theological controversies and refinements of the 3rd and 4th centuries.

In his second chapter (Chapter Eight), Father Kurz provides a contemporary example of engaging Scripture as an arena for disputed interpretation within a pluralistic culture. The "voices" raised on the moral issue of abortion are not only "in the church," they are also outside the church in a variety of religious and secular discourses. Once more I am reminded of the situation faced by interpreters like Origen and Augustine, who had to make arguments for the proper understanding of Scripture in a context in which such readings, and the validity of the Scriptures themselves, were in dispute. This chapter reminds me as well of the lesson derived from Augustine, that it is not enough to deal with Scripture's "meaning"; we must also take up the question of its "truth." Scripture is not adequately engaged when we simply describe its sense in terms of antiquity. We must also ask about its pertinence for today.

In his discussion, Father Kurz ignores the contemporary equivalents of Celsus and Porphyry (people who argue their case with no reference to Scripture), and debates with a prominent Protestant biblical scholar who has made a major statement on the use of the New Testament in Christian ethics, and who has made abortion one of his testcases. Father Kurz's main goal is to show a "biblical worldview based on Scripture," which assists Catholics in thinking about hard moral issues. The issue of abortion serves to show how "different preunderstandings [in this case denominational] can predispose readers to diverse interpretations and applications of the Bible to contemporary concerns."

In particular, Father Kurz shows how a more generous embrace of the scriptural witness as a whole with regard to the creation of humans and the sanctity of life, together with a reading of Scripture within the rich and consistent teaching and practice of the church concerning abortion, enables a "scriptural" grounding to an antiabortion stance in today's world that is not available to those who have fewer resources for filling the gaps in Scripture's explicit instructions. He makes a number of effective observations concerning the inconsistency shown by Professor Hays's argument: although he is generally opposed to abortion, he ends by granting that a decision to abort in some "hard cases" may be a legitimate matter of discernment; although he grants the need for "mediating" agents between Scripture and moral decisions (Tradition, reason, experience), he is inconsistent in their application. In this case, for example, Hays does not allow for any reasoning concerning "right to life" to enter the discussion. Father Kurz argues in response that the Catholic Tradition of moral reasoning based on humans being created in the image of God leads appropriately to language about a "right to life" even for unborn children, and that the overwhelming weight both of Scripture and tradition makes the absolute prohibition of abortion nonnegotiable in any circumstances.

I happen to agree with Father Kurz that Hays's difficulties in reaching clarity on this matter have something to do with an implicit *"Sola Scriptura"* sensibility: if Hays can't find an explicit statement in Scripture, he will not accord the prohibition the same weight as one that has explicit scriptural warrant. And I agree that appeals to the overall sense of the world revealed by Scripture — what I refer to as "imagining the world that Scripture imagines" — are more effective in shaping our sensibility in some hard moral issues than appeals to specific texts (especially pulled from their original contexts). Thus, Father Kurz's argument that the killing of innocent human life is always and everywhere declared unacceptable both by Scripture and tradition is difficult to controvert. And here also I want to applaud Father Kurz's important distinction between innocent and all life, a distinction not made in the recent Roman Catholic shift with regard to capital punishment. There is a fundamental difference between the situations of the unborn who cannot yet have done either good or evil and the criminals who may have taken other human life. Failure to make that distinction, and to assert the ultimacy of all human life, can also lead to the sort of pacifism that proclaims fidelity to Jesus' Sermon on the Mount, but that fails to do the hard moral reasoning required when communities must face organized forms of evil that specialize in killing the innocent.

Also attractive is Father Kurz's suggestion that women's experience in today's world can serve as a form of "analogy of faith" that helps direct our reading of Scripture. One of the things I have learned from my Methodist colleagues is the importance of "experience" together with Tradition and reason as a lens for the reading of Scripture. Indeed, Richard Hays also explicitly endorses this hermeneutical principle, although his use of it is inconsistent. It is an important principle especially if we hold that revelation is not over and certainly not adequately contained in a book, that instead we stand before the Living One who continues to work and therefore also to be revealed in the fabric of human freedom. But it is also a tricky principle. Not all "human experience" is necessarily revelatory of God's work and will. Experience must therefore be interpreted as carefully as Scripture itself. The example Father Kurz cites is to the point. His work with postabortion women in situations of repentance suggests that their "experience" serves to support the position that abortion is both destructive and distorting. The argument made by proponents of abortion (under the rubric of "freedom of choice"), however, uses the criterion of experience to make the exact opposite point: they relate the tales of women who have suffered because of unwanted babies. Now, I have already stated that I agree with Father Kurz on this issue, and on the use of experience, but I remind him as I remind myself, that it is as slippery as Scripture itself and must be discerned as carefully.

In his third and fourth chapters (Chapters Nine and Ten), Father Kurz turns to John 6, considering it in turn under the rubrics of "intertexuality" and "actualization." I see these chapters as profoundly continuous with the instincts of patristic interpreters. In the first case, a passage of the New Testament is read within the unity of Scripture; in the second case, a passage is read within the unity of the "rule of faith" enacted in the Eucharist. The main difference from the patristic practice is that what once came by instinct must now be painfully regained through theoretical justification. Thus, Father Kurz shows at every turn how his own reading is informed by the statements of the magisterium and various scholarly arguments. I applaud Father Kurz's patient engagement with the contemporary voices, but I also wonder whether we might regain our sense of living within the imaginative world of Scripture more quickly and surely simply by imitating our teachers in the faith rather than by working out positions within academic debate.

A good example is Father Kurz's useful discussion of the hermeneutics of suspicion and the hermeneutics of understanding — which I earlier called the hermeneutics of charity or generosity. I consider Father Kurz's position correct: we shall not attain a true and deep (transforming) understanding of Scripture unless we are willing to suspend suspicion and embrace Scripture with trust and love. But among those who have been hurt badly by readings of Scripture that are themselves characterized by suspicion rather than charity — readings that justify intolerance or oppression of humans, for example — the move from suspicion to trust is not going to be accomplished by theory, or even by exhortation. We must find a way of reading together, a way of reading that empowers all readers, a way of reading that allows hurts to be healed in a community of acceptance. The way to trust and the hermeneutics of charity is through practices of reading in community in which the power of some is not exercised at the expense of the many. This way is not easy, is in fact extraordinarily difficult, for it involves the reorganization of time and space and the formation of habits as well as the changing of mind. But unless we can begin to read "as church" together, we shall not overcome suspicion of the text or our mutual suspicion. Thus, in addition to the question posed by Father Kurz in Chapter Ten, "What Is God's Message to Me?" we must learn to ask, perhaps even first, another question, "What Is God's Message to Us?"

The examination of the theme of the Bread of Life in John 6 through the use of intertextuality provides a contemporary example of the patristic habit of reading the New Testament in light of the entire Scripture, specifically the version of Scripture found in the Septuagint. As also in his discussion of John's prologue, Father Kurz reminds us of the point made by Augustine in his discussion with Jerome: the Septuagint was the Bible "used by the Apostles." The Septuagint, not the Hebrew, is the "intertext" for the writers of the New Testament. The symbols of the Greek Scripture shape their perceptions, and the compositions of the Greek Scripture are the ones with which they interact as they seek to express their experiences of and convictions about Jesus the Christ. As Father Kurz notes in his first chapter (Chapter Seven),

John's prologue "actualizes" the Septuagint of Genesis 1, that is, it uses the language and sense of Genesis 1 in speaking about the "word" who is Jesus, and thereby at once clothes Jesus with the symbols of Genesis (so that we see the depth of his being) and gives new sense to Genesis itself (so that we can see Jesus already there in God's creative act). Similarly in John 6, language about the bread of life "actualizes" in a fairly obvious way the Septuagint of Exodus and the Psalms. And in a move that would be natural to Origen, Father Kurz suggests that the words of the Prophet Isaiah (specifically Isaiah 55) provide a still deeper layer of significance to the discourse, as well as a possible exegetical clue to its specific wording. The richness of this exposition presses the issue of the status of the Septuagint for Catholic biblical interpretation. Everyone acknowledges that the New Testament itself is unintelligible without reference to the Septuagint. But this recognition has no effect on anything else. Catholics who do not have Greek have no sense of these interconnections. But even when they are pointed out by scholars, ordinary Catholics cannot find them in their Bibles, or hear them in the liturgy, for all modern translations are from the Hebrew.

Mention of the liturgy leads me to a short and appreciative comment on Father Kurz's fourth chapter (Chapter Ten) on John 6 and the Eucharist. Just as the New Testament actualizes the Greek Scripture, so does the ritual practice of the community in its sacred meal actualize the New Testament. John's language about bread of life not only gains in significance from its allusions to Torah and its focus in the person of Jesus, but it takes on astonishing depth from its being enacted somatically in the life of the church. Catholics "eat the word" as well as "eat the body" of the Lord in the Eucharist. Father Kurz points us to a powerful way in which Catholics have always experienced Scripture. As I also suggested in my opening chapter (Chapter One), Catholics not only learn the Eucharist from Scripture, we also learn Scripture from the Eucharist. This happens most obviously in the readings from the Old and New Testaments. The fragmented form of these readings in the lectionary implicitly invites "intertextuality" in the practice of preaching, an invitation always accepted in patristic homilies and still heard from many Catholic pulpits. Catholics learn Scripture in the Eucharist also in the chants, prayers, and anaphora of the liturgy, all of which are fashioned from Scripture. A Catholic attentively present at the eucharistic liturgy is in an ideal position to "imagine the world that

Scripture imagines." Finally, Catholics learn the truth of Scripture (not simply a "word about God" but a "word of God") by taking the eucharistic body and blood of Christ into themselves, not simply as physical nourishment but above all as spiritual transformation.

Father Kurz's final chapter (Chapter Eleven) applies Scripture with the Catechism of the Catholic church, using as a test-case the promise in John 20:23, "whose sins you shall forgive will be forgiven them." The discussion contains a number of important elements. It focuses, for example, on a dimension of the life of faith that has always been important for Catholics, but in its specific manifestations (i.e., the sacrament of Penance/Reconciliation) has also been disputed by Protestants. It also raises the important question of the role of ecclesiastical authority, both for the interpretation of Scripture (in an authoritative text like *CCC*), and for the exercise of ministry (in the "administration of sacraments" like Penance). Because of the specific way in which the *CCC* discusses the forgiveness of sins, this chapter provides me the opportunity to pose a question that has run through several of Father Kurz's discussions but has special pertinence here. The question concerns the necessarily dialectical relation between tradition and Scripture. Father Kurz has properly emphasized the positive pole of that dialectic, the way in which tradition can be seen as legitimately developing and deepening the sense of Scripture through its statements of faith (the Creed), its collection of Scripture (the canon) and its ritual practice (the Eucharist). He has, I think, given less attention to the negative pole of the dialectic, which is the way in which Scripture also must challenge the tradition so that tradition does not seek to constrain and control the power of Scripture through its normative readings.

The forgiveness of sins truly is a "test-case" for this issue. I think that all Christians agree that "only God can forgive sins" in the fullest sense — only to God are we ultimately answerable and immediately known. All Christians agree also to some degree that "forgiveness of sins" ought to include not simply a "vertical" dimension (God and humans) but a "horizontal" dimension as well (humans among themselves). Scripturally, this conviction is expressed equally by the Lord's Prayer ("forgive us as we forgive others") and Paul's letters to Corinth and Ephesus (reconciliation with God is real only when manifested in reconciliation among humans).

The problem with the discussion of the forgiveness of sins in the

CCC is twofold. First, it tends to focus on the vertical dimension and gives very little attention to the horizontal. Second, it places the agency of forgiveness exclusively in ordained ministers. Father Kurz has shown how these emphases can be supported by the New Testament, including John 20:23. But he has not challenged the adequacy of the CCC with regard to the entire issue of the forgiveness of sins. Granted the legitimacy of the sacrament of Reconciliation administered by ordained priests, is that administration an adequate expression of what Scripture teaches concerning forgiveness of sins? Has the CCC, in other words, achieved an institutional shrinkage of the scriptural witness? I think, for example, of Jas. 5:14-20, which I will quote in full in my own (Anchor Bible) translation:

> Is anyone among you ill? Let that person call the elders of the assembly, and let them, after anointing him with oil in the name of the Lord, pray over the person. And the prayer of faith will heal the sick person, and the Lord will raise him up. And if the person has committed sins, he will be forgiven. Therefore, confess sins to each other and pray for each other so that you may be healed. A righteous person's prayer is able to have a strong effect. Elijah was a human like us in nature. Yet he prayed fervently for it not to rain. And it did not rain upon the earth for three years and six months. And he prayed again, and the heaven gave rain. And the earth produced its fruit. My brothers, if any among you wanders from the truth, and someone turns him back, let him know that the one who has turned back a sinner from his erring way will save that one's soul from death and will cover a multitude of sins.[1]

This canonical text clearly recognizes the role of "elders of the assembly" as leaders who come to the side of the sick to anoint and pray. And it connects the forgiveness of sins to this practice. But it also calls for the mutual confession of sins and mutual prayer within the community, as well as mutual correction of wrong-doing. This is a simple example of a scriptural text that presents a richer understanding of an ecclesial practice of forgiveness and healing than that presented by the CCC.

---

1. Luke Timothy Johnson, *The Letter of James*. AB 37A (New York: Doubleday, 1995), 325.

If the reading of Scripture in individualistic and idiosyncratic ways in order to support subjective life-styles is a serious problem, so is the reading of Scripture by ecclesiastical authorities to support institutional arrangements. The power of Scripture to challenge the human tendency both to subjectivize and to objectivize needs somehow to be maintained. In a word, the *critical* function of Scripture needs to be heard. And while Catholic scholars (in the full sense of the term) must do everything in their power to encourage and enable the formative and transformative reading of Scripture, they alone have the training and skills — and therefore the responsibility — to articulate that critical function of Scripture. How we understand "critical," of course, cuts to the heart of our contemporary crisis. I hope that we can return to this question in our final discussion, to which I look forward with particular eagerness because of the way Father Kurz has provided a rich and challenging set of essays on our shared concern for the future of Catholic biblical scholarship.

PART THREE

LUKE JOHNSON AND BILL KURZ

CHAPTER THIRTEEN

Opening the Conversation

In this final part of the book, we want to open up to our readers the conversation about the future of Catholic biblical scholarship. To provide some "conversation starters," each of us responds to a series of questions that have either been touched on in our separate chapters or have lurked just below the surface. We finish our part with each of us making a closing statement. We hope that these do not close the conversation but help to enable it.

1. Why is it important to claim a distinctive Catholic identity within biblical scholarship?

Johnson: I have always had a deep love for what is particular and embodied. I have tended to distrust the abstract and universal. Part of the joy of being Roman Catholic has for me been embracing Catholicism's very definiteness, its strong sense of boundaries, its ease at being exactly what it is. To be Roman Catholic means to have a specific place in the world and in history. So one reason to claim a distinctive Catholic identity is simply to celebrate being this odd and different way of being Christian that we call Catholic.

But more than tribal loyalty is involved. I am convinced that the Catholic Tradition contains sensibilities and practices that are true, that are threatened in today's practice of scholarship, and that therefore need to be nurtured. My sense of urgency is connected to the realization that scholars in my generation represent both a distinctive danger and opportunity. We are the last link with the sort of interpretation that preceded *Divino Afflante Spiritu* (1943) and are capable of bearing living witness to what was good and valuable in that earlier Tradition. But by the same token, we are capable of definitively rejecting that Tradition, so that future efforts to recover it will (like the clumsy gestures toward the Tridentine church evident in many forms of Catholic piety today) be forced and distorted. My sense is that, if we do not think long and hard about "what is Catholic about Catholic biblical scholarship," there will be a grievous loss both to the study of Scripture and to the spirit of Catholicism itself.

Kurz: I share this urgency to preserve a distinctive Catholic identity within biblical scholarship. Much of Christian biblical scholarship in the 19th and early 20th centuries has been more pertinent to the sensitivities and needs of Protestantism (e.g., some of the trend-setting German scholarship had a distinctively Lutheran set of concerns and presuppositions). More recently, as a much larger percentage of biblical scholars have been trained in nondenominational institutions or approaches, biblical scholarship has diversified to the brink of chaos and has been practiced from increasingly nonreligious academic, liberationist, and/or ideological commitments which are independent from and unrelated or sometimes even hostile to Catholic and other Christian beliefs, practices, and attitudes.

Many acknowledge the dictum, *"lex orandi lex credendi,"* namely that the ways people worship and pray have a major effect on what they believe. Since it is intuitively obvious that Catholics differ from Christians of other denominations in how they worship, pray, and emphasize sacraments, it stands to reason that Catholics will always have at least some significantly different beliefs from members of other denominations or religions, as well as from nonbelievers, no matter how ecumenical they may endeavor to be. If the Catholic church and Catholic believers have significantly different spiritualities and beliefs and forms of prayer and worship from others, then for Catholic scholars to serve their own church and fellow Catholics they will have to focus at least some of their efforts on addressing explicitly Catholic concerns and needs and to do so from Catholic sensitivities and vantage points.

Ideally, Catholic exegetes would experience a genuine reciprocal relationship between study and worship.

I also agree that Catholic approaches to biblical interpretation have important contributions to offer to biblical scholarship in general. To repeat examples mentioned earlier, Catholic approaches can contribute a more explicit and congenial partnership between faith and reason and between Scripture and tradition (including all aspects of church worship, pastoral care, and life).

2. What are or should be the positive characteristics of Catholic biblical scholarship?

Kurz: Both of us have emphasized the distinction (and complementarity) between the relatively more inclusive "both/and" emphasis of Catholicism and the accentuated "either/or" critical priority of both Protestantism and most historical criticism. This "both/and" approach is found in Catholic traditions of interpretation going back to medieval and patristic times, as well as in Catholic liturgy, sacraments, and worship. Exegetical insights can abound even in Catholic liturgical prayers, as when a preface prayer in honor of St. Peter sets Peter's naming Jesus "the Christ" in parallelism with Jesus' naming Simon "the Rock" (or Peter, as in Matthew 16).

Furthermore, Catholic doctrines have tended more than Protestant beliefs to emphasize the goodness of creation, in spite of sin and the fall. As a result, Catholic exegetes and religious thinkers have tended to put greater emphasis than their Protestant counterparts on the validity and importance of reason as well as of faith, of reasoning from natural law as well as of citing biblical evidence and revealed law, and of learning from culture as well as from revelation. Consequently, Catholic liturgies and forms of prayer, worship, church architecture and decoration all over the world have generally been less hesitant than Protestant counterparts to incorporate significant elements from the contemporary or indigenous culture. Catholic biblical scholarship should reflect some of these variegated emphases, even for the sake of a richer ecumenical dialogue.

Johnson: Catholic biblical scholarship should, I think, be characterized by a spirit of inclusion and generosity — both terms are encompassed by the term "catholic." By inclusion, I mean first the participation of all Catholics in the serious and critical study of Scripture. Second, inclusion means the willingness to balance the "both/and" so typical of Catholicism at its best. Catholic biblical scholars are concerned with Scripture, yes, but also with Tradition. They are fascinated by the questions posed by Christian origins, but no less so by the questions of the development of Christianity through time. They seek the historical sense of the text but do not restrict the text's meaning simply to the historical. They engage in historical criticism but embrace other ways of being critical as well. They are open to Scripture's capacity to speak in many ways and at many levels, starting with the literal but also including a variety of figural or imaginative senses. They engage the technical discussions of the academy, but are also deeply engaged in the existential questions of the church. They yield to no one in their pursuit of knowledge *(scientia),* but they are as passionately committed to the pursuit of wisdom *(sapientia).* I do not suggest that any single Catholic scholar can combine all these elements simultaneously or even sequentially. My point, rather, is that the conversation of Catholic Scripture scholarship should include in principle, and as often as possible in fact, all these dimensions.

By generosity I mean that Catholic biblical scholarship should be characterized by positive attitudes both toward the church and toward its Scripture. I say "its Scripture" deliberately, as a reminder that these ancient texts become Scripture only by being taken up into the canon of the believing community. The Bible is, in the strictest sense of the word, the church's book. Only by extension has it historically and today exercised a broader influence in the world. The Catholic scholar's spirit of generosity, then, means first a love and loyalty to the community whose Scripture the scholar studies, a willingness to serve the faith community through the ministry of learning and teaching, a dedication to shaping a scholarship of, for, and by the church, and not only a scholarship of the academic guilds. Such loyalty is the appropriate context for the expression of critical inquiry. The spirit of generosity or love also applies to the reading of Scripture itself, in a willingness to patiently wait for the wisdom that God wishes to speak through these often difficult and even repelling texts, a readiness to recognize both the ways in which Scripture wounds us and the ways in which it also can heal us.

3. In what ways should Catholic biblical scholarship also be ecumenical?

Johnson: Catholic biblical scholarship should be ecumenical in four ways. First and foremost, it must relinquish any vestiges of triumphalism, which show themselves in forms of exegetical special pleading, or in readings that are slanted to support specifically Catholic positions (and refute other interpretations) even at the cost of violence to the plain sense of the text. Second, Catholic scholars should gladly join the common discourse and labor of biblical scholars of whatever persuasion with an attitude of full respect and equality. They can do so because they recognize that a great deal of the work of interpretation involves methods and procedures that cut across denominational boundaries and even the boundary between believer and unbeliever. Historical inquiry, at least in the ideal, can enable scholars of quite divergent perspectives to see and evaluate the same evidence on the basis of agreed-upon criteria. Care must be taken, however, not to reduce biblical scholarship to those tasks which can be carried out in relatively neutral fashion.

Third, Catholic scholars ought to have deep respect for different faith perspectives that are brought to the study of Scripture and be willing to learn from, perhaps even be corrected by, such perspectives. Catholics cannot find in Paul's language about justification by faith the same depth of significance that Lutheran scholars do. Reformed readers cannot appreciate Paul's language about sanctification in the same manner as Catholics. Ecumenism does not demand the removing of differences, least of all in the reading of Scripture, but it does demand the willingness to enter into conversation with readings different than our own in a process of mutual gifting. Fourth, ecumenism means that Catholic scholars should celebrate the sensibilities that are distinctively Catholic (e.g., the concern for development as much as origins) and be willing to offer them as gifts to their Protestant colleagues.

Kurz: I second many of the observations above concerning dialogue with (both learning from and contributing to) scholarship from other denominations and backgrounds, and the importance of bringing to this ecumenical dialogue what is distinctive and important to Catholics. I would also like to add further emphasis on the *universality* of Catholicism (even in the denotation of the term "catholic"). Catholicism has always been a worldwide religion, to the extent that most people in the West would have been aware of the populated "world" in any particular age (cf. the Greek term *oikoumenē*). With admittedly widely varying degrees of sensitivity, effort, and success, Catholic missionaries have had to make at least some significant adaptations to the new peoples (and their languages and customs) among whom they preached the Good News.

In Western Catholicism (the type with which most of us are more familiar), there has long been a great variety of different, sometimes keenly competing, spiritualities (e.g., Benedictine, Franciscan, Dominican, and Jesuit) and even theologies (e.g., from traditional Augustinian, Thomistic, Suarezian theological systems to more contemporary competing theologies such as those of Rahner, Lonergan, von Balthasar, and Schillebeeckx). In many Protestant denominations a new theology might periodically result in a schism and consequently a new rival affiliation. But Catholicism for centuries has taken into its tent sharply diverse theologies, often in spite of even quite heated controversies among them.

The media and popular opinion have long placed an exaggerated concentration on the intolerance of diversity by Catholic authorities and on examples like the Inquisition and Index of Forbidden Books (all of which have historical foundation but also ought to be evaluated in relation to their respective historical contexts and situations). I certainly follow the lead of Pope John Paul II in expressing contrition over these and other examples of intolerance and the violence of religious wars and crusades in which Catholics have been guilty of participating over the centuries. But it seems also worth mentioning that some of the worst of these examples are more illustrative of the sinful mindset shared by humans of all (and no) religious affiliations than of bigotry peculiar to Catholic belief and practice. Fairness also might require that if one is to focus on Catholic intolerance, one also acknowledge similar phenomena in other religions and Christian denominations. In comparison to recurrent lack of mutual acceptance and division of many Protestant denominations over theological or interpretive emphases deemed mutually incompatible (such as opposing varieties of millenarianism), one could make a reasonable argument that perhaps

Catholicism is today one of the more tolerant forms of Christianity and of religions which have dogmatic content, and even generally has been. Over the centuries up to and including our post–Vatican II time period, the Catholic church has routinely included many rival and sometimes even mutually hostile approaches to Catholicism. The church has been slow to deny the name Catholic even to approaches not currently favored by the hierarchy, unless and until ecumenical councils have judged that these teachings could no longer be reconciled with the apostolic and creedal faith passed on by the church.

4. What do we mean by "critical" scholarship? Does it mean one or several things?

Kurz: One important meaning of "critical" scholarship must be its contrast from "uncritical" interpretation or scholarship. Much damage can be done to the life of believers and to the church from uncritical interpretations of Scripture that interject the reader's bias into the biblical message in the name of piety or "orthodoxy" or "political correctness," from either the "right" or the "left." In both my graduate and undergraduate teaching, I emphasize the need to read scriptural passages carefully and critically. One must first listen intently to the point of view in the biblical text without presuming that it is either identical to one's own or utterly irreconcilable with it. Only when one pays close attention to the actual meaning of the words and the grammatical and rhetorical structures in their original context (both textual and cultural) can one read Scripture in a receptive and simultaneously intelligent and nonabusive manner. Carefully rooting one's readings of Scripture in the written text of the passage also provides perhaps the most important common ground from which readers from differing religious and ideological persuasions can begin their conversations about the topic treated in that passage.

A related aspect of "critical" reading might be its contrast from "lazy" or careless reading. A careless reading would not take the trouble to look closely at all the textual evidence, nor to use relevant tools of critical exegesis according to the person's level of academic training, nor (for students and scholars) to apply strict scholarly standards in their use of languages, methods, and argumentation from evidence.

Both of these senses of "critical" scholarship will always have foundational importance for interpretation in the church.

A separate sense of "critical" scholarship might refer to the location of that scholarship on a spectrum of interpretation, ranging from
a "hermeneutics of suspicion" to a "hermeneutics of understanding (or
consent)." Although it is fervently to be hoped that even a "hermeneutics of consent" would be exercised in a manner befitting critical scholarship (in the senses above), the term "critical" can also relate to differing levels of distance from the point of view in the biblical text. Some
critical distance is always necessary, in order to ensure that one is truly
listening to the text's point of view and not just presuming that one's
own viewpoints are being reinforced by the text.

However, beyond a certain point, "critical" distance can become
skeptical, alienated, flippant, or even arrogant, in ways that ultimately
close the reader's mind to what the biblical text is communicating. No
matter what the text says, a truly alienated or hostile reader might either reject it as unacceptable or even unthinkable, or might make
moral judgments about the text that can often (uncritically) presume
the unquestioned moral superiority of the reader's view or contemporary cultural perspective over the viewpoint expressed in the text. For
example, an important biblical criterion of measurement, attributed to
Jesus himself, is "by their fruits you shall know them." By this standard, can one simply presume that contemporary moral or family practices or structures, which are correlated to something like a 50-percent
rate of broken families, are in all cases morally superior to traditional
mores recommended in Scripture, whose "track record" for family fidelity, stability, and happiness has been significantly higher?

Johnson: There are any number of ways to read Scripture. Liturgical
reading, for example, is not the same as the sort of reading we call
"spiritual," or "lectio divina." The Holy Spirit has no constraints on
how Scripture can communicate truth. A passage from the Psalms or
from the Gospel taken completely out of context can transform a person's life. An inadequate translation can nevertheless express Scripture's truth to the discerning mind and heart. God does not need
scholarship to do God's work. But the church needs scholarship in order to do its work faithfully in witness to God. This is why "critical
scholarship" must be a reality within the life of the church and not sim-

ply within colleges and universities. For the church faithfully to discern God's word in the fabric of human freedom, it must read and think critically, that is, it must learn to think in the way that scholars do at their best.

The term "critical" should not suggest adopting a superior position that enables one to render judgments on the adequacy of Scripture or distancing oneself so that Scripture has no claim on one's life. "Critical" means, rather, the practice of close, sustained, careful, attentive, disciplined reading that is characterized above all by the posing of hard questions rather than the harvesting of obvious and easy answers. When reading is genuinely critical, the process of questioning is turned both on the text and on the readers of the text. And because both texts and readers are complex and multidimensional, critical reading should also take many forms. Because the Bible was written by humans in another time and place in languages not our own and within social realities different than ours, the practice of historical criticism is of fundamental importance for any responsible reading. But the texts (like us) also have an anthropological dimension, and a literary dimension, and a religious dimension. Critical thinking is possible (and indeed required) from each of these perspectives. It is appropriate as well to think philosophically about the text and readers. Philosophy includes metaphysics. The lack of any sense of ontology severely limits contemporary scholars reading Scripture. Philosophy also includes moral discourse. Scripture must be tested for its moral adequacy, just as readers need to test themselves for their moral attitudes. In my view, "critical" has many dimensions rather than simply one, but all these dimensions involve a passionate engagement in the form of active and persistent questioning.

5. Of what value is historical study for the theological reading of Scripture?

Johnson: If the question was about the value of studying history for understanding Scripture, it would be easy to answer. Although I am skeptical about our capacity to do an adequate reconstruction of the world that produced the Bible or to recover everything we would want to know about the historical Jesus, a skepticism based in a respect for the potential as well as the limitations of history as a way of human knowing, I also think that undertaking such efforts is legitimate, so long as they operate within the appropriate canons of historical criticism. Even more, I think that all readers must seek to learn as much of the history of the ancient world as they can manage, so they can better understand the words of Scripture. To put this distinction neatly, I think we need to do good history in order to encounter responsibly the Jesus of the Gospels, but I don't think we should dismantle the Gospels in order to do the sort of bad history that generates countless "historical Jesuses." History is to help us understand the words of Scripture, rather than Scripture as simply the sources for us to do history.

The question, though, is harder than that. It asks about the connection between historical study and the theological reading of Scripture. It is precisely on this point that scholars today divide, in part because "history" became over the past several centuries the dominant paradigm for all biblical study. An extreme is represented by those who consider historical reconstruction itself to be theologically normative: if we could "find" the historical Jesus, he — and not the Jesus of the Gospels — would be the measure for Christian identity. Less extreme, but still strong, is the position that the "historical sense" of Scripture must be the basis of all theological appropriation within the church. The exegete, then, who controls the original languages and knows history and can "determine" the "original" meaning of the text, becomes the gatekeeper for theological discourse. Theologians within the church (including preachers) must rely on professional exegetes. They are not empowered to read on their own. They need to learn "what the text meant" from the experts, and their ability to say "what the text means" must continue to be guided by those expert opinions.

I find the extreme position that history is itself normative to be wrong. Even when communities of faith agree on what the story of the past was, that story forms only one element in a community's discernment of what God demands now. And I find the strong position that the historical sense of the text itself shapes all theological appropriation overly restrictive, and contrary to the Catholic spirit of both/and that I have tried to celebrate in this book. First, we must be careful not to identify the "literal sense" of the text (which must always remain primary for all discourse) from the "historical sense." The literal sense is that meaning which is made accessible by the structure of the grammar and syntax and diction of the ancient Hebrew and Greek texts, only imperfectly represented by "literal" translations. The historical sense is what the language of the Bible might have meant in its original context. Note that I say, "might have meant," for our grasp of those circumstances is as partial as our comprehension of the total linguistic systems of the original languages. It seems to me, on one hand, to be contrary to Catholic sensibility to make the "historical meaning" determinative for all subsequent readings. On the other hand, all subsequent readings must find some basis in the "literal meaning," even though such readings can range far beyond either what the first authors intended or the original hearers would have understood, so long as such readings respond to the actual language of the text.

Finally, the historical study of the text can serve two important functions for theology. First, if theological claims (as I think they should not be) are based on supposed historical evidence, they can be disconfirmed by other or better historical evidence. History can and should challenge bad theological claims made on the basis of inadequate history. Second, the historical study of Scripture preserves the *otherness* of the text, enabling it to resist theological appropriations that seek to collapse its voice into that of a contemporary ideology, even that of the church. History can help Scripture maintain its prophetic voice.

Kurz: In addition to these distinctions among literal and historical senses of Scripture, I would refer readers to scholars' arguments in my chapters above. They include further reasons not to simply identify the "literal sense" of Scripture with the results of historical criticism. One such reason is the fact that religious texts like Scripture include some of the "spiritual sense" within their very literal sense.

History and theological interpretation also intersect because Christianity is not a merely mythological religion, but a historical religion grounded in Jesus of Nazareth and on what happened to him and what he did and what happened to his disciples after his time on earth. Many refer to this "scandal of particularity" about Christianity. How can so much salvific importance for so many people (for all humans in fact) be claimed to ride on one particular individual from one time and place in history? Christian theological claims have their historical grounding in this particular person who lived in this particular time and place. Obviously, to deal with these particulars, a historical element will always be indispensible even for theological interpretation of Scripture.

The historical moment in biblical interpretation is also needed to prevent collapsing together the message of Scripture and one's preconceived notions and biases, as I too have argued above in slightly different ways. Historical awareness grounds the "prophetic" function of Scripture for challenging and calling for reform and renewal regarding current practices and beliefs of individuals or the church. In addition, my reference above to the application of Jesus' "woe" in Luke 11:52 (par. Matt. 23:13) to those who monopolize the key to scriptural knowledge and hinder others from entering without entering themselves provide a similar caution against historical scholarship being overly restrictive regarding others' use of Scripture.

6. What is the role of the teaching office of the church with regard to the interpretation of Scripture? Where is it located, and how does it relate to other sources of authority in the church?

Kurz: The two of us probably overlap in at least some of our perceptions about the role of the teaching office of the church in biblical interpretation and its location and relationship to other sources of authority in the church. But I would not be surprised if we also have some disagreements, or at least differences of emphasis, in answer to particular questions. I would expect us to accentuate different aspects of this question because of the rather dissimilar ways we respectively have experienced church authority and problems stemming from its misuse or its deficiency.

Since 1975, I have encountered numerous serious pastoral problems among ordinary Catholics because of confusion about or simply lack of authoritative church teaching, including lack of pastoral oversight of how Catholics interpret Scripture. I have experienced this lack of pastoral oversight by official church teaching authority on two very different levels. One is the level of pastoring simple believers. Urgent pastoral problems have occurred among nonprofessional lay Catholics who were attracted to the use of Scripture by movements like Charismatic Renewal, or by their association with Evangelicals and Pentecostals in prolife activities. Lack of oversight by bishops and parish priests left many such Catholics vulnerable to anti-Catholic fundamentalist forms of biblical interpretation. I know many enthusiastic Catholics who became alienated from the Catholic church in this way. In many such cases, although the pastoral responsibility for their parishioners rested primarily on the parish priests, these priests in turn felt inadequate to guide their people's biblical interpretation because of deficiencies in their own seminary training. Thus, both professional scholars who were the seminary professors (as many of them were lay as clerical) and priests in pastoral roles appear to share some of the responsibility for this failure in oversight of vulnerable parishioners' use of Scripture.

The more controversial circumstance regarding oversight by the official teaching office of the church (bishops with pope) has been its task of overseeing what professional scholars have written and taught, especially for popular and pastoral settings. It is unquestionably part of a Catholic scholar's responsibility to argue with other scholars about serious historical and interpretive issues, even those which have the potential of dramatically affecting the faith and traditional teachings of the church. When, however, their controversial interpretations (such as those which seem to deny the bodily resurrection of Jesus, or assert that the bodily resurrection of Jesus is not important for Christian faith, or claim that probably dogs ate Jesus' bones) are presented without disclaimer by scholars, or by teachers and catechists dependent on them, to untrained undergraduate or high school students or to ordinary parishioners, their potential (and actual) damage to the faith of these "little ones" can be devastating.

A serious pastoral problem has arisen because of an acute lack of "self-policing" by professional exegetes, who have been exceptionally reluctant since the 1960s to criticize their peers, no matter how problematic their pronouncements might be. Another implicates the realities of modern media: the former scholarly ideal of interchange in academic journals among only serious scholars of ideas which do not get simultaneously promoted in the popular media, until after they have passed scholarly muster among peers, no longer obtains, if it ever did. However, when ideas which are potentially and actually destructive of the innocent faith of untrained faithful are promoted on a pastoral level by Catholic exegetes without either some public challenge by their professional peers or counterbalancing instruction in the tradition by church authorities who are responsible for protecting the faith of their people, the result is and has been for decades mass confusion among ordinary Catholics.

Scholars ought to take some responsibility for mutual correction of their peers as part of their professional obligations as scholars (regardless of denomination). Still, in my judgment the primary responsibility for protecting the integrity of what gets taught to ordinary Catholics as Catholic teaching (or as compatible with Catholic teaching) seems logically to lie with those authorities who have been explicitly and publicly entrusted with oversight of Catholic teaching — bishops who were ordained by the church particularly for this pastoral role. For example, although as an educated scholar I have been entrusted with university teaching, still in my function as teacher-scholar no one has given me authority to judge or be responsible for the faith content of what Catholics are taught in pastoral, popular, and ecclesial settings. Whatever ecclesial authority I may have over others in the area of faith stems more from my authority as ordained priest and official helper of the bishop to make judgments in the internal forum of the sacrament of Reconciliation (Confession) or to preach the Gospel in Catholic liturgical settings with the mandate originating from my ordination as deacon and priest.

As priest I in turn am subject in principle (though rarely in practice unless I were notorious for teaching falsehood) to not inconsequential oversight from my bishop or equivalent superior over what I preach or publish especially on the popular and pastoral levels. As scholar and teacher, on the other hand, I enjoy academic freedom from most such oversight over the content of what I teach and write as an academic and university teacher. For me to have authority over what affects the faith of other Catholics, it seems that I myself would need to have someone else in authority over what I teach. That simply does not seem applicable to a scholar as scholar the way it is applicable to those who have been accepted, tested, and ordained to be part of the church's pastoral and teaching hierarchy, in which authorities are themselves accountable to higher church authorities.

It is for such reasons that I hold to a special authority of the church's magisterium or official teaching authority, and why I have serious reservations about most theories which claim or imply the existence of a "double magisterium" in the Catholic church — one, ordained bishops and pope; the other, professional theological scholars. I see the role of the magisterium regarding interpretation as protecting the apostolic revelation from errors and misinterpretations and approaches harmful to the faith life and worship and moral teachings of the church and its members. The main reason I resist notions of a "double magisterium" is that it is not private scholars but only bishops and pope who are publicly commissioned by the church for their office to oversee and guide and protect the faith and morals of the community as a whole. Obviously, both charisms of scholar and authority are essential for a healthy church, and ideally they will work closely together with mutual respect. Scholars are needed by the church to help the magisterium by their research and contributions and even criticisms. But scholars as scholars have not been commissioned by the church with any authority over the faith and moral teachings of the ordinary laity. How the recently inaugurated "mandatum" in Catholic schools might affect this state of the question remains to be seen.

Johnson: The Catholic Tradition recognizes the teaching office of bishops as well as the symbolic and real teaching authority of the Bishop of Rome. But the Catholic Tradition has also always honored the special authority intrinsic to the charisms of learning and holiness. Just as great sanctity of life demands that the church pay heed to its witness, so does profundity of theological learning demand that the church pay attention. Catholic biblical scholarship, therefore, should be critically loyal to the teaching of the hierarchy but also loyally critical. In the ideal, Catholic Scripture scholarship and the hierarchy remain in a positive and mutually beneficial conversation. Indeed, many of the great patristic interpreters of Scripture were themselves bishops. Catholic biblical scholars can serve the teaching authority of bishops by engaging those dimensions of Scripture that are theologically important and challenging, by rendering their learning in a form intelligible to readers outside the academic guild, by seeking to interpret for the sake of transformation rather than simply explanation, and by encouraging biblical literacy and interpretive abilities among the laity. Bishops can exercise their teaching authority creatively with respect to biblical scholarship by themselves becoming competent interpreters and preachers, by nurturing and enabling scholarly talent among clergy, religious, and laity, and by taking the best of contemporary biblical scholarship into account in their formal teaching.

Alas, the tradition of a learned hierarchy, even one that is biblically competent, has almost completely vanished, just as fewer Catholic biblical scholars show themselves primarily concerned for the instruction of the church. As a result, mutual suspicion has too often replaced the ideal state of trust and cooperation. It is a sad fracturing of the Catholic ethos when scholars are contemptuous of the Rule of Faith, and when bishops seek to impose ideological conformity. One longs for a situation like the one that obtained briefly during the Second Vatican Council, when scholars and bishops learned together and from each other and, as a result, composed documents that both richly interpreted Scripture and tradition and edified the faithful. Unless that happy state of cooperation is again seriously pursued by all, tension between theological scholarship and the hierarchy seems inevitable. In this situation, it is at least important for scholars and prelates alike to remember that they are all members of Christ's body, in which no member possesses all the gifts, and in which all members are to serve the greater life of the whole.

7. What is the proper critical function of Scripture scholarship vis-à-vis theology and church life?

Johnson: I think that Scripture scholars best serve theology by engaging the text theologically themselves, and by joining in the larger theological conversation. It is a remarkable aspect of contemporary seminary education, both Catholic and Protestant, that the part of the faculty most resistant to joining theological conversation tends to be the Bible scholars. Scripture scholars can enrich theology within the church by opening the texts to a theological, and not simply a historical, reading. Methods such as literary analysis and rhetorical criticism are helpful, but only when they transcend the technical analysis of biblical texts and engage the implications of the stories and arguments thus identified. Scripture scholars can also contribute to theology by forcefully presenting the powerful and prophetic voice of Scripture. Although historical Jesus research is both historically and theologically suspect, for example, it can serve to remind theologians how central the humanity of Jesus — as depicted in all the writings of the New Testament but above all the Gospels — should be. Likewise, serious consideration of the religious claims of the New Testament letters and the book of Revelation demands recognition of the resurrection not simply as a historical event of the past but as the on-going eschatological premise of all Christian existence, not an event of the liturgical year on which to preach once a year but the theological basis of all preaching and all prayer "in the name of Jesus."

Scripture scholars can remind theology of the relative weight of scriptural testimony. How much saner would contemporary conversations be if the weighty witness of Scripture on the use of material possessions were given more attention than its relatively slender directions concerning sexual behavior. And Scripture scholars can offer criticism of theological developments that are excessive or dangerous, such as supersessionist theologies that serve to delegitimize Judaism, or the use of the polemical language of the New Testament in support of the demonization of Jews or other non-Christian religions.

Scripture scholars, it should be emphasized, also join the theological conversation by learning from other participants in that conversation, rather than simply dictating to them. Scripture scholars have much to learn about the reading of texts from other theological disciplines, and for that matter, from all other readers of the texts, not least those powerful readers among nonspecialists that God always raises up in each generation. In the same way, if biblical scholars can offer useful criticism of a number of ecclesial practices — as in my own work, for example, I have tried to show how the process of decision-making that does not involve discernment among the faithful is theologically inadequate — it is also the case that biblical scholars can and should be involved in the practices of the community and learn from them.

Kurz: As a complementary perspective to these responses, I suggest focusing on the roles of Scripture and interpretation in any religion which has a canonical set of authoritative writings. If biblical scholars are primarily responsible for articulating the scriptural input into any issue, theologians take relatively more responsibility for finding appropriate applications and interpretations of the fixed canon to the changing circumstances of the living religion. Ideally, collaboration between biblical and theological scholars can help overcome the limits of one's own expertise and specialization in attending to these cross-disciplinary concerns.

The fixed scriptural norm, which was established in the distant past, provides correctives and limits for applications to the present and guarantees continuity in Catholicism with its origins. But a text which is millennia old also has to be recontextualized and applied to new times and circumstances. The special training and linguistic, historical, and literary skills of Scripture scholars serve theology in the ongoing comparison of contemporary theological developments especially with the apostolic origins of Catholic faith. We can help establish the original context and sense of the church's biblical norm, against which all subsequent developments are measured.

However, we Scripture scholars can overstep our bounds if we act as overeager "censors" of ordinary piety and theology, which are not simply rationally and logically constructed from the text of Scripture. Catholic piety and theology have also grown and accumulated novel elements from centuries of living worship, doctrinal development, Tradition, church life and practice. As a result, popular piety and devotions and even liturgical growth tend to be more haphazard and "messy" than any particular historical precedent or contemporary liturgical theology. Even the great medieval Catholic cathedrals accumulated elements that were not altogether and mutually consistent over the years and decades that it took to build them. Nor is the Roman Canon (now the first Catholic Eucharistic Prayer) as neatly constructed and liturgically consistent as the early form which now serves as the second Eucharistic Prayer. Yet ordinary people have long received remarkable devotion from many of these practices of piety or liturgical rituals which grew somewhat haphazardly over time. As scholars who function primarily with the rational, we need to respect those religious elements in popular and liturgical piety that have accumulated and been assimilated in nonlogical ways.

8. What factors inhibit Catholic biblical scholars from directing all their efforts to the building up of the church?

Kurz: Both of us have observed in the chapters above how the rewards and strictures of academia are quite foreign and unrelated to the needs of the church. Even in Catholic universities, promotion and tenure will generally be attained not by serving immediate church needs but by publishing articles and books that appeal to secular academic journals, institutions, groups, and tastes. One consequence of this is simply the limitations of time and energy for many biblical scholars and teachers to expend many efforts toward explicitly building up the church; many of their undertakings are devoted initially to academic survival and then to further promotion and salary increases for support of their families.

Within Catholic universities, where my academic career has been spent, it is mostly such everyday considerations of time, energy, salary, promotion, and tenure that appear to me to limit extra service of the church at large, beyond the genuine service which exegetes' authentic research and publishing already provides to the church. I have not noticed any limitation in principle on lay Catholic colleagues from serving in virtually any capacity within the university, or on diocesan and ecumenical offices, advisory boards, commissions, or the like. Although some church positions are currently limited primarily to clerics, at least in the diocese where I serve I have not seen any lack of opportunities for lay exegetical colleagues to exercise as much meaningful service and advisory and teaching functions on both diocesan and parish (not to mention national) levels as they possibly have time for. For example, one of my current Catholic colleagues is playing a prominent role in the current national New American Bible translation project: she heads one of the translation subcommittees.

Also, although in the mid-20th century Catholic biblical scholars have had justifiable fears of church censorship and were in fact sometimes forbidden to publish, such concerns today do not generally seem to correspond at least to anything that I have observed in teaching at a Catholic university since my doctoral studies. Perhaps others have suffered such censorship, but I personally have not been aware of much more than perceived fears which I have not seen realized. Though I have repeatedly heard apprehension about church censorship of biblical scholars, I have never experienced any confirmation of such concerns. Ironically, the only scholars whom I personally know who have had one or more of their articles forbidden publication have been some "conservative" religious priests censored by "liberal" superiors.

Johnson: Even if Catholic scholars wanted all their scholarship to be in service of the church, they would be blocked from two directions. The first and most serious barrier is that erected by the church itself. Ever fewer biblical scholars are among the ranks of the clergy or religious. Ever more of them are laypeople, and among them ever more are women. As laypeople, they have no official voice or recognized role within Catholicism's hierarchically-defined structure, even if they teach within Catholic universities or colleges. On the plus side, such lay scholars would seem to have more freedom to speak boldly, since they are not subject to the same sort of direct ecclesiastical discipline as clergy and religious, but that freedom is limited precisely by the degree of official ecclesiastical involvement in the life of those academic institutions. Indeed, the increased presence of such lay scholars in Catholic theological faculties was undoubtedly one of the factors leading to the creation of the *mandatum*. Whatever the final consequences of this instrument, it has a chilling effect on Catholic scholarship, signalling that not creativity but control is the main concern of the church's hierarchy. The deep disinterest in biblical scholarship among the Catholic clergy is attested as well by the sparse attendance of priests and bishops at the sort of advanced scriptural workshops that scholars provide. This past summer, at workshops I gave in Detroit and Denver, there were, I would guess, no more than 15 priests among some 300 lay and religious participants.

There is blockage also from the side of the academy. The more Catholic scholars are lay, the more they are found in non-Catholic faculties. Roman Catholic biblical scholars today hold major chairs at Yale, Harvard, Chicago, and Emory. These also happen to be the major producers of Ph.D.s in Bible in this country. But such scholars naturally are pulled away from the sort of communication of scholarship that most benefits the church, to the sort of technical scholarship that best pleases promotion and tenure committees in universities. The academy has its own laws and logic. Increasingly, as universities in this country become more secular in spirit and in fact, biblical scholarship (insofar as it can be called that at all) necessarily responds to that social setting rather than the existential needs of faith communities. And there is little incentive to overcome this inertia toward the purely academic when the Catholic faith community, at least in its official hierarchy, shows little interest in and much suspicion toward the efforts of biblical scholars.

9. How should Catholic biblical scholarship relate to the liturgy and preaching from the lectionary?

Johnson: The public worship of the church has always been the central locus for scriptural interpretation in the Catholic Tradition, through the elaboration of the liturgy itself and through scriptural preaching. With the eucharistic celebration now in the vernacular, the challenge is to recover some of the richness of the interpretive Tradition that was developed in the antiphons and graduals, the versicles and responses, of the medieval liturgy. Catholic scholars who participate in liturgical and musical appropriations of Scripture learn something important about the power of the imagination to see (and hear) things in texts that logical analysis can miss. Catholic scholars ought also to participate in the constructing of the common lectionary. They should be concerned not only with the accuracy and felicity of translation, but also with the theological appropriateness of selections. They are in a position to protest the now-common practice of abbreviating scriptural passages to accommodate reduced attention spans, with abbreviations often also involving the excision of parts that are deemed offensive to contemporary sensibilities. If biblical scholars do not argue for the integrity of Scripture as it is read in the assembly, who will?

The most obvious way that Catholic biblical scholars can help improve the dismal state of Catholic homiletics is by providing, as do their Protestant colleagues, first-rate interpretive materials in easily accessible form. A more enduring contribution would be to produce biblical commentaries and theological readings of Scripture that are aimed at common readers rather than academic peers. Good biblical scholarship need not be loaded down with endless footnotes and technical disquisitions. The classic and influential studies of scholars in both testaments in the last century prove, indeed, that the most significant interpretations are often those that are written with simplicity of thought and style. Finally, the most important contribution of all that scholars can make is to take seriously their role as teachers. In their seminary and college classes, they have an unparalleled opportunity to shape the minds and the practices of future pastors and lay leaders in the church. If their pedagogy produces powerful readers who can in turn empower others to read, then the entire culture of the church can change. Pastors can become better preachers because they read Scripture with others and learn from them, and congregations can grow in maturity as they learn to read critically together.

Kurz: I do not have much to add to these eloquent suggestions, which I would primarily "second." I am quite proud of the fine service Catholic biblical scholarship has provided for the church's liturgy in the form of translations, commentaries, guides, and many materials used in the the church's worship. Scholars have also been quite active in providing materials for Catholic preachers. However, I would like to express a personal *caveat* from my pastoral experience. For effective homilies that move parishioners' hearts and change their attitudes and behavior, there comes a point when preachers have to use their own resources, spiritual and life experience, prayer, and study to prepare truly personal (not "canned") homiletic reflections on the lectionary, for which no preaching aids can substitute. In this regard I suggest that biblical scholars' contributions come more in the remote preparation and education of the homilists themselves (usually in seminary Scripture courses or in publications read by them) than in immediate homily preparation aids. Another personal caution I might add: biblical scholars need to be careful not to intimidate preachers from doing their own prayerful meditation on lectionary texts and personally applying them to their listeners' lives. When simple parishioners hear biblical texts and their homiletical expositions, it is not primarily biblical scholars but God who should be speaking directly to their hearts and minds.

10. How important for the future of Catholic biblical scholarship is the empowerment of the laity as readers of Scripture?

Kurz: The desire to help educate and prepare lay students to be intelligent readers who nourish their faith and lives through Scripture has been one of the chief motivations behind my 27 years of academic teaching of Scripture. In my undergraduate classes I have persistently desired to open students' eyes to the power and meaning of Scripture for their lives. In my graduate classes I have wanted to prepare new generations of teachers of Scripture who, if they wished to do so, would be capable of doing likewise for their own future students. On the few occasions where I was visiting professor of New Testament at seminaries in Milwaukee and Nairobi, Kenya, I also had the privilege of trying to empower future priests and preachers to find in Scripture God's word and to interpret it intelligently for those whom they would serve.

Even pragmatically, if many students and laity can be empowered and encouraged and have their apprehensions overcome so that they can themselves read Scripture intelligently and responsibly, this will result in more of such laity deciding themselves to become Scripture scholars. It will also provide a larger ready audience for the publications, teaching, and presentations of Scripture scholars, especially when they are pastorally attuned.

Johnson: I think that the creation of strong lay readers of Scripture is key not only to the renewal of Catholic biblical scholarship but to the renewal of the church as well. The great tragedy of the present moment is that the proper and organic connection between the study of Scripture and the life of faith is frayed to the point of breaking. The dream of a Catholic laity capable of active and mature engagement with the Scripture has been realized only sporadically. The best pastoral efforts have not been directed to this goal. And the best Catholic scholars seem less and less interested in or able to engage in such pastoral activity; their own desires and the logic of their careers make their labor ever more purely academic and removed from the life of faith.

In response to the previous question, I touched on the importance of having other powerful readers in each parish besides the preacher. Having a community of disciplined, persistent, and questioning readers in each congregation makes for a more mature and capable community and, not incidentally, saves the mind of the pastor, who does not need to die mentally because of intellectual loneliness. Note my use of the adjectives "disciplined, persistent, and questioning," the same terms I used to describe "critical" scholarship. I believe that a critical biblical scholarship is possible — indeed, necessary — outside the framework of formal educational institutions (the academy) and in, of, and for the church itself. The place where such scholarship is embodied is in groups of laypeople (and, one hopes, also clergy) who join regularly in such informed and transforming reading of Scripture. The creation and nurturing of such communities of readers ought to be a project on which Catholic biblical scholars and hierarchy ought to be able to collaborate. For scholars, such communities of readers ought to be the "ideal readers" toward whom their scholarly work is most directed. Bishops, in turn, should see such communities of readers as the seed-bed of future leaders and future scholars who will understand how Scripture is at the heart of a transformative community of faith.

Final Comments

Johnson: It is our hope that this book is the opening rather than the closing of a conversation about the future of Catholic biblical scholarship. The conversation is truly needed, for the situation is urgent. At stake is also the future health of the church, and in this future, all of us have a stake. We do not pretend to have provided any recipe, but only the best thoughts we are now able to give to the question. We have no greater wisdom than others and therefore ask that others share their wisdom. We recognize that our lives are as implicated in the ambiguities we describe here as are the lives of our colleagues. We are not privileged observers but compromised participants. So we offer these thoughts in the hope that others will take them up, test them, improve them. More conversation among those deeply committed to the Catholic Tradition is needed. And something more than conversation is required. Also demanded of us, I think, is the willingness to change some of our practices as scholars, to undergo something of an intellectual and moral conversion, making the life of faith the starting point and goal of our scholarly efforts. Catholic scholarship will again be truly Catholic, I think, when it uses all of the tools of critical inquiry as a means of strengthening authentic faith, of transforming minds into the mind of Christ, and of building up the church in love.

Kurz: I too hope that this book and this final "conversation" might contribute to the beginning of a further conversation about the future of Catholic Scripture scholarship, and not simply be an end to the conversation that went on between its covers. I have often tried in my responses not merely to echo our common positions but rather to contribute divergent insights that originate in significantly different experiences which I have had. To the extent to which this may have contributed to some negative-sounding observations on my part, I am sorry. Nor do I pretend to absolve myself and the record of my own scholarly and teaching efforts from remarks of mine which might be perceived as criticisms.

The truth is that I too am extremely concerned about preserving and recovering treasures from our Catholic heritage of biblical interpretation that can bless the entire ecumenical church. I too have been profoundly persuaded for decades of the importance for myself and for other Catholic scholars of approaching Scripture study, teaching, and writing from our own faith in service of the Catholic community's faith. I'm not in this profession of teaching and biblical scholarship for the money (which is certainly nothing special). I teach and write and preach from a strong desire to share treasures with which I have been gifted — my Catholic faith in God and his merciful love, my academic and priestly training, and my experience studying, teaching, and preaching Scripture as God's loving and healing and saving word for a world that urgently needs it. I hope others will share with us from their treasures.

INDEX OF SCRIPTURE AND OTHER ANCIENT SOURCES